"Erika Schurchardt . . . frames her 'questions to theology' such that theology has to return to the suffering. . . . This book is full of experience and insight. It points to a more humane society."

Prof. Dr. Jürgen Moltmann
Faculty of Protestant Theology
Tübingen University, Federal Republic of Germany

"I have found your book an insightful, even prophetic, statement about pastoral ministry. . . . I read your book not only in the light of my pastoral experience, but of my personal experience as well. . . . Your book is an open door and invitation to such companionship."

Arie R. Brouwer
General Secretary
National Council of the Churches of Christ

"Here, too, Erika Schuchardt has broken new ground. She not only faces the socio-ethical challenge to give people support, but in all she does, she is living evidence of harmony between theory and practice."

Prof. Dr. Sporken
Chair of Medical Ethics
Maastricht University, Netherlands

"Rarely have I felt so grateful to an author, so well understood. . . . I was surprised to see my life and the development undergone by many parents described in this way."

Waltraud Ruprecht
mother of an autistic child
Oberhausen, Federal Republic of Germany

"For theology and education, for pastors, professional care-givers, adult education teachers, and religion teachers, Erika Schuchardt's book is a challenge. The suffering, and all of us, will find it a personal help, a piece of work to be grateful for."

Prof. Dr. Karl E. Nipkow
Faculty of Protestant Theology and
    Institute of Educati~
Tübingen University,

Erika Schuchardt

WHY IS THIS
HAPPENING TO ME?

Dedicated
since the second German edition
to my sister,
Annelie Stegemann, née Schuchardt,
March 12, 1944—August 14, 1983,
who died after a tragic accident,
and to her children, Thorsten, Tanja, Christian,
and her husband, Ulrich.
Philippians 4:4

Why Is This Happening to Me?

Guidance and Hope for Those Who Suffer

Erika Schuchardt

Translated by
Karen Leube

*Including alphabetical and classified (annotated) bibliographies
of more than 500 life stories from 1900 to 1989*

Awarded the German Protestant Literature Prize

Augsburg • Minneapolis

WHY IS THIS HAPPENING TO ME?
Guidance and Hope for Those Who Suffer

First North American edition published 1989 by Augsburg, Minneapolis. English translation copyright © 1989 Augsburg Fortress.

Translated from the fourth German edition, published 1987 under the title *Warum gerade ich. . . ? :Leiden und Glaube*. Copyright © 1981 Burckhardthaus-Laetare Verlag GmbH, Offenbach.

Scripture quotations unless otherwise noted are from the Revised Standard Version of the Bible, copyright 1946, 1952, and 1971 by the Division of Christian Education of the National Council of Churches.

Library of Congress Cataloging-in-Publication Data

Schuchardt, Erika.
    [Warum gerade ich— ? English]
    Why is this happening to me? / Erika Schuchardt ; translated by
Karen Leube.
      p.   cm.
    Translation of: Warum gerade ich— ? 4th German ed. 1987, c1981.
    Includes bibliographies.
    ISBN 0-8066-2309-8
    1. Suffering—Religious aspects—Christianity.   2. Empathy—
Religious aspects—Christianity. I. Title.
BT732.7.S3713   1989
248.8'6—dc20
                                        89-6562
                                        CIP

The paper used in this publication meets the minimum requirements of American National Standard for Information Sciences—Permanence of Paper for Printed Library Materials, ANSI Z329.48-1984. ∞™

Manufactured in the U.S.A.   AF 10-7160

93   92   91   90   89   1   2   3   4   5   6   7   8   9   10

Contents

Foreword by Alvin N. Rogness 9

Preface by General Secretary Gunnar Staalsett, Lutheran 11
World Federation, and Emilio Castro, World Council of Churches

Part One: A Study of over 500 Life Stories

1   The Experience of Suffering 15

2   Coping with Crisis as a Learning Process 24

3   Pearl S. Buck: The Child Who Never Grew 43
    A Case Study in Crisis Management

Part Two: Voices of the Suffering

4   Luise Habel: Lord, Tear Down the Staircases! 52
    Physically Disabled

5   Ingrid Weber-Gast: You Did Not Fear My Fear 62
    Emotionally Disturbed

6   Jacques Lusseyran: And There Was Light/Life Begins Today   70
    Visually Disabled

7   Ruth Müller-Garnn: Hold On to My Hand 79
    Silvia Görres: Life with a Handicapped Child
    Mentally Retarded

8   Laurel Lee: Walking through the Fire 89
    Terminally Ill

9   The Problem Created by "Helpless Helpers" 97

Part Three: Theological Background

10 A New Theology of Suffering 113
    Reflections on Suffering and the Ability to Endure Affliction

11 Summary: Not Knowing the Answer, but Finding One's Own
    Way 139

Bibliography of over 500 Life Stories

Notes 146

References 152

Alphabetical Bibliography 158

Classified Bibliography 174

Foreword

How do we as human beings, and especially as Christians in congregations, relate to one another in the crisis situations of life? This is a question that presses for insight, if not for answers.

More than any I have ever read, this book probes into suffering, fear, loneliness, rejection. Few books haunt me; this one does.

In this study, Erika Schuchardt, by the use of stories, lets suffering people speak for themselves. Silvia and Albert Görres and Ruth Müller-Garnn speak as parents of mentally retarded children, as does Pearl Buck. Laurel Lee speaks as a woman suffering from cancer. Representing the physically disabled is Luise Habel, whose mother committed suicide. Ingrid Weber-Gast speaks for the emotionally disturbed, Jacques Lusseyran for the blind.

Normally I am not intrigued by the use of stages and steps in dealing with crises or disabilities, but this author does it admirably in what she calls "crisis management as a learning process in eight spiral phases."

Her insights led me to self-examination, and to an awareness of where I have fallen short. I found myself drawn into the pathos of these people who bared their hearts in their call for understanding.

It is apparent that many of us are of little help in these instances of life's shocks. Failing to understand, and fearful of blundering, we withdraw, and deny the very relationships which should be God's gifts to us in these hours. Or, using shallow phrases, we only reveal how far we are from the one who suffers. And we are blind to the more profound fact that all of us in one way or another are the disabled. So, we isolate ourselves from one another.

The book reflects a sound and sensitive use of the theology of the church. God is seen, in Christ, as a suffering God, our companion who in his love is a constant presence against loneliness, and who gives courage and hope.

I was often tempted to lift out one striking phrase or paragraph, but there are too many gems to make a selection. I leave the reader to the joy of finding them.

The book should be in every pastor's library. It could well be a book for continuous study in a congregation. If it were, our congregations would have the wisdom and warmth of a newfound ministry.

ALVIN N. ROGNESS

Preface

Too often in the 20th century have the churches been required to say, "Late we come—but we come!" This has been true, paradoxically, in respect to the struggles of many people for justice and fundamental human rights. Sadly, too, it is true of the movement to condemn and compensate for the countless violations of the rights and dignity of so many disabled persons, who are still excluded from full participation in society. Yet there are now clear signs that the church is expanding and deepening its ministry to the disabled, often the persons least accepted by society.

At its Sixth Assembly, held in Vancouver in 1983, the World Council of Churches introduced concrete recommendations concerning ministry to persons with disabilities:

> We are all created in the image of God; all of us, including persons with disabilities, are living stones of the house which God is building, which is the church. Persons with disabilities cannot be isolated; they are part of the house (oikos), and essential for the wholeness of the life and worth of the church.

And the Lutheran World Federation, at its Seventh Assembly held in Budapest in 1984, stated the challenge like this:

> If the ministry of Christ is to be one that allows the transforming power of grace to bring hope out of despair, new humanity out of inhumanity, it must be carried out in those places where human dignity and rights are most consistently violated, the community of disabled people.

11

But as with all important declarations, such statements need to be amplified by concrete insight and guidance. This we feel is done in a remarkably helpful way by Prof. Dr. Erika Schuchardt in her book, now appearing in English, *Why Is This Happening to Me?: Guidance and Hope for Those Who Suffer.* Using vivid personal accounts written by people undergoing crisis—a kind of "narrative theology"—and bringing to bear penetrating insight into the religious, psychological and educational dimensions, the author illuminates how persons suffering crises, illnesses or disabilities can, with dignity and integrity, become part of a free and truly human community. What is required is not simply a ministry "to and for" suffering persons, but rather a ministry "of, by and with" them. This book contains clearcut guidelines for the liberation of innumerable people with disabilities, individuals who are in reality often the outcasts of our world. We will also find there new forward-looking and hope-giving insights on suffering itself, that manifold and deep-seated reality.

The cry of this book is loud and clear. The churches—and the ecumenical movement—must come.

GUNNAR STAALSETT
General Secretary
Lutheran World Federation

EMILIO CASTRO
General Secretary
World Council of Churches

Geneva, Switzerland, May 1987

Part One:
A Study of over 500
Life Stories

*"Listen carefully to my words,
and let this be your consolation."*
Job 21:2

1

The Experience of Suffering

Those who frequently have the opportunity to speak with suffering persons and their families, or perhaps live with them, quickly sense that above all these people want to be understood and to be part of a community. Often they direct these unfulfilled expectations at other Christians. They tend to think, "After all, the church is there to help us!" This thinking is not unfounded, since various church bodies and church agencies have given attention to this need and have begun to establish programs of service.

Several times the church has said that "the well-being of the sufferer is a major concern":

● At its Nairobi Assembly in 1975 the World Council of Churches adopted a statement on "The Unity of the Church—the Unity of Humankind: Disabled people and the Wholeness of the Family of God";[1] the European churches followed with a statement in 1978.

● In 1979 the World Council of Churches took up the challenge of the United Nations Year of the Disabled and began its work with a special desk for these questions, staffed by a disabled expert. Critical questions were posed on the way the church sees itself.

● In 1983 the Vancouver Assembly of the World Council of Churches decided that "persons with disabilities were to be included in the decision-making process of the church on all levels."[2]

● In 1984 the Assembly of the Lutheran World Federation took up the call for participation. But the gap between decisions on paper and lived reality still exists in everyday life. At the Lutheran World

Federation's Assembly in Budapest, I was the spokesperson for the working group "participation of people with disabling conditions," and my report turned out to be a provocation for the 12,000 people listening. I began: "Has the working group for the 'disabled' been a 'disabled group' itself? . . . Out of 315 delegates only three registered for the working group on disabled persons; the others were advisors, and these three delegates were themselves directly or indirectly affected by the problem. . . ."[3]

This brings us right to the heart of our study:

● What impression does the church make on people with disabilities and afflictions?

● What kinds of experiences have they had with support and care in relation to fellowship and Christian faith?

As lay Christians or as ordinary people, they primarily encounter the church at their own local level. Their neighbors may be church members or they may be visited by trained parish workers, community nurses, pastors or their lay assistants.

Three trends became evident in the answers given:

First experience

We see ourselves as objects of good works and only rarely as active members of the congregation. "The church works *for* us, but seldom *with* us!"

Second experience

We are preached at, and told to see our affliction or crisis as a kind of privilege that can lead to great benefit. However, the consolation we are supposed to be given is seldom the result of examining the crisis objectively, neither does it encourage an open dialog, one in which we can express ourselves freely. "The church tells us to be consoled by the thought of the next world and requires the transfiguration of this world, but it prevents and passes over our anguished laments and cries."

Third experience

We experience congregations and pastors—all those who try to give pastoral care—as people who have been assigned official roles within the church. We rarely get to know them as human beings who have been touched themselves and who are prepared to suffer with us. "The church hears us, but it is no longer able to listen to our actual questions. We are left to find our own way in coping with our crises."

People with problems or disabilities have not just talked about themselves but have also put pen to paper. In the following paragraphs, some examples are provided from my analysis of over 500 stories.

On the first experience

"We see ourselves as objects of good works and only rarely as active members of the congregation."
Luise Habel,[4] who is physically handicapped, wrote:

> It is a cold, rainy October day. The telephone rings. It is my parish pastor, whom I barely know. He says, "Next Wednesday two boys will be coming to see you. They'll take you for a ride through the city in your wheelchair." Period. He doesn't bother to ask whether I feel like going out with them, or if it is a convenient time for me. Nothing.

Her attempts to say no to the proposed plans, by mentioning her upcoming trip to the hospital or the cold October weather, were brushed off with rather strange reasoning:

> But the pastor is so filled with his mission that he explains to me at length that his confirmands must become familiar with the idea of Christian service, and it would really be good if they could take me for a ride through town.

Luise requested that the pastor send two girls instead, who could be of real help with her housework. Then this service project would be of some use to her and not just make her an "object of good works." Furthermore, she suggested that he send the boys to help some people who had heart problems with their yardwork. However, these suggestions fell on deaf ears as the pastor told her that all he wanted was to present a versatile type of service concept within the church:

> You know, the main thing here is for us to show the congregation how multifaceted our practical assistance has been.

This woman ended up suffering from this "good intention," and she felt how threatening an institution could be. Luise entitled the chapter, "Objects of Charity." It is depressing that we often unwittingly contribute to the self-aggrandizement of this type of service setup. The author pointed out that this particular case was not unique and that such offers can become a sort of "permanent prescription" for "care":

A year later, his successor, whom I had never met, gave me a call. He wanted to send two boys to tape an interview with me. I told him that it wouldn't be a particularly fruitful discussion, since as a person in a wheelchair I don't see much of the Christian congregation in my parish. I told him I would prefer him to visit me before the conversation with the children took place. But he told me that I should go right ahead and criticize the congregation.

Predictably, the task of conducting a formal interview was too much for the two confirmands. In addition to the stress of the interview itself, they were under pressure to produce a tape. As we read further, we learn that the pastor himself took three years to find time for a visit. Luise reported:

His slick way of responding to problems made me so angry that I ended up taking the offensive. I said that the people in our congregation were left so alone—so alone that I sometimes wondered if this congregation existed at all. The pastor responded to this comment very tersely. "That problem isn't limited to the disabled. There are many lonely people in our congregation." I insisted that it came close to being a scandal that the church saw the problem but did nothing about it. At this, he merely shrugged his shoulders. Instead of addressing my concern, the pastor chose to tell me in great detail how actively he had participated in our city's historical festival. He left me with the feeling that I had failed to get through to him on any level. Based on conversations with other disabled people, I know that my experiences are in no way unique. Frequently, the disabled remain objects of one-time special projects.

In an attempt to underline her personal experiences, Luise quoted some victims of the church's work with young people. They described the church's failure as follows:

It has failed to truly accept the disabled as real people. We are just objects of pity.

They don't need disabled people and don't try hard enough to put themselves in our places.

That church social halls, ironically, were *always* in the basement.

The church has always conformed to society instead of trying to shape it.

A survey conducted by Andreas Hämer[5] came up with some "Open Questions for the Church." Here are five examples:

1. When will the disabled person be accepted and no longer be referred to patronizingly?

2. Church members say, "our disabled people" and "our home residents." What right do we have to treat the disabled as if they were children and otherwise refer to "our brothers"?

3. When will the church and its staff give up the reserved or negative attitude they have toward the disabled? This makes any kind of partnership or participation on the part of the disabled impossible. (Note: Pity is also a way of keeping one's distance!)

6. Christians call each other brothers and sisters. Yet when Christians say, "I serve the handicapped person for Jesus' sake," they render this person an object of their good deeds. How can disabled persons feel as though they are "brothers" in this case, since they are reduced to taking, never giving? Don't brothers and sisters help *each other*?

8. When will people realize that they should not work *for* disabled persons, but rather *with* them?

On the second experience

"We are preached at and told to see our affliction or crisis as a kind of privilege that can lead to great benefit." However, the consolation we are supposed to be given is seldom the result of examining the crisis objectively. Neither does it encourage an open dialog, one in which we can express ourselves freely.

> The few times that I . . . articulated my heretical thoughts, there was always some pious person who demonstrated to me that God is not powerless. I began to fear these advocates of God's law, who always knew everything so precisely. . . . I decided no longer to expect anything from God. . . . Years went by in which I didn't read the Bible at all.[6]

Heinz Zahrnt[7] reported on a pastor's visit to a woman who was suffering from cancer. This pastor told her at her bedside that she had been chosen to "be allowed to suffer":

> I recall the story told by one of my theology teachers, a truly religious man, about the visit a pastor paid to his cancer-stricken mother. When the pastor had gone, the son asked his mother how it had been and what the pastor had said. This was her account of his message: "There are three stages of suffering: To have to suffer, to be able to suffer, and to be allowed to suffer." And the elderly lady added, "The only thing I could think about while he was there was that *he* should try to bear my pain sometime."

Christa Schlett,[8] who has cerebral palsy, described the visit of a parish worker who had decided that she had to convince Christa that it was her mission in life to be sick:

> . . . but I defend myself against the general opinion that suffering automatically leads to faith. Some of the most bitter atheists I have met have been disabled people. There is nothing that can lead to inner opposition better than the message of joy brought us by an elderly deaconess labeling us as martyrs in suffering. . . . I could hardly believe it when, during a visit with me, a deaconess in our former congregation tried to talk me into believing that it was my mission in life to be sick. Sick, so that other people could see how good they have it. Let's assume that she meant something different from what she said. . . . Yet the disabled must be on the alert when some type of cult is made out of their problem, and when others assign more importance to their weakness than to the fact that they are human beings.

Denise Legrix,[9] who is also physically disabled, wrote of her own resistance:

> Now and then we talk . . . about our fate, about "the good that God wanted for us." My hair stood on end at the thought of writing about something that seemed false to me. I had to keep repeating it—I couldn't accept it!

André Miquel[10] reflected on the death of his son Pierre:

> . . . I have never been able to accept the fact that I have had to give up my son. The thing that is intolerable is that suffering of the other person, of the dying child. That is the huge obstacle. . . . Only God can give up his son. A human being is not capable of giving up his own child. I refused to do it, as did my wife. Death took him from us by force. Yet we did not agree to it. Is it possible for parents to give up their children? . . .
>
> We are not God. Abraham is an unusual figure who is often unbearable for us. We felt more at home in the book of Job. Even the gospel was a burden for us at certain times.

Ingrid Weber-Gast[11] reported on her experience with an emotional disability, depression:

> Over the course of time, my expectations of preaching have disappeared. I feel as though I have been superabundantly blessed if something is said which is able to reach down into the darkness of my illness. Yet I no longer sit around waiting for that to happen. Instead, I assume I will be disappointed as usual. Perhaps it is something like growing a thick shell to protect one from new disappointments—disappointments which are especially intolerable at times of illness.

Andreas Hämer's[12] survey, "The Physically Disableds' Open Questions for the Church," emphatically recalled two widespread ideas:

12. What does the church say about the fact that disability is still often seen or felt as punishment by God (be it against the parents or against the disabled themselves)?

13. The church must stop emphasizing the promise that life after death will be better. Instead, the church should help create a more humane life for the disabled in *this* world.

Christy Brown[13] described his struggle with the Christian belief in salvation in the next world:

I remembered Lourdes and the people I had met on the way to the Grotto, and again I tried to be like them—patient, cheerful, resigned to their suffering, knowing the reward that awaited them in the next world. But it was no use. I was too human. There was too much of the man in me and not enough of the humble servant who submits willingly to his Master's will. I wanted to see and to know more of this world before I thought about the next.

It is enlightening to hear what one interview brought to light: an employee at a rehabilitation school made clear how great the gap is between the official preaching style of an institution and how people are treated:[14]

We received an unexpected response from the teacher of a remedial class: There was a great deal of interest in religion among her students, in spite of what the director of the school had said. Nevertheless, they rejected the type of sermons given—because the director tended to avoid conflict with the residents. So this type of Christianity was downright negative.

On the third experience

"We experience congregations and pastors—professional support-givers—as people who have been assigned official roles within the church." We rarely get to know them as human beings who have been touched themselves and who are prepared to suffer with us.

Based on the experience of her own depression, Ingrid Weber-Gast[15] sought someone who would be able to share in her suffering rather than someone who, in the pastor's role, had been officially assigned the task of providing support. She looked for someone who would allow a shadow to fall on his or her own life and could learn to replace self-confident assertions with the more low-key, uncertain language of a person sharing in the search.

> Of course, I think that pastors are always coming into contact with people like that (from groups with special needs), but usually only in their role as pastors, as people who have been called to this position by the church. They do not treat them as if they were friends, or could relate to this difficult kind of life on the basis of their own experience. That would require them to let shadows fall on their own lives and would mean that they would bind their own lives to the lives of those people who have to "die down there. . . ."
>
> The method of proclaiming the gospel has to take into consideration the listeners' melancholy. It should never just radiate faithful assurance, but should always address the dark and difficult side as well.

The father of two mentally retarded children, Albert Görres,[16] posed the question, "What can a congregation do?" He dedicated an entire chapter to the topic "The Disabled Child and the Christian Congregation":

> What can an individual or a congregation do? Let's look at an example: How does a congregation act on Sunday when a family brings its disabled child along to morning worship? Will the parents be spared the curious and astounded looks they would normally receive? Can they feel they are supported by loving compassion for their situation? Will the occasional noises made by their problem child be tolerated, or must the parents feel that Sunday worship with their child is an exercise in humility which only increases their feeling that they are left alone, by God and man, with their burden.
>
> Unfortunately, one rarely hears compassionate, encouraging words from the pulpit for the often embarrassed young mothers who decide either not to attend church or that they have to take their offspring out again, if he or she is not able to behave "well" and sit still. Even more difficult is the situation of parents with a disabled child who always attracts attention, and who has trouble learning the rules of proper church behavior. Sometimes these parents are told that they would be better off staying at home with the child.

Edith Meisinger[17] had a similar experience when she attended a worship service:

> I understand completely. It is not easy for a healthy person to bear the sight of a paralyzed person. And yet I would like to tackle Christians on this point. . . .

Theoretically, we Christians know all this—that Christ had standards that are completely different. But what are things really like? It went without saying that I went to church with my attendant. We sat down in the third pew from the back. Then a friendly woman came to us and spoke to my attendant in what was supposed to be a whisper: "Would you be kind enough to sit in the back pew with the little one so that she doesn't distract anyone from the sermon? . . ."

The next worship was to be a communion service. On that occasion, my attendant was kindly asked to see to it that I not participate in communion.

Analyzing these stories, it is hardly possible to balance the negative tendencies in the writers' answers with examples of hope. These results, however, may bring about change. On the basis of over 500 stories, the following observations can be made:

● There are relatively few stories referring openly to the church or pastoral care. This could suggest that the church had little significance in the lives of most of the disabled.

● The writers who do report on their experiences with the church or with pastoral care make mostly negative judgments.

● In contrast to the findings about the role of the church, the writers mentioned here, as well as others, say that their personal experience of faith was decisive and meaningful for their way to cope with crisis (see Part Two: Voices of the Suffering).

The overall result of the analysis could be summarized as follows: Despite the problems that suffering people and their families or friends have had with the church and with pastoral care, they stand by their positive experiences with religion.

2

Coping with Crisis as a Learning Process

The evaluation of the stories of suffering points to a quality of relationship that seems to be rare nowadays—the dimension of humanity. Despite the fact that the suffering persons are often given support, their helpers often lack the ability to develop meaningful relationships with them. This survey gives some insights into the different phases in which others can be of assistance in the process of coping with crisis. In order to do this, it would be good to first analyze the various motives of the writers. What prompted them to write?

Almost without exception, the writers pointed to their isolation. Their own history had to take on the role of a friend or support-giver who was near. Writing turned out to be like turning to a person whom they could trust completely on the difficult path of coping with crisis, that is, in the process of learning to live with suffering or crisis.

Most of the writers had to live through the different phases of the learning process (see pages 28-37) on their own without any support. So it is shocking, but no accident, that for two-thirds of all the writers the process came to a premature stop. They lived their lives in social isolation, while barely one-third reached the goal of social integration. These results are in keeping with the experiences with church workers described in Chapter 1. The feeling shared by all writers was that they were not accepted.

And therefore I would like to raise the question, "What can or must the church do?" However, if we consider the numerous ways[1] in which the church is actually involved—it may be that the church does too much *for* the suffering through its various service agencies—then the following question seems more appropriate: "How can the church and church members do their work better, that is, primarily *with* the individuals with problems? How can the members of the church prevent social isolation and help to ease the additional burden of *social* suffering, with the goal of integrating everyone into congregations?"

The question of which ways might lead to social integration or to social isolation was one of the subjects of a study in which I analyzed all available stories of incapacitated persons, and people close to them, written between 1900 and 1987. (See Figures 1–5.)

The result was the discovery of certain patterns, which correspond to typical trends in learning processes. These patterns may be used as starting points for coping with crisis. The target stage in the "process of learning to cope with crisis," if it took a positive course, turned out to be social integration. Using many practical examples, long-term case studies, and learning situations from adult education sessions with both affected and not yet affected persons, the study indicates the difficulty of the journey. At the same time, however, it shows how promising this kind of process of learning to cope with crisis can be.[2]

It seems helpful to imagine the long path of infinitely difficult learning that suffering persons and their contacts have to tread if they want to handle their existential crisis, at least to the extent that this path opens up new possibilities of life in accepting their situation. In examining the stories, it was fascinating to see that in order to reach social integration it seemed necessary for the stages of the learning process to be lived through and mastered no matter what led to the crisis. This crisis may start with the onset of physical, mental, or emotional handicaps, or hearing or visual disabilities, as well as by chronic illness or affliction brought on by terminal illness. It is important to note that people who have not yet been affected by disability or crisis live through the same learning process as the others when they experience major crises, such as unemployment, loss of their partner, or fear of death.

In order to illustrate the learning process associated with living through a crisis, it may be helpful to imagine what it would be like if we ourselves were confronted with the diagnosis: "Cancer!" Sooner or later, We would naturally ask ourselves, "Why me?" Yet we seldom or never allow the opposite question, "Why not me?" While Elisabeth

Fig. I: Year of Publication* and Number of Life Stories

These figures include biographies, autobiographies, and books that are a combination of the two, since parents and/or partners who write biographies often write about themselves as well.

*Based on the first German edition

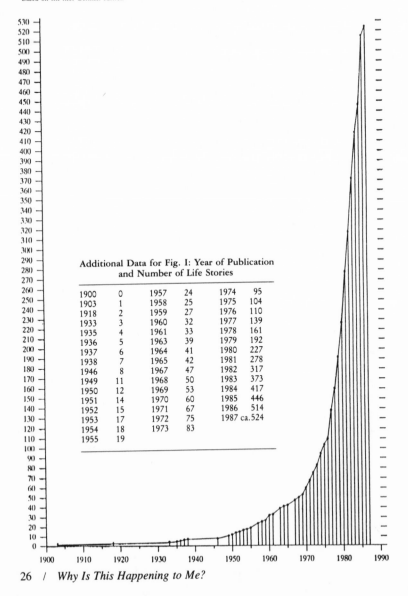

Additional Data for Fig. I: Year of Publication and Number of Life Stories

1900	0	1957	24	1974	95
1903	1	1958	25	1975	104
1918	2	1959	27	1976	110
1933	3	1960	32	1977	139
1935	4	1961	33	1978	161
1936	5	1963	39	1979	192
1937	6	1964	41	1980	227
1938	7	1965	42	1981	278
1946	8	1967	47	1982	317
1949	11	1968	50	1983	373
1950	12	1969	53	1984	417
1951	14	1970	60	1985	446
1952	15	1971	67	1986	514
1953	17	1972	75	1987	ca.524
1954	18	1973	83		
1955	19				

Fig. II: Socio-Political and Educational Backgrounds of Writers

| | European Countries | | | | | | | | | | | Countries outside Europe | | | | | | |
	Federal Rep. of Germany	Denmark	German Dem. Republic	France	Great Britain	Italy	Netherlands	Norway	Austria	Sweden	Switzerland	Israel	Japan	Colombia	Mexico	Soviet Union	USA	Total
German	281		26						8		9							324
German Translations		1		39	45	2	4	4		4	1	2	1	1	1	6	89	200
Total																		524

Fig. III: Writers and Their Disabilities* and / or Disruption in Their Lives

| | Types of Disabilities | | | | | | Long-term Illnesses | | | | |
	Mental Retardation	Physical Disability	Learning Disability	Psycholog. Dis./ Emotional Disorder	Sensory Dis. Blind a. Deaf	Speech Dis.	Cancer	Multiple Sclerosis	Addiction	Others	Total
Persons Affected	–	60	–	38	39	7	43	7	50	38	282
Parents	35	7	–	12	3	1	10	–	4	10	82
Partners	–	–	–	5	1	–	12	–	1	8	27
Professionals	11	11	1	38	16	3	12	2	5	34	133
Total	46	78	1	93	59	11	76	9	59	90	524

* Types of Disabilities according to the Classification ot the German Council of Education, Bonn 1973.

Fig. IV: Status of Writers

Persons Affected	Women 154	Men 123	Together 5	Total 282
Parents	Mothers 54	Fathers 21	Together 7	Total 82
Partners	Female 12	Male 7	Together 8	Total 27
Professionals	Women 46	Men 62	Together 9	Total 117
Persons Affected together with Professionals	Women 6	Men 4	Together 6	Total 16
Total	272	217	35	524

Coping with Crisis as a Learning Process / 27

Kübler-Ross asks, "How can one learn to die?" we seek to answer the question, "How can I learn to live under conditions that seem to make life no longer worth living?"[3] If we dare to really face up to this question, we end up anticipating the phases of the process of learning to cope with crisis. We need to go through with them as a spiral in order to undergo the dynamics of the struggle to find our identity. This process often lasts a lifetime. In my study, I have used the term "spiral phases." In this struggle, sufferers live through three stages involving the total experience of head, heart and hand: the *initial* stage, cognitive and externally directed; the *transit* stage, emotional and non-directed; and the *target* stage, one of considered action ("I'll handle it"). These three stages can be seen in terms of eight spiral phases.[4] I attempt to describe this journey below.

Spiral Phase 1: Uncertainty

At the beginning of a crisis, shock overwhelms a person. The trigger of the crisis—an accident, a piece of news, or an event—strikes like lightning, destroying a life that has been structured according to norms and oriented toward them. Completely unprepared, one is confronted with a life situation that deviates completely from the norm. The crisis has been triggered and affected persons are panic-stricken, afraid of the unknown. They automatically fall back on patterns of reacting which they developed earlier in life. They resist, build up fortresses of defense, set rational rituals in motion, and do everything in their power, omitting nothing, to repress the cause of the crisis. For them, this cannot exist because they will not allow it to exist. They cannot bear it yet and fight for time by continuously producing defense mechanisms.

"Implicit denial" becomes the chief characteristic of all people who are in this state of suspense as they circle around the crisis. Elisabeth Kübler-Ross calls this state of *uncertainty* "denial and isolation." However, this act of "denying" the crisis is a conscious process, while the term *uncertainty* refers to the fact that this phase is more a semiconscious state or the inability to recognize what is going on, including the tendency to deny the crisis. On the level of verbal expression, the question that corresponds to this state is *"What is really going on?"* To one trained in psychoanalysis, it becomes clear that hidden behind the word *really* are thoughts the person is not yet acknowledging and that the recognition of the crisis is already being latently prepared.

It will help support-givers if Spiral Phase 1 is divided into three typical intermediate phases. They alternate with each other, can be present simultaneously, and last for various periods of time.

Intermediate Phase 1.1: Ignorance

"What is this supposed to mean?" With this question, any doubt that arises is played down, since one should not always assume the worst. This phase of not yet knowing creates the emotional space of *ignorance* (1.1) and is the transition to the *uncertainty* phase (1). Yet this ignorance must inevitably give way. In view of the ever-increasing signals and the changed reactions from the world around, these clues crystallize into worrisome facts which burden the individual.

Intermediate Phase 1.2: Insecurity

"Does it really have any significance?" With this question, ignorance gives way to *insecurity* (1.2). There are two basic characteristics of this phase: 1) doubts that arise are no longer denied; 2) the individual's unstable emotional condition prevents the person from recognizing the reality of the situation. It requires a lot of time to learn to accept what has happened. Insecurity means that a higher degree of sensitivity is at work, and it seems that everything is being registered seismographically. The question of what is certain and true is posed much too directly and is thus overstated. Comparisons are made and attempts at explanation are considered. These steps have one, and only one, purpose: to deny the *insecurity* (1.2) by saying, "No, it doesn't have any significance for me!"

In this intermediate phase, often one or more other persons are already aware of the potential crisis: for example, the doctor, the neighbor, or fellow patients. They may know more than the person concerned. This creates a strained atmosphere. The possessors of information about the situation bear responsibility and, in the way they act, set the course for future relationships of trust or distrust. It is clear that the knowledge other people have of the situation always begins to play a role in their relationships with the unwitting victim of the crisis. In turn, this knowledge distinctly influences the recognition process by the individual. Also, contrary to what one would expect, this growing insecurity typically does not increase the person's ability to accept the truth. Instead, in view of the threat that is experienced, massive defense intensifies and foreshadows the next intermediate phase (1.3).

Intermediate Phase 1.3: Inability to accept the facts

The question, "Couldn't this just be a mistake?" denotes the inability to accept the loss of certain possibilities for living. This intermediate phase is called the *inability to accept the facts* (1.3). At this point, active attempts to fend off the impending certainty begin to accumulate. A further sign of this phase is selective perception. The individual sees only that which nourishes the calming state of *ignorance* (1.1). In other words, they overlook anything that could reinforce their doubts. Over and over, the attempt is made to forcibly convince oneself and others that by relapsing into the phase of *ignorance* (1.1), everything is actually all right.

Again, the knowledge that others have of the situation accompanies the ups and downs and increasingly becomes a part of the unquenchable thirst for reassurance: "You think so too, don't you?" or acceptance with an escape clause, "Well, that's true, but . . ." This intermediate phase is the final attempt to find emergency exits that will help one escape the absolute truth. The final point of the first spiral phase, uncertainty, at the end of these three intermediate phases, is the unspoken desire for a redeeming *certainty* that will put a stop to the unbearable strain.

Where support is lacking in this process, the length of time it takes to discover the truth is drawn out beyond normal proportions. At first this discovery does not take place at all. It finally needs to occur so that it communicates the truth in various doses, a process that brings to the surface what has already been latently recognized. Yet it is clear that this early phase of introducing or recognizing the facts influences the entire process of coping with the crisis. When appropriate support is given, the course is set for moving through each phase. This support can help to prevent the individual from breaking off the process altogether, which tends to bring about social isolation. Companionship at this stage instead can be a means of learning to develop meaningful relationships.

Spiral Phase 2: Certainty

The *certainty* that some possibilities for living no longer exist, already implied in the phase of *uncertainty* (1), now logically follows as Phase

2. This phase is emotionally articulated in the exclamation, *"Yes, but it can't be true!"* This statement sounds like a negative affirmative and looks like the continuation of denial, which, in fact, it is!

Even individuals who have recognized their crises are forced to deny them now and then in order to continue living at all. In this case, they are prepared to accept the undivided truth. Yet emotionally and in actuality, they continue to hope against hope that the signs they have seen so far will turn out to be wrong. This ambivalence between the rational "yes" and the emotional "no" is the characteristic of the phase called *certainty* (2). The ambivalence in the statement "Yes, but" is used whenever a buffer is needed between the individuals and their terror of the diagnosis. It gives them space in which they can get hold of themselves and begin anew in order to continue on their journey.

Nevertheless, in view of the irrefutable certainty, each conversation about the actual situation can provide clarifying relief, because it builds up a connection between rational recognition and the emotional state one is in. The crucial factor here is the willingness of the individuals themselves. *They* must give the signal that they are willing to speak openly. This is the only way they can discover the truth themselves. The truth can be accepted when someone else helps them—in measured doses—to get to the point of wanting to "talk about it."

The search for truth is not really the search for correct information, or for theories, nor is it a one-time act of transmitting news. It is much more complex and manifests itself as a problem of communication between the transmitter and the receiver. It is thus a question of the medium and a question of how close the relationship is between the person who is suffering and the one who is not (doctor, professional, support-giver).

In this way, true statements, "You have cancer," "You have a child with Down's Syndrome," "You may be paralyzed from the waist down," are not isolated in a vacuum. Hence, a statement like that occurs in a specific situation in the context of a relationship between human beings. However, the following question remains open: "Is the truth accepted only rationally with defense mechanisms suppressing one's emotions, or is the afflicted person already emotionally capable of bearing the truth?" How do both the suffering person and the support-giver together face the fate that has been inflicted on them? This is not least a question of how durable the support-givers are or how competent they are in communicating and providing therapy. It is a question of the inner stability of their ego identity in borderline situations. The suffering have the right to the whole truth if they are capable of immediately facing it and dealing with it.

Spiral Phase 3: Aggression

Following the "rational" and externally directed phases of *uncertainty* (1) and the still ambivalent phase of *certainty* (2) come the "emotional" and "nondirected" phases of strong emotional outburst.

It is not until this point that rational recognition starts seeping down into awareness as something experienced by the heart. "It's just beginning to hit home!" Hurt and stunned, the stricken person cries, *"Why me?"* The agony of this realization is overwhelmed by such strong rushes of emotion that people think they will either suffocate from them or, at best, they use the energy from these emotions to lash out at their surroundings. This volcanolike protest can most aptly be termed *aggression* (3). The tragic element of this phase is that the actual object of the aggression, that which triggered the crisis, is neither comprehensible nor assailable. As a result, these aggressions search out other objects. The target can be anything that lends itself to attack.

Thus it seems to people outside the situation that, for no reason at all, the aggression is released in all directions and against anything and everything. Wherever persons who are in this phase look, they find an opportunity to let others know how they feel. Unaware of this themselves, they look for outlets for their high emotional energy so they can go back to acting normally. At this point, another vicious circle begins.

During the phase of *uncertainty* (1), denial of the crisis is often reinforced by the well-meant attempt on the part of others who are aware of the gravity of the situation to spare the afflicted individual. If, in the *aggression* phase, the suffering individual's protests are misinterpreted and are not recognized as an emotional release when they occur in the form of personal defensiveness, there is an even greater tendency for them to lash out at others who are already involved as fellow sufferers in the situation. People who are overwhelmed by their suffering take this lack of understanding from others to mean that everything and everyone is working against them. They feel abandoned and isolated.

This phase makes particularly clear the types of risks that affected people run if they do not have appropriate support. They either suffocate from the aggression through passive or active self-destruction, or they succumb to the undertow of isolation which is fostered by the hostile reaction of others who were targets of the outbursts. On the other hand, owing to their internalized control of negative feelings, they often fall into a state of apathetic resignation. In this phase, we clearly see the significance of aggression as the introductory phase to the emotional aspect of learning to cope with crisis.

Spiral Phase 4: Negotiation

The emotional energy that was released in the aggression phase now presses for action. Almost haphazardly, every conceivable measure is considered that could pull the individual out of the powerlessness of the inescapable situation. These attempts to "abort the problem" are produced in an incessant stream. The game is played for ever higher stakes. The individual bargains and negotiates.

Depending on the person's financial situation and particular sense of values, two different courses of action can be recognized: the use of "department-store shopping for doctors" and the search for "miracle cures." Paradoxically, the two courses often run parallel, perhaps because they are nondirected. The haphazard consultation of different doctors, from foreign consultants to the most remote healers, is intended to buy the hope that it is possible to put off the final diagnosis. These attempts are made at a considerable cost, often driving a family to financial ruin. At the same time, every possible means of discovering a miraculous cure is undertaken, such as pilgrimages to Lourdes (made by two-thirds of all the writers in the study), saying mass, the laying on of hands during worship, taking vows, willing one's entire possessions to the church or to some humanitarian cause, the vow to enter a monastery, or the promise that they will turn their lives around completely. Attached to these promises, of course, is the condition, *"But if . . . , then . . . !"*

This undirected emotional spiral phase can be seen as a final attempt to fight back against the crisis and has been designated *negotiation* (4). In this phase, we can also recognize how dangerous it can be for those who are suffering to have to go it alone. The result can be material and spiritual bankruptcy. By the same token, it is obvious how many disappointments can be diminished if the people suffering in this phase can understand their own reactions and learn to deal with them.

Spiral Phase 5: Depression

Sooner or later most people fail in their attempts to find a doctor who has a secret remedy, or to be granted a miracle. Persons suffering from terminal cancer are no longer able to avoid the knowledge that they will die. Accident victims whose limbs have been paralyzed can no longer deny the numbness of their legs. The mother of a mongoloid child can no longer ignore the child's behavior and facial expression.

The externally directed emotions are spent. They are replaced by internally directed emotions that bury the individual's hope, leading to silence. The failure of suffering individuals to find solutions in the previous phases is often experienced in this phase as total failure. They sink into the abyss of despair or resignation as they ask themselves, *"What for? It's all pointless."* They are in a state of depression. Yet sadness and tears are still part of language and are signs that those who are suffering are continuing to experience what is going on and that they feel injured. The tears are a sign of passive resistance within the feelings of terrible loss. What is gone is now registered not only rationally, but emotionally. There is a conscious effort to leave behind the memories of what could have been. Yet the individual recognizes what remains and what can be done with it. The mourning of what is lost has so many faces. On one hand, there is the grieving over what has now gone for good: the knowledge that one can no longer walk; the healthy child that one continues to yearn for; and fear of the threatening consequences of loss (in other words: what we call "retrospective grieving"). On the other hand, there is grieving over vocational and social goals that can no longer be reached; the feeling that one's value as a partner, as husband or wife, is diminishing; friends who fade from sight; and the feeling that one's goal in life has been completely destroyed (in other words: "anticipatory grieving"). Both kinds of depression— retrospective and anticipatory grieving—are indications that the individual is letting go of unrealistic hopes and that he or she is bidding a final farewell to utopia.

The act of giving up and the threatening fear of being given up pave the way for the ultimate relinquishment of all attempts to deny the irretrievable losses. This is accompanied by a boundless sadness, the process of dealing with grief. This process serves to prepare sufferers to accept their fate and includes the steps of turning around, turning inward, and encountering one's self. Out of this process of finding one's self grows the freedom to distance one's self from the experience of suffering and to personally decide what steps must be taken next to cope with the crisis.

Spiral Phase 6: Acceptance

Characteristic of the spiral's coils is the conscious feeling of reaching one's limits. Enduring the crisis—suffering through the phases of battling against everything that exists in both the rational and emotional spheres—has by this time exhausted all capacity for resistance. The sufferers feel empty and almost without willpower. Yet they feel as if they have been liberated and are standing on the brink. They have let their minds wander in every direction in order to think of every possibility for coping with the crisis. They have fully suffered loss in both the present and the future by retrospective and anticipatory grieving. Now that they have reached the end, spent, it is as though they have been relieved of their burden. They are ready to open up to new insights. In being open, totally at one with themselves and at the same time being totally rid of themselves, a new feeling begins to grow.

It becomes evident to sufferers that they are still there. They are moved by the fact that they are not alone and that they are still able to use their senses. These individuals become ashamed that they had forgotten their thoughts and feelings, as well as their total humanness. An abundance of perceptions and experiences pours over them, which boils down to recognition. *"Now I begin to realize. . . I am, I can, I want to, I accept myself the way I am. Now I am living with my individuality."* This phase is referred to as *acceptance* (6).

I'll accept myself with my limiting conditions, my paralyzed legs! I'll accept myself as the mother of a mongoloid child! I'll no longer live *against* the crisis, but *with* it. I am a human being just like everyone else. Each of us has to learn to live with his or her crises and limitations and each of us is alive! I want to live my life and learn how to!

Acceptance, however, does not mean resignation, nor is it yet a state of pacification. *Acceptance* is not approving affirmation. No one can willingly affirm hard knocks. However, one can learn to accept the inevitable when coping with crisis. Thus, *acceptance* is stepping over the border of one's awareness, which unexpectedly, is beginning to extend itself. With this step, the individual has become capable of accepting.

Spiral Phase 7: Activity

The personal decision to live *with* one's limiting conditions releases energy which up to this point has been used in the fight *against* them. All this energy wants to burst out. *"I'll handle it!"* is the spontaneous expression for this turning point. The first steps of Phase 7, *activity,* are actively reflected and are taken with the complete use of rational and emotional capabilities. The suffering individuals recognize that the deciding factor is not *what* they have, but what they *make* of what they have!

A kind of regrouping occurs both directly and indirectly in suffering individuals. Values and norms are recast based on experiences they have worked through. They establish these standards for themselves based on the value system that is valid for the society in which they live, and not based on a new system. The values and norms remain the same, yet they are regrouped according to the new perspective.

It is inevitable that action and thought now alter reality itself. What is significant is that suffering people primarily change themselves and that, on the basis of this learning process, they can become the impulse for "changing the system" as a result. Doing so is not their goal initially. In this case, however, change means the possibility of being different through alternative action as the result of redefining one's self within fixed limits. One dares to act independently.

Spiral Phase 8: Solidarity

When suffering people are appropriately supported in the phases described above, at some point there begins to grow the desire to act responsibly within society. The individual area of social contacts and the limiting conditions are recognized within the broader framework of the person's life. The disability begins to fade into the background, while the area of social interaction becomes part of consciousness and challenges the individual to interact with others. *Solidarity* (8) is the final step in the process of learning to cope with crisis.

"We're handling it together; we're taking the initiative." This is the expression of successful crisis management and the indication that appropriate social integration has been achieved. There can no longer be any doubt that this final spiral phase is reached by only a small number of disabled people and only rarely by people without disabilities.

If one compares the way disabled and incurably ill people cope to the struggle undergone by others who are in the grip of crisis, a common feature becomes evident: in the end, there is no salvation in the sense of being relieved of the weight of the problem. The only possible solution involves no longer trying to fight *against* what seems unacceptable, but living *with* it. This is a new task, requiring the individual to cope with the problem both on a personal level and in solidarity with others.

With reference to situations that are discussed later in the book, it can be said that this method of "taking control" can be experienced as personal meaning, even as a form of happiness. The ability to take the upper hand by actively participating in life together now takes the form of "self realization" through daring to be different in the midst of the inappropriate norms our society sets for achievement. The act of encouraging someone to continue following this difficult path is justified by the premise that none of us is without gifts and that each person is a part of the whole. Yet the whole is more than the sum of its parts.

The Image of the Spiral

In these eight phases we can recognize that the disabled and those stricken by suffering have to struggle their way through a spiral-like set of contradictory experiences, their own reactions and the reactions of their environment until they reach the point where they feel clear about their new vision of life.

The image of the spiral illustrates both that the inner processes are not yet finished and that various turns in the course of daily life and action are superimposed on each other. The image conveys the fact that this difficult learning process is one that will continue throughout life, even if those who are suffering have succeeded in affirming that their lives are worth living despite difficult limitations. Thus, this spiral should not be simply viewed as a technical means of explaining this process, but rather as a symbol of the struggle through the imperceptible twists of the path. They are not directed toward annihilation, isolation, or the abandonment of the meaning of life. The spiral is a symbol of the "narrow gate which leads to life" (see Matt. 7:14), a path through endless uncertainties that still allows us to anticipate what we will become (see 1 John 3:2).

Why have we dealt in such detail with the way in which suffering people experience crisis? Can an awareness of the eight spiral phases in the learning process of coping with crisis ease the situation of "being disabled" or "having incurable cancer"?

The discovery of certain characteristics in the learning process of coping with crisis offers a challenge to everyone as individuals, as church members, as pastors, or as teachers to support people in crises more appropriately and with more sensitivity.

As will be shown, the people involved in crises are both those who are suffering and the people in their lives (see Chapter 9: The Problem Created by "Helpless Helpers"). An example: We visit someone who is suffering—a neighbor who has incurable cancer, someone who has been widowed, the mother of a handicapped child—and we become the target of their *aggressions* (3): "Why do you bother coming at all?" "No one visits me!" "Everyone has written me off!" Familiarity with the various spiral phases in the process of learning to cope with crisis now puts us in the position to decide whether the aggression is actually directed at us personally or whether we have become the unwitting object of random aggression as in the third spiral phase, *aggression*. Thus, along with the other person, we can look for possible ways to interpret their aggression or our own. The analysis of the over 500 stories brought to light a total of nine different reactions (guilt, suicide, flight from reality, and others). Through interpretation and reinterpretation, a chance to change the situation can evolve. From an educational perspective, support-givers can strive to "make it possible to be different" through crisis intervention and prevention. From a theological perspective, we can help sufferers encounter "the mystery of the cross and the resurrection" through the basic experience of *acceptance* (6).

One thing is clear: we cannot do away with either the crisis or the cross. In our examples, cancer, loss of a partner, and a child's disability remain lifelong problems. However, we can change the conditions and the way in which people are affected by crises or by the

Fig. V: Crisis Management as a Learning Process in Eight Spiral Phases

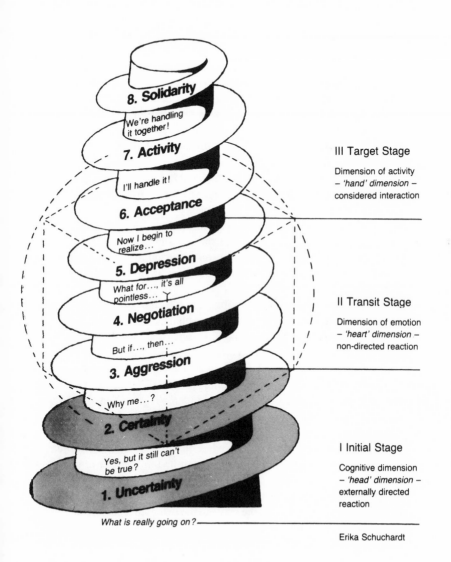

8. Solidarity

We're handling it together!

7. Activity

I'll handle it!

6. Acceptance

Now I begin to realize…

5. Depression

What for…, it's all pointless…

4. Negotiation

But if…, then…

3. Aggression

Why me…?

2. Certainty

Yes, but it still can't be true?

1. Uncertainty

What is really going on?

III Target Stage

Dimension of activity – 'hand' dimension – considered interaction

II Transit Stage

Dimension of emotion – 'heart' dimension – non-directed reaction

I Initial Stage

Cognitive dimension – 'head' dimension – externally directed reaction

Erika Schuchardt

cross, and we can change ourselves. In that way we overcome our limitations.

With mutual support, we can break through the additional handicap of social isolation, which results from disrupted or nonexistent social relations. We can do this by initiating interaction and by daring to be the ones to begin relationships, as well as by untiringly searching for contact with others. In so doing, we make human support available to those attempting to cope with crisis in the spirit of the gospel, the good news told through the church and its members. Unfortunately I cannot describe all the aspects of coping with crisis or how these findings have been worked on in adult educational courses and training sessions.[4] Instead, we shall now further develop the points made so far in the context of suffering and faith.

In analyzing the stories, I found that to achieve social integration each person had to live through the phases of the coping process regardless of the type of disability or crisis.

To illustrate this point, the following case studies have already been presented in previous books: a child's mental retardation described by Pearl Buck, a physical disability in an account by Christy Brown, a visual disability as told by Helen Keller, and an emotional disorder in the case of Clara Park.

Furthermore, it was established that the third spiral phase, *aggression* (3), has a key function as catharsis. There is a close connection between the ability to be aggressive (3) and the capacity for *acceptance* (6). Using evidence from the stories, I was able to demonstrate that the absence, interruption, or denial of the *aggression phase* can mean the termination of the learning process. Cutting off the process like this often condemns the individual to remain in lifelong depression, as in the case of Käte Keller, who suffered from an impairment of one of her senses. In the case of Christa Schlett, who was physically disabled, the disruption led to resignation, while in the case of Majorie Shave, mother of a mentally retarded child, it resulted in the refusal to accept the situation. In the case of Richard d'Ambrosio, who suffered from an emotional disorder, therapeutic intervention enabled him to release his aggression and deal with the crisis to the extent that social integration was achieved.

How do suffering people and their friends and families experience their crises if they believe in God? Expressed in another way, What role does Christian faith play in the process of learning to cope with crisis? Formulated even more precisely, Does Christian faith help?

There is no question that Christian faith is more than a conditioning factor. It defines our equation of life. Faith is a basic quantity, a constitutive element that alters both attitudes and interpretations as well as the process of coping with crisis.

Hence, the basic hypothesis that *aggression* (3), seen as catharsis, plays a key role in the coping process, can be expanded by the theory that: Christian faith can embrace *aggression* (3). It has been recognized as catharsis when the suffering accuse God and pour forth their laments to him.

This means, on the one hand, that Christian faith can enable persons to "obediently" accept their suffering and crises by unquestioningly taking them as "given" by God. This is the so-called *naive-apathetic reaction* on the part of the believer.

On the other hand, Christian faith can enable people to release their *aggression* against their suffering and crises. It enables them to bring those feelings to God in dialog with him as they develop the capacity to positively *accept* the situation (phase 6; see Heb. 5:8). This is the so-called *critical-sympathetic response* on the part of persons who believe in Christ (see Chapter 10: A New Theology of Suffering).

In the first form of the learning process, people who believe, with their *naive-apathetic reaction,* seem to "obediently," unquestioningly, unresistingly, and unconditionally accept the fact that they are handicapped or are involved in a crisis. They see their condition as a punishment or as a test imposed by God. People who believe in God, whether they are stricken with problems or not, are sure that God loves them unconditionally. This enables those in trouble to bear the seemingly unbearable burden that God has laid on them. Faith in this sense enables them to continue to live with their crisis; the *naive-apathetic reaction* can even bring about *acceptance* (6).

The writers tell us that Christian faith:
- liberates disabled or suffering people from their loneliness and leads them to dialog, leading, in turn, to community;
- provides them with a partner who can be reached day and night;
- gives them someone to talk and pray to, a patient listener;
- gives them an advisor who does not simply hand out pat answers and gives them a companion who shares in the search for answers;
- offers a message that I myself must hear, consider, and absorb;
- liberates me from myself to find myself, to turn to Thou (my neighbor), to God in prayer, worship, and in fellowship.

Christian faith can compensate for *aggression* (3) and bring about *acceptance* (6).

In the following analyses of the stories, I will now examine what effect Christian faith and human companionship have on the life stories of people stricken with different kinds of crises (disability, illness, disruption of life).

3

Pearl S. Buck: The Child Who Never Grew

A Case Study in Crisis Management

Pearl S. Buck wrote a book that can be used to illustrate the phases in the process of learning to cope with crisis. Her autobiography, *The Child Who Never Grew* (New York: The John Day Company, 1950), tells of her life as the mother of a mentally retarded child. A Nobel Prize winner, she lived through her crisis just as every other mother in a similar situation. The way she deals with her experiences is typical of all 500 stories I studied for this book. She reported that for 10 years she had no support while going through this difficult process of learning. Pearl S. Buck represents the majority of the women who reported on their experience with managing crisis. Pearl S. Buck approached the situation as an intellectual, but revealed that coping with crisis is not so much an intellectual problem as a problem of the heart. It is a question of one's willingness and ability to change one's views and to alter one's attitude and behavior in relationships with others.

> To learn how to bear the inevitable sorrow is not easily done. I can look back on it now, the lesson learned, and see the steps; but when I was taking them they were hard indeed, each apparently insurmountable [p. 27]. . . .
> But it is interesting to me and may be of some small importance to some, merely as a process, to speak of learning how to live with sorrow that cannot be removed. Let me speak of it so, then [p. 29]. . . .
> Again, I speak as one who knows [p. 62].

With her wonderful art of narration and infinite mother's love, Pearl Buck described the life of her only child, a child who never grew up. At the same time, she confessed that she had to learn something that was extremely difficult, "to live with sorrow that cannot be removed." As early as 1952, Pearl Buck saw two distinct phases of her 10-year-long "process": the first phase, in which she experienced her own destruction as she had to learn to comprehend "the inevitable knowledge that was forced upon me," and the second phase, in which she experienced "the turn . . . out of (her) self," in which she accepted her fate as "given" and recognized it as something which she had to "give in" to.

> The first phase of this process was disastrous and disorganizing. As I said, there was no more joy left in anything. All human relationships became meaningless. Everything became meaningless [p. 29]. . . .

Her analysis of the turn toward *acceptance* (6) shows how she was able to find herself again once she could live with her grief:

> I do not know when the turn came, nor why. It came somehow out of myself [phase 2]. . . . It was in those days that I learned to distinguish between the two kinds of people in the world: those who have known inescapable sorrow and those who have not [p. 30]. . . .
>   It was surprising and sad to discover how many such persons there were. . . . It did not comfort me . . . but it made me realize that others had learned to live with it, and so could I. I suppose that was the beginning of the turn [p. 31].

For Pearl Buck, the "stages of the process" began with the **transit** stage. Yet if we examine her story more closely, we can establish that it took more than three years of working through the recognition process in the **initial** stage for her to go from the feeling of *uncertainty* (1) to the feeling of *certainty* (2). Her experience corresponded to that of the majority of the 500 stories examined. Shaken, she wrote:

> I think I was the last to perceive that something was wrong. . . . She was three years old when I first began to wonder [p. 13].

She then described how sharply her discovery of the truth was hindered by the inappropriate behavior of the people around her and by lack of support. Pearl Buck portrayed the transition from the intermediate phase of *ignorance* to *insecurity* (1.2) as a restless quest for reassurance by friends.

> I remember asking friends about their children, and voicing my new anxiety about my child. Their replies were comforting, too comforting [p. 13].

Pearl Buck characterized the typical behavioral pattern of the "rule of irrelevance," "to act as if" everything was all right. She began to notice how inappropriate the words of comfort could be.

> They spoke all the empty words of assurance that friends, meaning well, will use, and I believed them. Afterward, when I knew the whole tragic truth, I asked them if they had no knowledge then of what had befallen my child.
>
> I found out that they did have, that they had guessed and surmised and that the older ones even knew, but that they shrank from telling me [pp. 13-14].

Owing solely to the habit of everyone around her to play down the difficulties of the situation, Pearl Buck was condemned to be stagnate in the transit stage of the *inability to accept* the facts (1.3) until her child was four years old:

> Thus my child was nearly four years old before I discovered for myself that her mind had stopped growing. . . . I was reluctant and unbelieving until the last [p. 14]. . . .
>
> I must have been more anxious than I knew, however, for I remember I went one day to hear an American visiting pediatrician give a lecture on the preschool child, and as I listened to her I realized that something was very wrong indeed with my child [p. 15]. . . .

At this point, she began consulting doctors, attending lectures and finally asked a group of doctors into her home. All of these attempts had the same ambiguous result:

> Something is wrong. . . . I do not know what it is. You must have a consultation of doctors! [p. 15].

With the *certainty* (2) that "something is wrong," Pearl Buck embarked on a torturous journey through every continent (spiral phase 4: *negotiation*), "shopping" in the "global department store of medical knowledge," in order to buy some hope:

> Then began that long journey which parents of such children know so well. I have talked with many of them since and it is always the same. Driven

by the conviction that there must be someone who can cure, we take our children over the surface of the whole earth, seeking the one who can heal [p. 17].

She described the end of the journey, as she suddenly recognized the inescapable truth:

> The end of the journey for my child and me came one winter's day in Rochester, Minnesota. We had been sent finally to the Mayo Clinic [p. 20]. . . .
> Now came the moment for which I shall be grateful as long as I live. . . . I have to thank a man who came quietly out of an empty room as I passed. . . . He came out almost stealthily and beckoned to me to follow him into the empty room. . . .
> He began to speak quickly in his broken English, his voice almost harsh, his eyes sternly upon mine. "Did he tell you the child might be cured?. . . Listen to what I tell you!" he commanded.
> "I tell you, madame, the child can never be normal. Do not deceive yourself. You will wear out your life and beggar your family unless you give up hope and face the truth. She will never be well—do you hear me? . . .
> "I tell you the truth for your own sake" [pp. 22-23].

This "brutal telling of the truth" led to despair; the child was now 5 years old and the opportunity for her mother to discover the truth "in small doses" had been ruined by the people around her. Pearl expressed it through *aggression* (3), manifested in a death wish against her child:

> Death would be far easier to bear, for death is final. What was is no more. How often did I cry out in my heart that it would be better if my child died! If that shocks you who have not known, it will not shock those who do know. I would have welcomed death for my child and would still welcome it, for then she would be finally safe [p. 27]. . . .

She openly added:

> For the sake of others who are walking that stony road, I will say that my inner rebellion lasted for many years. . . . But common sense and duty cannot always prevail when the heart is broken [p. 28-29].

Pearl Buck reflected that the *depression* phase (5) was the first stage of her "process." Yet one should note that she herself described her experience as consisting of two types of depression—anticipatory and retrospective grieving. *Anticipatory depression or grieving* was the fear of the uncertain future of the child whose fate it would be to be given up on by others in the future. *Retrospective depression or grieving* was described as the process of mourning the glamorous life which had already been given up and the sorrow caused by her isolation:

> I found myself with two problems, both, it seemed to me, intolerable.
> [The first was the question of her future (p. 24).] In addition . . . there is the problem of one's own self in misery. All the brightness of life is gone, all the pride in parenthood. There is more than pride gone, there is an actual sense of one's life being cut off in the child. The stream of generations is stopped [p. 27]. . . .

The "turn" toward *acceptance* (6) as the beginning of the *target* stage, which for Pearl Buck could not be rationally explained, has already been presented as a second phase in her learning process. At the same time, she described how intensively and repeatedly she experienced the phases of the spiral model:

> The first step was acceptance of what was. . . .
> But practically this step had to be taken many times. I slipped into the morass over and over again. . .
> The sight of a neighbor's normal little daughter [p. 31]. . . .

Similarly, Pearl Buck describes the phase of *acceptance* (6):

> This is my life. . . . [I began to realize] there were other things I could enjoy—books, I remember, were first. Flowers, I think, came next. . . .
> It all began, I remember, in a sort of wonder that such things went on as they had before, and then a realization that what had happened to me had actually changed nothing except myself [p. 32].

Phase 7, *activity*, ("I'll handle it . . . !"), on the one hand took the form of her search for room in a home for her daughter to ensure that she would be cared for in the future. On the other hand, Pearl Buck's activity phase manifested itself in her intensive work of lecturing and giving information to parents, as well as of setting up and financing research. She wrote:

> Knowing what I was going to do and thinking how to do it did not heal the inescapable sorrow, but it helped me to live with it [pp. 35-36]. . . .

She demonstrated her achievement of phase 8, *solidarity* (8) "We're handling it together!" in the writing and publishing of her autobiography, which can be distinguished from many other autobiographies by its frankness. On the basis of this openness, the author built a relationship with her readers.

It will not be easy to tell it all truthfully, but it is of no use to tell it otherwise [p. 9].

Thus, Pearl Buck entered into solidarity with all such suffering people and accompanied them on their journey from a death wish to an affirming "yes!" to decision making in a common, neverending learning process. She concluded:

There must be acceptance and the knowledge that sorrow fully accepted brings its own gifts. For there is an alchemy in sorrow. It can be transmuted into wisdom, which, if it does not bring joy, can yet bring happiness [p. 5].

Pearl Buck experienced her crisis as an opportunity to learn. We recognize that we are dependent on one another if we see life as something more than plain survival. The interaction model for coping with crisis as an open learning process can make a contribution to this area.

The results of the analysis of all the stories (over 500) can be summarized as follows:

1. Writers with various types of afflictions (disability, illnesses, disruptions of life) described similar developments in the process of learning to cope with crisis.

This means that this process of learning to cope with crisis is similar for people with mental, physical, emotional and other disabilities as well as for people with cancer, multiple sclerosis, drug addiction and long-term illnesses. The process can thus be diagnosed accordingly and any intervention will depend on the individual situation of the person concerned.

2. Within the process of learning to cope with crisis, aggression as catharsis plays a key role.

This means that if *aggression* is lacking in the learning process, tendencies toward *nonacceptance* and *social isolation* are shown. If, on the other hand, one undergoes the *aggression* phase, tendencies toward *acceptance* and *social integration* are reinforced. Accordingly, the missing phase of aggression has to be released through crisis intervention in order to enable the learning process to continue toward social integration. (On points 1 and 2, refer to the case studies presented in my studies: Schuchardt, Erika: "Biographische Erfahrung und wissenschaftliche Theorie" [Biographical Experience and Scientific Theory]. *Soziale Integration Behinderter,* Band 1 [The Social Integration of the Disabled, Vol. 1], Heilbrunn 3rd printing 1987. Schuchardt, Erika: "Weiterbildung als Krisenverarbeitung" [Continuing Education as Crisis Management] *Soziale Integration Behinderter,* Band 2 [The Social Integration of the Disabled, Vol. 2] Bad Heilbrunn, 3rd printing, 1987.)

3. Religious faith as a means of determining values can replace or compensate for aggression.

This means that faith as a passive attitude can lead to an *apathetic reaction* to the crisis. On the other hand, Christian faith as a critical answer can become the *sympathetic response* to the crisis. Both of them are an appropriate means of learning to deal with crisis and can eventually lead to social integration.

4. Support and human companionship appear as a conditional factor in the process of learning to cope with crisis.

This means that when support in the midst of the crisis was nonexistent or inappropriate, the process of dealing with the crisis is abandoned, interrupted, or not undertaken at all. This inevitably brings about a tendency toward social isolation. In contrast, through appropriate support to intervene and prevent this isolation, the learning process can be directed toward social integration.

Part Two:
Voices of
the Suffering

4

Luise Habel: Lord, Tear Down the Staircases!

Physically Disabled

Data: Luise Habel[1] was afflicted by polio as an infant of 15 months. (The German title of her book is *Herrgott, schaff die Treppen ab!*, 1978.) From then on she was physically disabled and dependent on a wheelchair. She experienced the threat of Hitler's National Socialism both as a member of the Protestant Youth Group and through the unemployment of her father, who lost his job as a cabinetmaker for political reasons. This forced her mother to support the family by selling vegetables from their garden. In spite of this, the parents bought their daughter every piece of equipment she required to be able to stand and walk. In addition, they insisted that she attend an academic high school and that she take the examination for a vocational qualification. On top of this, they took two orphans into the family. This psychosocial overload caused the mother to commit suicide.

The background of Luise Habel's family social situation motivated her to pose this vital question:

Filled with rage and bitterness . . . I have thought, "What can God do when his people refuse to serve him?"
    This became a question which has accompanied me my whole life long. If you are always dependent on the help of other people, in every practical respect, [posing] this [question] can become a great temptation.

I have done a lot of thinking about the God who is powerless, who is unable to help even if he wanted to [p. 64].

She turned her anger, bitterness, and *aggression* (3) against this powerless God, who apparently has no influence on his "bad ground crew." It became her main theme in life! Whenever she posed the question this bitterly, pious people pushed her away and God's all-knowing attorneys told her to fear God.

When I expressed these heretical thoughts openly, there was always some pious person or the other who proved to me that God is not powerless. I began to fear these spokesmen of God who had an answer to everything [p. 65].

On her own, Luise Habel became acquainted with a completely different God, not the one that Christians, "his people," had described to her. She became increasingly convinced of that which she had worked out herself. Her perception of God seemed closer to the New Testament than all the "talk about omnipotence":

For me, he was not the triumphant God to whom everything is subject. I saw the suffering Christ, who failed in this world, who helplessly let himself be nailed to the cross and who cried out that he had been forsaken. I felt at one with him [p. 65].

As expected, *aggression* (3) at first drove Luise Habel to radically break off all her relations to the church and to God: no more prayer, Bible reading, or attending worship services:

I decided to no longer expect anything of God, to no longer ask anything of him. I was afraid that my expectations and my disappointment in God and perhaps in his people, as well, would make me fall apart. I couldn't risk that. And so, after having soberly thought about it, I decided to accept the life that was beyond my power to deal with and to either get a grip on it or fail in it. Then it would be my own failure, the failure of my capabilities and possibilities. This seemed more bearable to me than to be at the mercy of this unknown God [p. 65].

However, emotional searching can accompany rational renunciation. Luise Habel's penetrating criticism, as a sign of *aggression* (3), pushed for a *critical-sympathetic response* in the form of *acceptance* (6).

Luise Habel told about the way she experienced this struggle in her book, "Lord, Tear Down the Staircases!" Three experiences from the book will be dealt with here: the mother's suicide, the author's desire to train as a parish worker in her congregation, and correspondence with a pastor.

The suicide of the mother suggests that she was unable to cope with her crisis—the result of the many burdens she had to bear. In contrast to her daughter, who was able to direct her rage and bitterness at her surroundings and against God in the form of *aggression,* we learn that the mother had "never spoken about it" in her lifetime but instead swallowed everything mutely. Day after day, she fought for survival, in addition to saving every penny for her handicapped daughter. She was smashed to pieces by the government's monetary reform policy, which overnight rendered her savings worthless.

Now everything was meaningless, and she fell into a paralyzing *depression* (5). More than ever before, she and the family were completely "left alone at the mercy of" the alienating conditions [p. 21].

In the introduction, we explained our proposition that *aggression* (3) as catharsis plays a key role in the process of learning to cope with crisis. The mother's missing out on the *aggression* phase (3) very probably led to *nonacceptance* of the crisis and therefore to the stagnation of the learning process in the *depression* phase (5).

It becomes clear how well this description fit the mother and what stressful consequences it had for the people around her. The mother, who remained silent her entire life, was incapable of aggressively coming to terms with the new misfortune which befell her (financial ruin, loss of meaning of life). Instead, she forced herself to direct the pent-up *aggression* (3) solely against herself: she attempted suicide for the first time. The failure of this attempt caused her concern for her daughter to reach "immeasurable proportions." "Dying with her daughter" was now her main concern, as she constantly informed her. Luise Habel described how she resisted being pulled into "the fascination with death with all my might." Finally, the mother tried to carry out her intention, although later she was completely unable to recall the act. She attempted to attack her sleeping daughter with a hatchet. A second failed attempt to commit suicide turned the mother's love into hate. Belatedly, too late, the *aggression* (3) that had been dammed up for a lifetime was now uncontrollably released during an illness. For hours on end the mother repeated:

"I would have had everything if it wouldn't have been for you." Morning after morning and evening after evening it was the same. "I would have had. . . ." I couldn't listen to it any more. I pleaded, begged, screamed, "Stop it once and for all!" [p. 57].

However, the daughter comprehended and apologized:

I knew that she had gotten nothing out of life. She had sacrificed more than a person can cope with. She had always been lonely, perhaps because she had a handicapped child [p. 57].

However, there was no chance that the *aggression* (3) could be dealt with in a way that would enable her to reach the stage of *acceptance* (6). Unleashed far too late, her aggression had taken the form of emotional illness for which she received no human support or professional counseling whatever. A third attempt at suicide was finally successful; the mother drowned herself. Luise Habel once more expressed bitterness:

If all the people who had paid respects to mother at her death had once in their lives visited her or had invited her to come over, perhaps her life would have seemed more bearable [pp. 60-61].

She encountered the failure of "God's spokesmen" once more:

The pastor didn't come to our house during the time before the burial. But he sent word that it wasn't clear whether mother would be given a Christian burial or not [p. 61].

Thanks to the official decision that due to her illness it was not an "actual case of suicide," the mother was buried with the church's blessing. Luise Habel wondered if it was a "coincidence" that the pastor unknowingly chose her confirmation verse for his homily:

Fear not, for I have redeemed you, I have called you by name, you are mine [p. 62].

For the first time, she discovered the continuation of this Bible passage:

For when you pass through the waters I will be with you [p. 62].

Suddenly God's word got through to her:

I was in such despair that mother had to die so alone. That no one was with her. And now there was someone who said, "I was there. She wasn't left alone. She isn't alone now. Do not be afraid." Here I was suddenly drawn into a reality which was stronger than death [p. 62].

She experienced the homily as a sharp contrast:

The pastor's words at the grave did not reach me. It was as though I were numb, I was unable to cry [p. 62].

Luise Habel makes us aware of the extent to which her faith in God had become alert and, in contrast, how badly she got along with God's "ground crew," the church. She became aware of this during a visit by a preacher from a Christian community shortly after her mother's death. He came with the following message:

I have the feeling that you have gotten off the right track. . . . I haven't seen you in church for a long time [pp. 63-64].

Vividly, Luise Habel attempted to explain her unusually needy situation to him, first in conversation, then in writing. She explained that as a woman in a wheelchair she was completely worn out by her job and by running the household for her father. She even dared to make a suggestion:

I referred to his Bible study group, to which about 50 women came each week. I was naive enough to suggest that if each of these women would come to me just once instead of to the Bible study, I would be free of the problem of finding someone to help me clean for a whole year. But instead, I received a letter from the preacher in which he wrote that he would fold his hands for me and ask God to send me someone [p. 64].

Once more, her *aggression* (3) toward the institution of the church burst out:

God sent me no one, and the man never visited me again. At that point, filled with rage and bitterness, I thought, "What can God do when his people refuse to serve him?" This turned into a question that accompanied me throughout my entire life [p. 64].

Luise Habel provided a variety of these kinds of examples. Particularly typical were the reactions to her desire to work as a professional parish worker in a congregation. As the daughter of Christian parents and a member of the Protestant Youth Group for many years, she applied to her regional youth pastor after the end of the second world war. She wrote that he was obviously pleased at the idea and confidently brushed aside her scruples about her disability, farewelling her with a smile and a firm acceptance for the first class at the Bible school. In order to explain her decision to give up office work and begin working for the congregation, she referred to the conflict between occupational and social integration:

Even if I succeed in becoming integrated in the working world, my place in society leaves a lot to be desired [p. 34]. . . .

Little by little I had begun to earn the respect of my fellow employees. . . .

My colleagues learned to judge me on the basis of my work rather than in terms of my handicap. I belonged there. Of course, that was only during the workday. In my free time I was alone. But because I had very diverse interests I never really noticed it [p. 45].

In a separate chapter entitled "Membership in the Protestant Youth Group," she illustrated how she felt totally accepted in the Protestant Youth Group:

Even today, I have the feeling that I was completely accepted as a member there. It was just assumed that I was taken along everywhere, even in the wintertime when there was snow and ice—even when the weather made it risky [p. 36].

Then, like a bolt from the blue, she learned through another woman on the same train, a lecturer at the Protestant Youth Foundation, that this woman was on her way to a course at the Bible school that had been going on for several months. When she made an inquiry to the Regional Youth Pastor, her chain of let-downs on the part of the church was only extended. She received in writing:

. . . that [the] handicap was too much after all. But at the same time, he said that if God wanted me to do this work God could open the door for me [p. 47].

Again, she was overwhelmed by *aggression* (3), and the concepts of faith and the church remained in conflict:

Filled with bitterness, I thought, "His people are slamming all the doors in my face. And God is supposed to see how he can get them open again." I was too realistic and perhaps I didn't believe strongly enough, to count on a real chance of anything happening. I knew what it had been like with my former employees and realized that church people would hardly be able to react any differently. For that reason, the negative responses that I received to my further inquiries did not surprise me a bit. Why should it be any different in church circles than in the rest of the working world? [p. 47].

The list of similar experiences went on. Each time they brought Luise Habel back to her existential question, "What can God do when his people refuse to serve him?" Again and again her sense of reason struggled with her denial of this impotent God. Yet she could not evict him from her heart.

Her correspondence with a pastor illustrated how by means of pastoral support her *aggressive struggle* (3) within the conflict between faith and the church could still be transformed into a *critical-sympathetic response* which would result in *acceptance* (6). The pastor who corresponded with her was different than the others mentioned. Instead of providing incomplete or pat answers to her questions, or showering her with special offers, he took her seriously, seeing that she was in need of assistance.

He didn't have any pat answers. He just let my questions stand and didn't attempt to force me into a kind of faith that I couldn't live out [p. 66].

From him she learned the difference between truth and truthfulness and between the objective preaching of the Bible teachings and the subjective message that must go through the preacher as an individual in order to reach us as the proclamation of the gospel.

I learned from him that there are phrases that dare not be used. Statements which are objectively correct, but when they are expressed verbally, have the effect of throwing stones. He seemed to be a person without any principles. A pastor without principles? I had to get to know him [p. 66].

Later, she used this experience against the false comforters who told her how wonderful people are "from whom one never hears one word of complaint."

Once a woman wrote to me, "How God must love you for him to demand so much of you." At that point, I wrote back bitterly that I would be just as content with a little less love and a little more health. Today I know that there are phrases that one just mustn't use. They may be theoretically correct. Yet in practice, they are destructive. How am I supposed to live with a God who expects me to fulfill my goal in life by suffering? How can I live with a God who will only accept me in a certain role and who will only love me because I suffer? [p. 204].

She illustrated how perceptively this pastor supported her in a serious crisis situation:

Once I spent my vacation in the place where he lived. I had to have an orthopedic examination and the results were disastrous. Actually I had known the truth for a long time. Yet when it was put on paper again, it gave me a lot to cope with. After the consultation with the doctor I visited the pastor. On the surface I gave the impression that I was quite calm. I told him about the results as though they were part of some other anonymous report about a sick person. But I thought, "If the pastor tells me that I have to accept God's will, I'll smash his face in!" [p. 67].

For the first time, Luise Habel talked with someone who could withstand her *aggression* (3). Instead of fending off her aggression, he unreservedly allowed it to flow out and even more took it upon himself and began to suffer *with* her:

The pastor sat there and didn't say a word. When the silence became unbearable I took my leave [p. 68].

His silence rattled her. She wrote to him and got a reply. The pastor wrote:

You were right. I was so helpless. I simply didn't know what I could have said to you. Even a pastor has to admit that one sometimes doesn't have any answer [p. 68].

Like Ingrid and Stephan Weber-Gast, who spoke of the twofold nature of the gospel and who allot space to the darkness in life, Luise Habel experienced how she was taken out of the dark: One of the pastors went to her in the darkness. He withstood it and bore it with her. For the first time she felt: "I am no longer living through this by myself. He is walking beside me, suffering along with me. When there are two of us, the darkness loses its burdensome loneliness." She could stand it, accept it, affirm it!

That was new for me, that there was a Christian who had no answer. That for my sake he chose not to repeat all the Bible verses which were available to him. He could have tried to make himself feel that he had a good conscience. But he didn't do it. For my sake. He took something upon

himself in order to spare me the burden. With that he became credible to
me [p. 68].

And here she noticed that the more the pastor knew of the
temptations of real life, the more intensively he counted on God. This
made it all the easier for her to begin asking about God again:

This pastor had a lot of patience with me. Thanks to him, I began to ask
about God again. This man did not forbid my doubts. He didn't admonish
me to believe. Once he wrote, "As long as you continue to grapple with
God I don't need to be afraid for you" [p. 69].

Luise Habel showed how her Christian faith permitted her
aggression (3) and held up under it. She had someone she could address,
namely, God. She was able to oppose him, to leave him, and to deny
herself a relationship with him. Yet in so doing, she was taking him
seriously and, as a result, herself. Consequently, she was saved from
breaking off her difficult learning process and ending up in apathetic
resignation, as her mother had done. Christian faith enabled her to use
her *aggression* (3) as the precondition for *acceptance* (6). There was
no point where she could leave God completely. Like Laurel Lee and
Ingrid Weber-Gast, she found out that "he doesn't give up on me!"
She affirmed her *critical-sympathetic response* as *acceptance* (6) with
the support of the pastor who shared the darkness with her:

Yet I listen very carefully when the discussion is about Jesus. About the
Jesus who suffered as we do. Who wasn't a superman, rather who was
able to cry, "My God, my God, why have you forsaken me?" He liberates
me from the feeling that I have to play a role, to always be brave. With
him I can also cry, question, complain [p. 205].

Her reactions were always seismographic. She had a horror of
Bible-thumping pastors, those people who forgot that even though re-
citing verses did not cost them anything, in the case of suffering people
it could result in denial of God, the loss of trust, and the plunge into
loneliness.

I loathe those people, including pastors, who have an appropriate answer
for everything and who do not notice to what extent they can thrust another
person into loneliness and even despair. Bible verses that are repeated at
the wrong moment rarely help people cope with their situation. On the
contrary, they often cause me to feel my misery even more intensively.

This is why I have begun to defend myself against the cheap phrases that do not cost those who repeat them anything [p. 206]. . . .

Thus, she recognized her task in life:

> In recent years, I have become something like a trash heap for all sorts of worries, a place where people can and may dump everything. . . . I try to accept everyone as they are. . . . Basically, I am attempting to be and do only those things that convey the feeling that there is someone there who listens to me, who takes me seriously and who stands next to me, not over me [p. 205]. . . .
>
> What we need are people—Christians—with whom we can cry and laugh, pray and lament according to our needs at a particular time. I need people who love me, not my role in life. Then suffering would be more bearable, God would be easier to know, and life would be more human. Of course, there would still be part of our lives that we would not understand, but it would make honesty possible and for that reason would be easier to put up with [p. 207].

5

Ingrid Weber-Gast: You Did Not Fear My Fear

Emotionally Disturbed

Data: Both spouses, Ingrid and Stephan Weber-Gast,[1] related the story of Ingrid's illness—depression. (The book's German title is: *Weil du nicht geflohen bist vor meiner Angst: Ein Ehepaar durchlebt die Depression des einen Partners,* 1978.) Both of them did this as theologians with training in pastoral psychology and as hospital chaplains at a special clinic for neurology and psychology. Although they were familiar with similar illnesses from their daily pastoral visits with patients and visitors undergoing rehabilitation, they were not prepared for Ingrid's emotional illness. In the end, they felt they had no choice but to have their preschool-aged daughter stay with someone else for a period of time.

Ingrid Weber-Gast's diary from the period of her depression is so lively, forceful, and direct that readers feel it is more like letters personally addressed to them than an objective report. The reader increasingly wonders to whom the title of the book actually applies: You Did Not Fear My Fear.

On the surface, it seems that the reader is merely presented with the story of yet another person's illness, one that was originally written at the advice of doctors in order to contribute to the recovery process. However, readers are, in fact, confronted with the main question of the two authors: "What role does (our) Christian faith play in depression?"

and how do we use "(our) experiences during depression in our sermons?"

In his review for a German Sunday newspaper *(Deutsches Allgemeines Sonntagsblatt)*, Franz-Josef Trost said,

Surprisingly, this faith played no role in their most difficult moments.

He concluded from this:

This observation provides food for thought. It demands that we exercise caution when offering religious consolation to those who are emotionally ill.

He entitled his review "Trained to Be Alone." Why then, did Rolf Zerfass decide to make the following comment on the book jacket?

This testimony of a young married couple's suffering is at the same time a moving testimony of their faith. . . .

The couple felt threatened from three different angles: 1) as partners: one an emotionally ill person, but both therapists; 2) as believing Christians, and; 3) as theologians whose job it was to preach the Word. They experienced the onset of illness as a "crack in creation" that ran through the middle of their relationship.

Ingrid Weber-Gast soberly began her third chapter, "The Role of Faith in Depression," with a negative inquiry:

First of all, faith played no role whatsoever in the most difficult hours. My sense of reason and my will may have continued to affirm it, but as far as my heart was concerned, it was completely out of reach. It was of no comfort, no answer to my desperately torturous questions, no help when I didn't know which way to turn. On the contrary, it was not faith which carried me through the crisis. Rather, I had to drag my faith along with everything else [pp. 32-33].

The chapter ended with her accusation (3) to God:

Even today, my prayer is often like that. As with my faith in general, prayer has lost its luster for me. I try to pray, regularly and patiently, but I continually have to overcome a certain inner distance while doing so. Maybe I simply can't forgive God so quickly for leaving me in the lurch— which is contrary to everything he promises [p. 38].

Her struggle became clear: "I am trying, but. . . ." To a psychoanalyst, her "but" subconsciously expresses an aggressive "no." She explained it herself:

I cannot . . . forgive . . . God so quickly . . . leaving me in the lurch.

The path of her aggression continued into the sixth chapter, "Sermons Drawn from the Experience of Depression." She treated her problem in a New Year's Eve sermon under the topic, "God, give me the courage to change what I can change." Using Hassidic tales, she told about Rabbi Susja, who said shortly before his death,

In the next world, I won't be asked, "Why weren't you Moses?" Rather, I will be asked, "Why weren't you Susja?" [p. 73].

In addition, she dealt with her own experience of *depression* (5) and wove it into her message:

I strongly believe that God has established an individual measure for each person that requires fulfillment: a measure for those who are not gifted, a measure for the fearful, a measure for those in sorrow, a measure for the sick. . . . You may ask me why I didn't do anything with the circumstances under which my life has gone by. You will not ask me, "Why were you sad so often?" Rather, you will ask me, "What did you do with your sorrow? Within your sorrow, did you gain the slightest bit of insight into how difficult and how depressing life can be for others, and did that make you a little more patient, a bit more sensitive and less quick to judge?"

You will not ask me, "Why were you will so often?" Rather, "What did you do with your illness? How did you use the freedom of movement that your illness allowed you? You weren't obligated to work and to earn a living, you had a lot of free time. How did you use it? For useless complaining like *if only* and *couldn't you*. . .? Or did you just try to make someone else happy occasionally? Even by just taking the time to listen to someone else?"

I want to repeat it again: I firmly believe that each person can achieve perfection [pp. 74-75].

It is not only the subject that moves us, it is the speaker herself. Ingrid understood what she was talking about because she was moved by it herself. In the fifth chapter, "Helpful Texts," she explains about this:

It may sound illogical, but that's still how it was. Although God remained out of touch, there were several verses from Psalms which I kept repeating, perhaps also in prayer. I clung to them so that I wasn't completely without support. Especially the verse: "God is our refuge" [p. 57].

With particular fervor, I continually read the verse: "So teach us to number our days that we may get a heart of wisdom." Becoming wise— that appeared to me to be the step to actual recovery. Becoming wise— that meant regaining my overview of the situation and not being consumed by dark confusion. To have reached the other shore, unable to be reached by the tortures of the illness. Yet also to have learned to live with my own past, however painful it may have been, to have exchanged the nice, delusive deception for reality. For me, being wise meant having looked at one's own abyss without despairing. I do not want to reflect on the extent to which I have reached that in the meantime, but I rather suspect that my journey actually went in this direction. I feel more clearly that I was right in searching for healing for myself in this direction and that the more I stick with it, the more easily I can achieve things in my life [p. 59].

She described her close relationship to the psalms of lamentation:

It was especially these psalms which seemed to particularly reflect what was happening to me and sometimes I thought that they should really be included in Sunday worship more often [p. 36].

The chapter, "Sermons Drawn from Depression," closed with the interpretation of Luke 9:18-25, "taking up one's cross daily." Her message:

I believe . . . that one neither resigns one's self nor rages, but that one tends more to look reality full in the face and say: "Yes, it has turned out this way, but I must accept it. How can I use it?" . . . Taking up one's cross, on the other hand, means accepting reality without driving one's self crazy on top of everything through illusions, but forcing one's self to use every element of one's imagination. . . .

It means not saying "all or nothing!" but rather trying to gain "a little bit. . . ." Because true imitation of Christ begins here. It begins at the point where, despite one's sadness, one has the energy to say something nice to another person, to give an encouraging smile or a helping hand. . . .

That isn't something that can be learned in a matter of days. It is a problem that one struggles to solve right up to the end, no matter how long life goes on. Yet it is a problem that must be tackled anew every day, just like daily prayer. In fact, it is something that could go hand in hand with daily prayer. Perhaps the way many of us say: "My best prayer, Lord, is my cross which I take up daily. Amen" [pp. 100-101].

She followed with a short passage entitled "Being Able to Show One's Pain." Her message was as follows:

> One possibility . . . would be that we allow time and room in our midst for people who would like to show their pain, in fact, who have to show it in order to cope with it. . . .
> Because we humans drown in our unwept, hidden tears [p. 101].

Ingrid Weber-Gast expressed her experiences with dealing with crisis in the image of a rainbow—God's bridge to his people. She built her bridge to God beginning with her initial experiences with faith and continued with her *aggression* (3) against God as she lamented, "I cannot forgive you yet. You left me in the lurch!" The bridge extended on to her confession, "My best prayer, Lord, is my cross which I take up daily." This is what encouraged her to say we should show our pain. There is no more impressive way to portray the central role played by her faith during *depression* (5) nor for her to prove our proposition that Christian faith can compensate for *aggression* (3)! Ingrid Weber-Gast did not need to randomly direct her *aggression* against her husband, her surroundings, her fate, or even herself. The power of her Christian faith permitted her to unload her aggression directly onto God. She called him to account for leaving her in the lurch despite all his promises. And she who was imprisoned by *depression* (5) and fear did this fearlessly, surprisingly full of courage:

> Strangely, I didn't have any fear at all of being sinful, at least I was spared that. . . .
> When I felt far away from God, I suffered, but I never thought that this distance to God could be a sin, nor my quarrel with him, nor my despair. . . . I saw myself as a beast of burden that had been loaded to the breaking point by God. Didn't he then at least have to bear the consequences of the breakdown? [p. 37].

She was able to be fearless because at no point could she willingly let go of her faith:

> . . . it was not faith which carried me. . . . Rather, I had to drag my faith along with everything else. Yet it was a help. In rare, but truly comforting hours, it meant a lot to me to know that others were praying for the sick and for me [p. 33].
> Except during the lowest period of the depression, I continued to preach. It was possible for me.

. . . and from the response to my preaching, I concluded that I had reached the hearts of the people [p. 35].

In her sermons, she told about her experience of not being able to leave God:

Sometimes I even think that for each of us, at some point in life the moment comes when all the enthusiasm and assurance disintegrates, where we become people who cannot leave God because we have heard of him once and now can no longer forget him. They have to endure the silence waiting at God's doorstep until he comes [p. 84].

In this manner, Ingrid Weber-Gast experienced how Christian faith can spur cathartical *aggression* (3) to grow into acceptance (6), here called the *critical-sympathetic response*. This the reader can gather from the points made in her sermons. Husband and therapist Stefan Weber-Gast took a stand on this change from *aggression* to *acceptance* and he was not afraid to speak openly about the temptation to commit suicide. Like his wife, he faced up to the challenging question of the role of his Christian faith in *depression* (5):

In a certain sense, I was at the mercy of my wife's depression. . . . At that point, we didn't repress any of our thoughts, not even the question of what kept my wife from taking her life. . . .

I lived through hours in which I myself felt overpowered by the feeling: "It's too bad that we cannot, may not escape together by this means. . . ."

Admitting this challenges me to think about what my faith meant to me at that time. It did not bring me any immediate relief. I saw how the person at my side, whom I love more than anything in the world, was ruthlessly tortured. My prayers became very emotional. The longer they were, the stronger the undertone of lament and the accusation and demand that God must vindicate himself. I do not know whether it was a coincidence or not that there were several times where my wife felt much better the day after an evening where I had prayed particularly fiercely [p. 30].

For him, the "indirect" support given by his faith was in the fact that he was allowed to "wrestle" and "quarrel" with God, who allowed himself to be "accused" without threatening revenge.

In this way, my faith did somehow help me, my faith and the example of many people in the ancient Judeo-Christian tradition. That our God is a God with whom we are allowed to struggle and who allows himself to be indicted without threatening revenge, a God who is greater than our hearts.

Quarreling with God may actually keep one's fight for life alive in cases where impassively accepting fate would have led to nothing more than mute resignation [p. 31].

Though only indirectly affected by crisis, Stefan Weber-Gast proves our proposition that Christian faith can liberate one's *aggression* (3), permitting it to be expressed and changing it into *acceptance* (6). He also chooses the *critical-sympathetic response.*

Neither partner wanted his or her suffering to be transfigured, yet both posed questions about their faith. For both themselves and ultimately for other theologians, they perceived that suffering expands the intensity with which we experience life. And because the "crack in creation" goes through me, proclamation of the gospel can have two sides. Thus, they suggested:

● Proclamation of the gospel should take into consideration the melancholy of the listener and offer more words that reach down into the darkness of their illness (p. 34).

● In addition to his or her official role, every pastor should experience this difficult life as a friend who is close to the situation rather than outside it (p. 34).

● More of the psalms of lamentation should be included in the service so that they become better known and are then available in a crisis to those who need them for support (p. 36).

● People who are on the fringe of congregational life because they are in doubt about their faith should be brought to the center of the congregation. They bring life into the church (p. 83).

● We should be more candid in our dealings with God, . . . talk and write to God more openly. . . , leave behind comforting half-truths . . . speaking our minds and no longer talking about God's "impenetrable decree" where there is nothing but pain and emptiness (p. 85).

Ingrid Weber-Gast was not contradicting herself when she said that God can "no longer be a companion" to the melancholy and "human contact" was the only thing that could "reach them." For her, human contact was of symbolic importance in her contacts with followers of Jesus. In contrast, in her sermons she told of God's presence in the midst of darkness because her brothers and sisters also allowed her to see God. For Ingrid Weber-Gast, human contact became the symbol of encounter with God because these people embodied the presence of Jesus.

> Whoever else becomes ill can attempt to use their faith to support them in their illness. But those whose hearts are heavy, the melancholy, are robbed of this support from the very beginning. . . .
>
> And the fact that for these people God is no longer a companion on their difficult journey means that we actually can no longer leave them alone for a minute, because human contact is probably the only thing that can still reach them. And it is precisely this, human contact, which is so difficult to guarantee [pp. 36-37].
>
> Yet I firmly believe that people who seek their place alongside those who can go on no longer, and who try patiently and unswervingly to share, even if they would often like to flee from it—such people are, in a sense, living out the discipleship of Jesus. . . .
>
> Yet those who are forced to live in darkness will also find their Lord there if their brothers and sisters show him to them [pp. 80-81].

At the beginning of this chapter we asked who was meant by the title of the book: You Did Not Fear My Fear [Weil Du nicht geflohen bist vor meiner Angst]. This question must be posed again. If we apply our proposition that Christian faith can compensate for *aggression* (3) as catharsis in the process of learning to cope with crisis and can lead to *acceptance* (6), we come up with three possible interpretations:

- Because you, my partner in life, did not fear my fear: You gave me warmth and acceptance!
- Because you, my congregation, didn't fear my heavy-heartedness, my melancholy: You prayed for me and showed God to me!
- Because you, God, didn't fear my laments: You let me struggle with you, but you never let me go!

Those who want to follow Jesus must know how they have to bear their burden in life so that they can follow him. Because only then does true imitation of Christ begin. . . . It is perhaps the way many of us say, "My best daily prayer, Lord, is my cross, which I take up daily. Amen" [pp. 100-101].

6

Jacques Lusseyran: And There Was Light/Life Begins Today

Visually Disabled

Data: Jacques Lusseyran[1] went blind. However, his sight impairment was an acquired one. The son of two physicists, he had an accident during an experiment, at the age of seven, which resulted in the complete loss of his vision.

Jacques's parents, who were lower middle class *(petite bourgeoisie),* fought to place their blind son in a regular school in Paris. In so doing, they provided him with the basis for the qualifications he later needed as a university professor, father, and writer in America and Paris.

Jacques Lusseyran's two autobiographies are documents of faith. If faith means saying yes to this life, to this limited finiteness, working on it and remaining open to the future which has been promised, then Jacques Lusseyran embodied this infinite affirmation of life. He lived in the *target* stage of *acceptance* (6) in the process of learning to cope with crisis: "Now I begin to realize!" The titles of his autobiographies witness to his unconditional affirmation of life with blindness: 1) *And There Was Light,* first autobiography, 1963 (A I); Life Begins Today, second autobiography, 1976 (A II).

Lusseyran wrote the following in the "epilog" of the first autobiography:

> Here my story ends. . . . His dearest wish was to show, if only in part, what these years held of life, light, and joy by the grace of God. . . . Joy

does not come from outside, for whatever happens to us it is within. . . . Light does not come to us from without. Light is in us, even if we have no eyes [A I, pp. 311-312].

At the end of his second autobiography, he confessed:

Inner life means being convinced that "seeing" consists of "contemplating," "knowing" consists of "understanding" and "possessing" consists of "surrendering to others." Our entire lives are given to us before we live them. Yet it is necessary to have a complete life—perhaps even more—to become aware of this gift. Our entire lives are given to us each second. Life begins today [A II, p. 132]. . . .

The analysis of Lusseyran's story serves to illustrate what the reality of acceptance means. In addition, I will now present five results of my analysis that confirm the model of coping with crisis as a learning process:

1. His visual disability did not cause him to be handicapped because his psychosocial condition was extremely good. He overcame his blindness through the opportunities for social integration that were given to him.

2. *Acceptance* (6) of his handicap did not come about without preconditions, rather it was built on the experience of acceptance that he already had:

● for Jacques as a child, acceptance by his parents was the foundation of his acceptance of himself.

● for the Lusseyrans as parents, acceptance by God included the acceptance of themselves as parents of a blind child.

● for Jacques as an adult, self-acceptance was never called into question because he was accepted by his parents and God.

3. Lusseyran as a Christian did not live his *acceptance* (6) as a silent fact, bowing to his fate in a *naive apathetic reaction*. Rather he shaped *acceptance* (6) using his own active hold on the situation, for example, by dissociating himself from his blindness. People called him: "The person who isn't blind!" as in *And There Was Light;* and describing his escape from death in the Buchenwald concentration camp: "The person who didn't die!" as in Life Begins Today.

4. Not accepting his reality rendered Lusseyran blind. He suffered from this refusal to accept the situation whenever he was "beside himself" in the grip of fear, rage, bitterness, darkness, disorientation,

and depression. He experienced it as the loss of trust with the feeling that everything was irrelevant. He fell back into the *transit* stage of the process of learning to cope with crisis:

> What the loss of my eyes was unable to achieve was accomplished by fear. It made me blind.

5. Lusseyran's Christian faith compensated for *aggression* (3) and led to the reality of *acceptance* (6). These basic thoughts on the reality of acceptance can now be studied in detail.

Both before and after he lost his sight, Jacques described the situation in his parents' home as one which was unusually good:

> When I think of my childhood I still feel the sense of warmth above me, behind and around me, that marvelous sense of living not yet on one's own, but leaning body and soul on others who accept the charge. . . .
>
> My parents carried me along and that, I am sure, is the reason why through all my childhood I never touched ground.
>
> I passed between dangers and fears as light passes through a mirror. That was the joy of my childhood, the magic armor which, once put on, protects for a lifetime (A I, p. 6).

For him, faith and God could not be treated as separate topics. They constituted his entire life. He counted on God. God was self-evident to him (which literally means that God made himself evident). God became the essence of his unconditionally endorsed and lived reality:

> My parents were heaven. I didn't say this to myself so precisely, and they never said it to me, but it was obvious. I knew very early, I am quite sure of it, that through them another Being concerned himself with me and even addressed himself to me. This Other I did not even call God. My parents spoke to me about God, but only later. I had no name for him. He was just there and it was better that way. Behind my parents there was someone, and my father and mother were simply the people responsible for passing along the gift. My religion began like this, which I think explains why I have never known doubt. This confession may be something of a surprise, but I set store by it because it will make so many other things clear [A I, pp. 6-7].

The author described his faith using the wonderful image of the "relay race from assurance to assurance."

> I was always running; the whole of my childhood was spent running. Only I was not running to catch hold of something. That is a notion for grownups and not the notion of a child. I was running to meet everything that was visible, and everything that I could not yet see. I traveled from assurance to assurance, as though I were running a race in relays [A I, p. 7].

Lusseyran experienced his first major calamity as a result of human error at the age of seven, when he was blinded during an experiment. Neither his parents nor he himself interpreted this disaster as destruction. His parents completely averted the potential psychosocial damage by allowing him and his brother to remain "normal." Jacques as a child did not experience emotional trauma because he accepted himself as a blind person. As an adult and a Christian, he characterized this part of his childhood under the title, "Revelation of Light":

> The next morning they operated and with success. I had become completely and permanently blind.
>
> Every day since then I have thanked heaven for making me blind while I was still a child not quite eight years old. I bless my lot for practical reasons first of all. The habits of a boy of eight are not yet formed, either in body or in mind. His body is infinitely supple, capable of making just the movement the situation calls for and no other; ready to settle with life as it is, ready to say yes to it. And the greatest physical miracles can follow from this acceptance. . . .
>
> These simple things I know, and I know that since the day I went blind I have never been unhappy [A I, p. 14].

A variation in the second autobiography describes a "love of blindness."

> I know only too well what kind of chain of gifts of grace I was given in order to love the blindness in me [A II, p. 114].

The fact that Lusseyran himself thought critically about the provocative challenge of total assent to his suffering here reveals even more clearly the transforming power of his unconditional *acceptance* of suffering.

For him, suffering as a result of human error had lost the sting of fatefulness. He no longer raised the question, "Why is this happening to me?" Rather his crisis opened him up to another inner way of seeing, "his light which was found again," as the German title puts it, which opened up a new dimension of perception and life:

> My theme—inasmuch as I have one—is life. Life of the soul, of reason, of the human reaction to the interior of the world and my own interest [A II, p. 69].

In complete contrast, Lusseyran also described extreme situations of fear, insecurity, rage, and bitterness in which his confidence abandoned him. He lost his light again, no longer accepting his blindness, but suffering under it instead:

> Still, there were times when the light faded, almost to the point of disappearing. It happened every time I was afraid.
> If, instead of letting myself be carried along by confidence and throwing myself into things, I hesitated, calculated, thought about the wall, the half-open door, the key in the lock; if I said to myself that all these things were hostile and about to strike or scratch, then without exception I hit or wounded myself. . . .
> What the loss of my eyes had not accomplished was brought about by fear [A I, pp. 19-20].

The *nonacceptance* of his disability and a long stay in the *transit* stages of *aggression* (3), *negotiation* (4), or *depression* (5) were torturous to him when he once was in the company of another blind boy:

> For a blind child there is a threat greater than all the wounds and bumps, the scratches and most of the blows, and that is the danger of isolation.
> When I was 15 I spent long afternoons with a blind boy my own age, one who went blind, I should add, in circumstances very like my own. Today I have few memories as painful. This boy terrified me. He was the living image of everything that might have happened to me if I had not been fortunate, more fortunate than he. For he was really blind. He had seen nothing since his accident. His faculties were normal; he could have seen as well as I. But they had kept him from doing so. To protect him, as they put it, they had cut him off from everything, and made fun of all his attempts to explain what he felt. In grief and revenge, he had thrown himself into a brutal solitude. Even his body lay prostrate in the depths of an armchair. To my horror I saw that he did not like me [A I, p. 31].

The most extreme threat brought about by suffering in its three dimensions—physical, emotional, and social—was exhibited in the other boy. Both suffered from physical blindness, yet only Lusseyran was spared the basic emotional and social trauma in his life. In faith, he overcame his physical suffering in the "relay race from assurance to assurance." Yet for Jacques, it also remained impossible to completely deny his suffering. As a result of *accepting* (6) the disability, he actively opened himself up to life. In other words, he entered into relationships entailing the inevitable risk of being hurt. Jacques also suffered crises at times when his life switched gears, just like anyone else. Yet unlike the boy, he was able to learn through his suffering instead of becoming bitter. He revealed his experience of suffering with extreme frankness. It seemed to him, the blind man, that it was solely due to his blindness that he might be excluded from the marvels of partnership. He learned to recognize that being human always means being lonely as well.

> I wondered whether Francoise would interest me. Was that possible? I was not as happy as I had been. No doubt about it, I had worries. . . . Frankly, I was frightened, and that was my trouble.
>
> I made it clear to him [his friend] that Francoise was only a pretext. Because of her I had remembered that I was blind. Or rather I had realized for the first time that this was so. I would never be able to see the girls' hair, their eyes, or their figures. . . . It frightened me to know that I should always be kept away from these marvels. . . . No doubt about it, the danger must be real if pity was the treatment I deserved.
>
> Without realizing it, I had just faced one of the toughest obstacles a blind person ever has to meet, and from here on I had to go from one fall to another for two years, until I regained my common sense [A I, pp. 112-114].

In response to these kinds of questions, Jacques talked about the reality of his acceptance in his first book:

> It [an inner voice] said I had fallen into a trap; I had forgotten the real world which lies within us and is the source of all the others. I had to think about the fact that instead of perishing, over the years this world would always grow—but only on one condition: that I steadfastly believed in it. The only way to be completely cured of blindness, and I mean socially, is never to treat it as a difference: The cure is to immerse oneself again and without delay in a life that is as real and difficult as the lives of others [A I, p. 36].

Lusseyran's answer in the second autobiography rang out even more clearly where he stated that nonacceptance of the crisis is the one and only infirmity of the crisis, comparable to Paul's message (2 Cor.

4:7-12) about the paradoxes of Christian faith, he allowed himself to be pulled through by "suffering in the freedom from suffering":

> There is no infirmity. I learned this by being blind. God—or you can say nature or life, if you prefer—never withholds anything from us. And if he seems to deprive us of something, it is only appearances and habits which he robs us of. We have to know that. The only infirmity that I know is neither blindness, nor deafness, nor paralysis—as difficult as they may be—rather, it is the *rejection* of blindness, deafness, or paralysis. I do not praise the act of doing without something, but I give credit to realism, and common sense, that is, love—love for what exists. In my blindness, I say "love for light," because light is present for me.
>
> In the same way, "life" is present in its totality at the moment when our life no longer seems to contain anything [A II, p. 113].

We could add to this Paul's message: "dying, and yet we live on" (2 Cor. 6:9).

A final situation of extreme suffering, which was brought about by the Buchenwald concentration camp, once more powerfully illustrates that it was purely by faith that he accepted his situation. Jacques, then a 19-year-old secondary school student and leader of a resistance group, was carried off, interrogated, and tortured. In the concentration camp, he survived hunger, cold, and seeming hopelessness in the course of illness, and then once more took over duties in the group called "The Defense of France" for his fellow prisoners.

Jacques acquired information about the military situation for his block and others in the camp. He also gathered news which he interpreted and translated. Most important for him, however, was what he considered most necessary—helping others:

> I could try to show other people [fellow prisoners] how to go about holding on to life. I could turn toward them the flow of light and joy which had grown so abundant in me. From that time on [after his illness] they stopped stealing my bread or my soup. It never happened again. Often my comrades would wake me up in the night and take me to comfort someone, sometimes a long way off in another block. Almost everyone forgot I was a student. I became "the blind Frenchman." For many, I was just "the man who didn't die." Hundreds of people confided in me. The men were determined to talk to me. They spoke to me in French, in Russian, in German, in Polish. I did the best I could to understand them all. That is how I lived, how I survived. The rest I cannot describe [A I, pp. 282-283].

It is remarkable that Lusseyran did not deal with Buchenwald and his learning process there until his second autobiography. This autobiography is reminiscent of Dostoyevsky's *Brothers Karamozov.* Here, his friend Jérémie the blacksmith was added to the account. He was the only person in Block 57 who lived without any fear, and explained it simply:

> For a person who can see, it is all just like everyday life. Now the Nazis have given us a horrible microscope: the camp!

Lusseyran's personal dialog with Jérémie reminds us of the indignation of Dostoyevsky's Alyosha at the suffering of the world. Characteristic of both is the role of lament as a mandatory phase in learning about their reality of *acceptance* (analogous to our proposition that aggression—spiral phase 3—has a cathartic function in the process of learning to cope with crisis):

> At first I didn't understand him [Jérémie]. I even sensed a feeling that bordered on indignation. Buchenwald was supposed to have a similarity to everyday life? Yet this was impossible. All of these hideous, terrified people, this screaming threat of death—all this was supposed to be just like everyday life! I remember that I did not want to believe that. Things were supposed to get worse, or better. Until Jérémie taught me to see. . . .
>
> For me it wasn't any revelation, no overwhelming discovery of truth. I do not think that we exchanged words about it. Yet one day I felt and recognized that Jérémie, the blacksmith, had lent me his eyes for a long period of time. . . .
>
> With his eyes, Jérémie taught me that Buchenwald was in each of us, that in each of us it was heated and reheated, incessantly caressed and loved terribly by each of us. And that, consequently, we could fight it if we only wanted to with all our power. . . .
>
> "How ordinary," Jérémie sometimes said. He had always seen people who were afraid. They were not able to conquer their fear because they had no object. He had seen the way they secretly had one ultimate wish: to hurt themselves. This was always the same—here, as well. Except that here the conditions for doing so were finally fulfilled. The war, Nazism, and the political and national insanity had produced a masterpiece of total suffering and hardship: the concentration camp [A II, pp. 24-25].

The power of *acceptance* (6) can transform. Lusseyran described it as the rediscovery of joy:

> In the midst of Block 57, he [Jérémie] found joy. . . . What a gift it was that Jérémie gave us. . . ! What joy was it? . . . It was the joy of being

alive, . . . feeling the life of others, at least of several others, pulsating against ours in the shadows of the night. . . . It was the—completely unexpected—pardon, only a few steps away from hell, it was the new possibility and capability of doing everything, the great joy.

It was the joy of discovering that joy exists, just as life is in us, and that it sets no conditions and that because of this, there is no condition—not even the worst one—that can destroy it [A II, pp. 25-26].

Jérémie helped the man who would later become a university professor to make an important discovery, that it was not his intelligence that had brought this about, since Jérémie was not familiar with the world of science. Lusseyran confessed:

I said that he [Jérémie] saw. I have spoken of him as I would say a living prayer.

Those who are hair-splitters will maintain that Jérémie's faith was undifferentiated. Does that matter? For him and—through him—for us as well, the world was saved every moment. Grace was unlimited. And when grace abandoned us, it was because we did not want it, because we—not it—had lost joy. . . .

But Jérémie had delved into his deepest interior and there he had laid open the supernatural—or if anyone is disturbed by this word—the essential, which is not dependent on any circumstances and which can exist at any time and any place, in pain and in joy. He had found the source of life. And at the same time, a cloak of transparency and purity surrounded him. I have used the word supernatural because Jérémie's behavior seemed to be a downright religious act: the discovery that God is there and that a return to him is possible. That was the "good news" that Jérémie proclaimed so simply [A II, pp. 27-28].

This was the "good news," the glad tidings of the gospel, here in the testimony of the witness, Jacques Lusseyran.

7

Ruth Müller-Garnn: Hold On to My Hand

Silvia Görres: Life with a Handicapped Child

Mentally Retarded

Data: As a result of a smallpox vaccination, Markus Müller-Garnn[1] suffered from a "severe abnormality . . . in the language of medicine" at the age of 10 months. (The German book is titled: . . . *und halte dich an meiner Hand*, 1977.) Shortly afterwards, his father became a complete invalid and then three daughters were born who were not handicapped. Ten years later—after the Second Vatican Council ended in 1970—the parents celebrated their Catholic (church) wedding (theirs had been a Protestant-Catholic mixed marriage). Together they provided all the requirements for a Christian family life so that Markus, who by that time was 15 years old, found security in his parents' home.

Silvia and Albert Görres were practicing psychotherapists and doctors. The birth of two mentally retarded children alongside their two healthy children, the older daughter Regina and the son Patrick, forced them to take on an unexpected parental role in addition to their role as professionals. (German book: *Leben mit einem behinderten Kind*, 1973.)[2] They lived and thought through their personal crisis as parents, as experts, and as Christians.

As Christians, both sets of parents, the Müller-Garnns and the Görreses, sought an answer to the question, "Our child is mentally retarded! How can God allow that?" Both found answers, not ultimate solutions. By interpreting the situation, they learned to live differently. The Müller-Garnns found the answer in a *naive-apathetic reaction,* whereas Silvia and Albert Görres came up with a *critical-sympathetic response.* Both demonstrated the capacity of Christian faith independent of formal theology. They learned to affirm their lives with a handicapped child. In accordance with our proposition, they provided evidence in their stories that their Christian faith can compensate for *aggression* (3) as catharsis and lead them to *acceptance* (6) in the process of learning to cope with crisis.

In the case of Ruth Müller-Garnn, we gain insight into the *naive-apathetic reaction.* Her strong religious ties were the basis for a childlike, accepting trust in the situation. She willingly put up with all her problems, such as her son's severe retardation, poverty, and social isolation, as burdens that had been especially chosen by God for her to bear:

> I had a very good basis for my positive attitude toward my seriously ill child. I had this attitude from the very start of his illness. The basis was my religious belief, which up until that point had always been able to show me a God-given reason for all the blows struck by fate [pp. 117-118].

The strength of her unwavering trust in God, which she herself described as "childlike and naive," underpinned her unrestricted acceptance of her severely retarded child Markus. Fully aware that she was a child of God, she was far from asking the age-old question, "Why is this happening to me?" as the expression of powerless *aggression* against some fate. She had always unburdened herself and her cross onto God and had let herself be carried by him:

> I accept the events from *his* hand as intended for me. For that reason, the question, "Why my child?" never occurred to me. For me this is a special form of trust in God, even though I otherwise have a considerable number of peculiarities despite being religious. I call this unwavering trust childlike. Skeptics may . . . call it naive. In any case, my trust, absolute as it is, often borders on presumption [p. 118].

This fundamental trust as lived *acceptance* also benefited the family and provided a "reason" for the situation:

> Markus implanted a reason for living in our family. He changed us and the people around him [p. 49]. . . .

Perhaps love for these created beings changes us so positively because it is a love which from the very start is always given without the expectation that it will be returned. Perhaps love simply becomes real in contact with these children. Here I am speaking of love as the willingness to help, to respect other people and leave them, or allow them to regain their dignity and not shower them with feelings of sympathy. . . . Perhaps it is also their unrestricted trust, their feeling of being totally dependent on us, that touches us to the heart [p. 123].

The change in her husband took place as he grew in faith. The change was expressed in his pride in his son Markus:

. . . George [was also able] to say "yes" to Markus from the very start . . . , although "at that time" he didn't have as much faith in God as I did [p. 118].

With George, in the course of time, a feeling of pride was added to his love for Markus. Today—it seems to me—in a certain sense he is just as proud of Markus as he is of his three pretty and intelligent daughters [p. 119].

An altered reaction on the part of the siblings was shown in their school life, when Sybille and Annette came home upset over a disparaging remark made by another schoolgirl:

"Your Markus isn't a normal human being—he's part animal." . . . Sybille was indignant: "Mommy, how can she say something like that! She doesn't know Markus at all. . . . She has no idea why we have Markus."

I thought about it. . . . And with a certainty that made me happy and almost ashamed, Sybille (7 years old) told me: "Why, to love him, of course!" [p. 112].

She saw her own transformation as the mother of a severely retarded child within the paradox of Christian existence: the bearing of burdens and, at the same time, the freedom from burdens.

In the years since Markus's illness began, I have surely wept more often and in more despair than mothers of healthy children normally do. I have certainly also cried more uncontrollably and bawled like a calf because my nerves were shot. The truth is that we perceive Markus as both an enrichment and as a burden. We love our "sick" child and would give anything to have him be healthy again. We know how much our entire family has to thank Markus for our experience of living with him, but we would also be happy if we had never had to go through this experience. That all sounds paradoxical. Yet every illness brings with it the opportunity to grow and mature. At every site of misfortune, happy episodes of human companionship can be seen [pp. 116-117].

She gave space to the burdens and dedicated a separate chapter to the problem, "And Suddenly You Are Isolated (p. 101)." She described how she suffered from the disturbed relationship with her surroundings. However, she also demonstrated how in a childlike, trusting relationship with God, everything could be unconditionally conceded to and allowed, yet at the same time it could be shared: there was the disgust for Markus, whose contact with others primarily consisted of biting and spitting, which as a Christian, Müller-Garnn saw as a symbol for Jesus' suffering on the cross (p. 102).

There was the accusation by people around her who said she was hard-hearted for locking up the poor boy. And yet others around her said their heart was too soft to stand the boy with his fits (p. 104). There was isolation from society when, for example, her company felt relieved by her resignation notice because she had been getting on their nerves for so long with her difficult fate (p. 105). We read of how she broke out in fits of weeping, during which "heaven" sent Sister Sofia, who for a few short moments broke through the mother's bondage to her household. Finally, the confession followed that during every parents' meeting or telephone conversation, her search for contact with others made her run the risk of chatting too much. She felt an even greater risk in the temptation to "escape into a kind of arrogance displayed by those who are tested by suffering, in which you wear your difficult fate like a halo" (p. 106).

Ruth Müller-Garnn told us that faith does not exclude doubt and strife. Yet one can turn trustingly to God, whose presence brings *acceptance* (6), and teaches one to stand suffering, even when it is undeserved. Her murderous doubts on the occasion of one of Markus's difficult fits threatened to cast her into despair:

> Why, why must Markus suffer like this? He has never had enough sense in his life to do anything bad. Is God truly so merciful if he allows this suffering? . . . After all, unconditionally accepting a child who is so severely retarded (with all the difficulties and sacrifices which go along with it) or seeing the child suffer so terribly is something else. That went beyond my strength and I began to get angry [p. 74].

Yet the faithful Catholic identified herself with Mary. "How in the world did Mary stand it under the cross, just standing silently? . . . How terribly she must have suffered!" She too was receptive to Paul's message of the sufferings of the present time that are not worth comparing with the glory that is to be revealed to us (Rom. 8:17-18).

> And yet at this time, in my deepest despair a vision of this eternal bliss came to me, because perhaps it is only within the dimensions of suffering that we can visualize the extent of its counterpart: the joy and happiness which have been promised [p. 74].

This certainty of faith within a *naive-apathetic reaction* is also mentioned in a verse of Psalm 73. It was used as Markus's confirmation verse and later was used for the title of the book:

> "Yet I always stay close to you, and you hold me by the hand" (Ps. 73:23, Today's English Version).

The situation of Silvia and Albert Görres was different from that of Ruth Müller-Garnn. They described their "radically different experience" as involved parents in the face of their roles as counselors in their professions as doctors and psychotherapists. Silvia Görres perceived life with her disabled children as a "thorn in her side" and reflected with distance in the third person because her shock and proximity to the situation were still too great:

> For every mother and every father, an impaired child, even if he or she lives in a home or institution far away, is the perpetual "thorn in one's side." This piercing shock will never be removed, not by anyone, by anything, not even by the death of their child. This child is their fate, from which they cannot exempt themselves for one minute in their lives [p. 8].

Silvia Görres dedicated her book to the two children, Regina and Patrick, "out of the long, personal effort to comprehend and master an apparently incomprehensible fate," in order to give parents some clear and useful assistance. She did this with an impersonal title, Life with a Handicapped Child, instead of saying "with our two handicapped children." As a psychotherapist and doctor, she commented on the situation and on the roles of the parents, the handicapped child, the siblings, and the spouses. She talked about the practical aspects of dealing with a handicapped child and about whether the child should live with the family or in a home. In conclusion, she cited several of her own situations in the chapter entitled, "Glimpses of Everyday Life." It was inevitable that in her account she hit on the crucial question of *acceptance* and *nonacceptance* of the handicapped child, along with death wishes, which she attributed to lack of help on the part of the world around, in particular the church.

> The strain and the continual demand one is under because of the handicapped child can lead to the fact that parents, especially the mother who is often most severely affected, no longer see any way out of the situation. They voluntarily seek death for themselves and for the child because they believe that they can no longer bear this lifelong burden and because they have received too little help. The unconscious expectation on the part of the parents . . . is that they will receive help . . . from the church and from God [pp. 78-79].

In the ninth chapter, "The Handicapped Child and the Christian Congregation," Silvia Görres envisaged how this sort of help on the part of the church—usually sought in vain—could look from a practical perspective (p. 129). She compiled a catalog of conceivable types of assistance. For her, the essence of these various possibilities was not the provision of funds, but it was kindness and the undoing of prejudices. As an example of the kind of assistance she suggested, she cited appropriate behavior in the church that would spare certain members the usual hassles and exercise in humility during Sunday worship. She referred to the "rediscovery of concerns for difficult situations in the prayers of intercession" in which the congregation would identify itself with the undeserved suffering of parents of handicapped children. At the same time, the church would avoid pushing off personal suffering into a noncommittal relationship by labeling it an accident or misfortune. If such concerns were included in the prayers of intercession, they would take on their vicarious purpose for the community of believers, the church, and especially for those parents who, "without merit and worthiness" had only healthy children. Finally, she appealed to the brotherly and sisterly *solidarity* (8) of the congregation, who alone could help to draw the sting of the terrible pain, and whose possible forms of expression—home visits, someone to talk to, various kinds of practical help, Sunday duty—could be so diverse, and as numerous as the church members themselves.

The crucial question, namely, "Our Partner—The Handicapped Person?" (p. 185) was posed in the epilog by the father, Albert Görres, who wrote as a Christian doctor and psychotherapist. He was not satisfied with a *naive-apathetic reaction.* Instead, he wrestled within a *critical-sympathetic response* to make sense of this kind of suffering, since mental retardation, much like an almost inconceivable catastrophe—in many cases worse than the death of a family member—prompts many parents to have torturous death wishes and fantasies of death for their child. As a Christian and father of two mentally retarded children, Albert Görres confessed:

> Those of us who are honest with ourselves realize that a primary and inevitable element of our relationship with disabled persons is that of rejection, fear, and even hate. . . .
> Christians are in no way spared the temptation of feeling and thinking, "Get out of here, so that I[!] do not have to suffer and get out of here for good so that my[!] life will be easier" [p. 137].

The risk of this public lament and the enormous courage, on the one hand, to openly admit as a practicing psychotherapist and doctor that he felt "an element . . . [of] rejection, . . . fear . . . hate" toward his own children and, on the other hand, as a responsible Christian to confess his own temptation to wish death upon his children brought Görres relief and encouraged him to release his *aggression* (3). According to the results of this study of the process of learning to cope with crisis, *aggression* as catharsis is an important requirement for *acceptance* (6) and for *solidarity* (8). Görres reminds us of Job, who protested against his undeserved suffering, the reason for which God did not reveal to him. Within his *critical-sympathetic response,* Görres raised his lament for others and as a fellow sufferer, put himself next to other such parents in his practice. He also stood alongside the large number of nameless people whom he had liberated from suppressed aggression, from their involuntary isolation from life and from any interruption in their coping process.

However, Albert Görres told Christians that they do not have to randomly lash out against the people around them as a result of their *lament/aggression* (3), thereby creating a vicious circle. In fact, he indicated that they can turn directly to God in inner dialog instead. Görres's most recent publication proved how this critical dialog drove him irresistibly deeper into thought about his faith. In the 300-page document, entitled Does Psychology Understand People? Debates between Psychotherapy, Anthropology, and Christianity [In German: *Kennt die Psychologie den Menschen? Fragen zwischen Psychotherapie, Anthropologie und Christentum,* 1979], Görres maintained that the more central and important an object is for existence, the less knowledge there is about it. Moreover, he confessed, "I need these reflections because I have not yet found any way. . . ." (p. 9). Görres said that it is our duty to question the shrill sounding dissonances of cognitive contradiction to see "whether they do not leave open a way after all, not just bearing God's burdens and praising him, but finding God in all things, in the good as well as the bad" (p. 13). The results of his own search for meaning are presented in the chapters, "Reasons for Faith," "Meaning and Meaninglessness of Illness," "Courage to Trust," and "Disappointment in God: On Tilman Moser's Book *God-poisoning (Gottesvergiftung)."*

In both publications, he derived his position of partnership with handicapped people from a definition of faith. For him, "faith [is] the recognition of a person's rights" (1979, p. 90). He referred to Martin Luther, who used what for him were obvious arguments to grossly characterize feeble-minded children as "massa carnis," who would be better off being drowned because they were incapable of recognizing or loving God and of living in freedom, which made it questionable whether God actually wanted these people to live (1973, p. 138). This was the source of his emphatic demand that we live in partnership with mentally retarded people, who do not demand pious feelings of sympathetic attention, but rather the effort of thought.

In 1973, Albert Görres's philosophical insight was still that all of us, no matter how severely disabled, are people and therefore have rights which no one can infringe. Yet at the same time we are people who cannot represent and defend our rights ourselves (p. 138). In 1979, however, he carried his argument one step further in developing the theological principle that the recognition of a person's rights include the recognition of God's rights. In so doing, Görres found the answer to the fundamentally insoluble question of "Meaning and Meaninglessness of Illness," namely that God should also be granted the right to a "downpayment of trust," which demands "an effort of courage" on our part (p. 163). This would inevitably promote the unconditional *acceptance* of "existence as it has been allotted." It would then, according to the theory of his teacher Sigmund Freud, include dispensing with the need of individuals to "appoint a substitute God for themselves on credit" (p. 167). Görres developed these thoughts in the context of the book of Job:

> The courage to trust, which God requests of us in this situation, seems to be so important to him that he does not make it easier for us intellectually. [The book of] Revelation teaches us about many things, but it does not provide us with a satisfactory answer to the question of the meaning of evil. It only tells us that it cannot all be meaningless, but it does not reveal the meaning to us. . . .
>
> In the trial Job is allowed to conduct against Yahweh, Job tells Yahweh all God's disgraces to his face. Yahweh is not too good to make a speech for the defense, but his argument is not an explanation of evil, rather it is an explanation of himself: My wisdom and power have been so clearly bestowed on the spirit and the mind that I can also reasonably expect a downpayment of trust from you even where the details of the meaning of my decrees remain veiled. You should not just follow me in the light of my presence but also in the darkness of my concealment, which is not absence [1979, p. 164].

Here Görres found the answer that is meant to help the lamenting parents in his psychotherapy:

> . . . even if they [the parents] do not admit it to themselves, frequently the lament is brought to the psychiatrist or psychologist: "Doctor, I can no longer love this child with its tremendous demands and aggression. The child is mean to me, he hits me and abuses me—I can no longer love this mean child!" For these people, it is a great relief when someone asks them, "Can you try to still give this child his or her rights and to recognize the child within his or her rights?" There are many people who say, relieved, "Yes I can, and I want to do it with my whole heart." They are comforted and can manage better if they are told, "If you seriously want to do that, then you are loving your child as best you can" [1973, p. 140]. . . .

He answered his questions by identifying with Job:

> But I let what was enough for Job be a message to me: God can answer for my suffering. I truly know enough of him to let this concern be his problem, since I am neither able nor called to solve it. My trust would be easier if it [my problem] were solved, but then not much would remain of the trust. Because it is only in this one point that trust is expected from me as a burden—actually as a burden—I think that God may expect trust from me as a burden. . . .
>
> I am not a judge who condemns [God] to nonexistence for the sake of evil . . . [I] have the most vital interest in victory. Victory in the trial decides on existence or nonexistence. . . .

Leaving the place of faith would be the loss of identity. . . . Faith is the only access to reality, to concealed introspection [1979, pp. 97-103].

Out of this *critical-sympathetic* attitude to faith, Albert Görres gained a new perspective on things: Mental retardation is no longer "a technical difficulty in life," which the doctor should do away with. Instead, it is a "necessary, salutary reality in our journey of life," which we can probably ease but not heal.

Healthy, strong, powerful, rich people need the poor, the weak, the sick, and those needing help and protection because, in partnership with them, and in no way without this partnership, they learn what they absolutely have to learn. The path to their salvation and to the salvation of humanity is a downward path [1973, p. 144].

He expanded on this in his 1979 publication:

Our fellow human beings who are sick are wonderful examples of the chances that we have to learn a selfless and downright superhuman maturity of love. For that reason or some other, we remove them from our homes, among other things, yet in so doing we neglect ourselves . . . we run away at the price of not finding ourselves [p. 169].

Görres saw our world in the image of Solzhenitsyn's cancer ward, in which it came to light how all internal hope and all meaning of life can be ruined by the suffering and death of incurably ill and disabled people. The disabled person emphasizes that the world always wears the face of the cancer ward.

It is not the individuals among us whom we can push into a ghetto who are damaged by life, rather we are all mentally handicapped children who are dependent on protecting hands to help us find the way [1973, p. 15].

Albert Görres concluded that we so-called healthy people are different from what we would be without the existence of illness and disability. This enabled him to resist the temptation to say "Get away!" and let him see the opportunity to ask, "Stay with me!"

Stay with me so that we can all become what we are supposed to be [1973, p. 148].

8

Laurel Lee: Walking through the Fire

Terminally Ill

Data: *Laurel Lee,*[1] incurably ill in the final stage (IV) of Hodgkin's disease, was the mother of three children. She went against the advice of doctors and chose to carry out her third pregnancy despite radiation therapy during the pregnancy. Then, almost simultaneously, she experienced the anticipation of her own death, the birth of her third child, the divorce filed by her husband, her isolating poverty, and her debut as a best-selling author.

The last story concerns the paralyzing certainty of approaching death through cancer. Since every fourth person dies of cancer today, this specific disorder must not be treated as a separate category alongside the four main types of disability, namely physical, emotional, mental disabilities and impairments of sight and hearing. After all, the chronic disruption of the normal flow of life also places people in a crisis situation that will not go away, one which they must learn to live with. In her diary, Laurel Lee sought an answer for this, which we could term a *critical-sympathetic response*.

Laurel Lee's account of suffering could be from the Bible. It would once again teach that miracle stories tend to tell less of concrete healing than that they attempt to change the reader's point of view. Laurel Lee also remained incurably ill with cancer and her time of death became foreseeable. Laurel Lee suffered illness, misery, poverty, abandonment, and loneliness. Yet she always felt close to God:

> I discovered wonderful things in death. It was a journey into my inner self. The more I deteriorated outwardly, the more my inner self was renewed day by day (cover).

Laurel Lee was happy to be alive, yet at one point she did not want to live at any price:

> I was in a place where it no longer made any difference whether I was alive or dead. I had caught a glimpse of heaven, and what I saw was wonderful. And if I hadn't thought about my children, I wouldn't have wanted to let go of that window to heaven (cover).

This was the attitude of her Christian faith, this is how she applied it to what she called "misadventure." The electrifying aspect of her faith was Laurel Lee's "intactness" and her "indestructible health," which we can sense in every line we read and about which her German editor writes during her trip to Germany:

> Laurel Lee . . . incurably ill—as we knew after our days with her— indestructibly healthy and incorrigibly positive. Her will to live is electrifying and blurs the boundary between health and illness.

And then we hear her own account:

> I had something I wanted my doctors to know. If I told them, they might later forget. If I wrote it down, they could remember. I wanted to make a gift for them and my family (cover).

In order to do this, she used impressive images to describe what was almost impossible to render in words. When, after the spleen operation, she was told that she was in the third and next-to-last stage of Hodgkin's disease, *aggression* began to break out of her:

> At War! [p. 79]. . . . I have three little children, not even old enough for school [p. 79]. . . . I was mad at every encouraging word and that I had believed them. We all stood two inches tall; I was set up for a fall. It was winter, and they took my only coat [p. 75].

She felt like weeping. Yet because she hated to involve strangers in her time of need, she turned on her "defense mechanism," put on her emotional armor, clapped the visor down, and asked "How will this affect my therapy?" In response to the confusing repetition of regular radiation therapy and testing of the liver and spleen, she could only say, "But I don't have a spleen any more!" After a short, "Oh yes, that's right!" she was left alone.

She appropriately clothed what happened to her in the image of an elevator. She saw herself in the role of the elevator operator. She alone could control whether it would be the up or the down button that she would choose to push:

I was alone. What could I do with my mind? It was like I was in an elevator and my will could push the up or down button. I sang a portion from a song that a minor prophet sang thousands of years ago:

"Although the fig tree shall not blossom, neither shall fruit be in the vines; the labor of the olive shall fail, and the fields shall yield no meat; the flock shall be cut off from the fold, and there shall be no herd in the stalls; yet will I rejoice in the Lord, I will joy in the God of my salvation. The Lord, My God, is my strength" (Habakkuk 3:17-18) [pp. 79-80].

The song could be turned up and sung out loud, but I could not turn it off. It was like the Holy Ghost Radio Station. My agony turned into a great joy that was beyond understanding: And joy is one with peace. I was in a very high place, and I wanted to look around [p. 80].

I wanted the doctors to come back so I could comfort them. But instead Clara came, and she knows how to weep with those that weep, and rejoice with those that rejoice [p. 81].

Against all reason, Laurel Lee's faith removed the mountains of fear of her death. She was once more free, free to continue her journey! *The New York Times* commented: "What Laurel Lee did was an answer to what happened to her. She counters death with patience, cheerfulness, a personal philosophy of life and faith in Jesus."

Her move into the hospital was like having landed on another planet, suffering something like culture shock. For example, she was panic-stricken when, owing to a malfunction in the equipment, radiation therapy was scheduled to begin instead of the slated sonogram to determine how far along the pregnancy was. She shared with us how, in a vision, the biblical story of Naaman occurred to her. With it she gained confidence and composure:

I was terrified. I felt I was being pushed in a little cattle car to Auschwitz, or some other extermination camp.

My fears all came upon me when I saw the corridor. I have never had an understanding of machines, small or great. Patients were treated behind lead-lined doors that read: "Danger Keep Out High Radiation Area."

Red lights were turned on while technicians turned knobs, watching the cancer victims on TV screens [p. 22]. I was taken into an examination room. I prayed with utter fervor. There I had a vision in which my mind could see a story: Naaman was a Syrian who had leprosy. He sought a prophet of God who told him to dip seven times in the Jordan river, and he would be whole. Naaman balked at the word; but he obeyed and was well. There was much more than this, but it was clear to me that I had a course to follow, and in my submission to radiation, I would be restored [p. 22-23].

Anticipating her radiation treatment, she submitted to the preparation procedure, which she compared to the torture scenes from the Inquisition. During the preparation, however, she was told that she would have a reprieve from the radiation therapy until the sonographic diagnosis had been received. Relieved, she turned down "the wheelchair transportation service, and went my way rejoicing" (p. 23). Afterwards the verdict: immediate radiation therapy was necessary:

I was not ignorant of the danger of radiation to the fetus. Dr. Montoya had been emphatic about the chance of retardation. . . Tears just welled in my eyes [p. 35].

The senior doctor again had doubts about the possibility of treatment in view of the upcoming delivery and wanted to transfer the decision to her alone, the expectant mother:

I was in real stress. All men were liars. If I had had any strength, I would have run away for the afternoon just to look at one solid thing, like a tree [p. 35].

However, she received the orders to come back and the radiation therapy began immediately. Once more she found herself directly caught in resistance, yet she experienced that God suffered along with her and stood alongside her.

I was rolled under its girth. Earphones were applied because the machine roared as it worked. They put small rice bags on my neck, and a lead apron over my abdomen. I could feel the baby moving within me and my mind was held constant to God.

The day of the second treatment, peace of mind rolled slowly back up and filled me. I spent the hours of that returning tide with my water colors, painting a little picture. I recalled the lines from Isaiah: "When thou walkest through the fire, thou shall not be burned, neither shall the flame be kindled upon thee" [pp. 35-36].

She described the struggle between "resistance and surrender" in shocking images.

These lions stayed in my room. At times they were very big, and I would tremble. Sometimes they were small, but they were always present, with teeth [p. 99].

Besides the concern of the cancer-causing agents, I did not want the top of my head to look like my knee. A disease and its treatment can be a series of humiliations, a chisel for humility.

My room had been an ice-skating rink. As I sat and wrote, I glided through the hours, leaped over barrels, and was exuberant. Now there were holes I had to maneuver around. My feet could get wet and cold, and I would shiver on the bed [p. 100].

The lengthy hospital stays triggered homesickness and death wishes:

When Dr. Mainer made his rounds in the morning, I told him in solemn tones, "I've lost my will to live," pause, "in the hospital" [p. 43].

And she encountered God's presence in the hospital as well. She experienced it while meeting with her doctors. For one of the doctors, Michael Mainer, she was first a person and not just any "case."

This was based on a feeling, not words.

It was rare for our conversation to go beyond what was medically relevant. He kept disclosures of his inner self on a strict budget [p. 44]. . . .
I once was a lot happier. I want to get back there again [p. 45].

And then this happened: he, the healthy one, was infected by the indestructible inner health of Laurel Lee. He questioned her:

He asked me about how I had become a Christian [p. 44].

The birth of Mary Elisabeth took on the meaning of the biblical promise:

I felt I could run the length and breadth of the world [p. 50]. . . . Saturday and Sunday Mary Elisabeth was mine for a brief season, with a circle just around us, and all the cares to come had to recede [p. 51].

And as the neonatal doctor reported on Mary Elisabeth, the book of Daniel came to Laurel Lee's mind:

> In speaking of Mary Elisabeth, he said the words from the book of Daniel, without knowing it: "After examining her . . . she appears more vigorous than the rest" [p. 54].

Then, almost abruptly, Dr. Stu, Mary Elisabeth's doctor, asked her the question:

> Just what are you into, anyway? [p. 55].

Her search for a *critical-sympathetic response* continued, and for the path between "resistance and surrender," to use Bonhoeffer's phrase; it was interrupted only by the outside commute between hospital and home.

> Within myself I was so exhausted that life lost all its colors, its past, and its future. I was pressed down by each day [p. 62].

In the midst of others who do not have cancer, she felt like a leper and suffered the running of the gauntlet that all disabled people have to go through:

> Did you see those red marks on them? It's for the radiation machines.
>
> It's like they were passing lepers and everyone whispered, "Unclean, unclean" [p. 63].

The worst experiences were her meetings with mothers of cancer-stricken children, whose suffering she wanted to scream out along with her own:

> I kept feeling a cosmic apology that mine had to emphasize the contrast of health. Anna loved to climb the coat rack to the top. The other mothers were at the other end of my tunnel. Their child was leaving them; I was leaving my children.
>
> > Where are words
> > That say good-bye
> > I'm just going
> > I will not die
> > I think it best
> > To shout it out:
> > See you later
> >   alligator
> > After a while,
> >   crocodile. [p. 64].

Alongside this "anticipatory grieving" (see phase 5, *depression*) for the lost future of these children and for her own future, she experienced "retrospective grieving" for that which she had already lost as a result of the illness. This she suffered through complete desertion by her husband:

> When I was back home I found that he had taken a portion of my clothes and deposited them in a grocery store lot Goodwill box. I shouted, "What do you think you are doing—getting rid of your dead wife's estate?" "I thought about that," he answered [pp. 85-86].

That was on March 13. Two months later, on May 27, she wrote:

> Home is said to be the one place you can go and they have to take you in. . . . I walked into someone else's house at my old-shoe address [p. 104].

She realized:

> I understood that to him I was dead. "We're in two different kingdoms," he said [p. 107].

In response, he painted a telling picture:

> "Have you ever seen two dogs and one has been hit by a car," he said. "The other just walks around it and howls, not knowing what to do" [p. 96].

Under the entry "Monday, Memorial Day," she described the final straw of the abandonment:

> Friends opened houses to me. Richard started to file for divorce. . . . I was in the wilderness of my life. I was a Gretel lost in the woods without a Hansel. There was a wicked witch who would eat me if I would listen. In my thoughts were my wars fought.
> Weeping may endure for the night, But joy cometh in the morning (Psalms 30:5) [pp. 108-109].

This "but" against all reason enabled her to rent an apartment, bring the children home, finish the diary and let her doctor, Michael Mainer, read it and circulate it through the doctors' mailboxes until it reached one of the consultants to the Surgeon General.

Laurel Lee's message was neither glorification nor transfiguration of suffering as a trial, or "visitation" by God, in the sense of a *naive-apathetic reaction*. In an interview with her editor in a German Sunday newspaper she explained:

> Yes, I wondered why I have to stand this misery. And I haven't been able to find anything positive about this suffering.

Laurel Lee's message was her witness, Laurel Lee struggled and wrestled with God her creator, she wailed, lamented, and wept to him. Yet God her redeemer fulfilled his promise to her: "I will be with you; when you walk through fire you shall not be burned." And Laurel Lee learned to accept her cancer within a *critical-sympathetic response*.

> There was something I wanted my doctors to learn. . . . I discovered wonderful things in death. It was a journey into my inner self. The more I deteriorated outwardly, the more my inner self was renewed day by day.

Laurel Lee, a female Job, went through hell, but stepped back out of it. She was pulled out by that indescribable, contagious faith which against all reason and medical prognoses could move mountains. Laurel Lee is alive and will continue to live in her diary as a witness.

9

The Problem Created by "Helpless Helpers"

In this study, I intended to provide the large circle of potential support-givers to suffering people with some insight into the processes of coping with crisis. I hoped to enable them to carry out their duties as partners more effectively. So far, I have portrayed the sufferers themselves with their experiences, needs, and desires. It became obvious that, in most cases, human support was inadequate, and in fact, tended more to burden them. This is not only because in most cases the support-givers were unaware of the thinking of the other sufferers. Rather, it is evidence that these potential companions are initially incapable of establishing contact with afflicted people. They become their own problem.

Bethel is a big church-sponsored rehabilitation center in northern Germany, founded in 1872 and called in German, "City of Mercy." Two visits there were rude awakenings for me. The first was in 1978 on the occasion of the Conference of the Synod of the Evangelical Church in Germany (EKD)[1] and the second was in 1979 within the framework of a project-oriented seminar with students from the education department of the University of Hannover.

The synod met in Bethel to discuss their topic, "Why do we live and teach?" and took part in a considerable program for meetings with staff members and disabled people during the proceedings. As a result, the discussion of the service of the church (diakonia) went beyond the limits of its usual framework. The synod had decided to tackle the problem of educational work, with the emphasis on work with groups with special needs. The students from the University of Hannover had chosen a project-oriented seminar in order to gain experience working practically with disabled people. However, in view of the concrete offers of "Visits and Encounters with Bethel Residents," both the synod representatives and the students were confronted with a personal challenge that they had not actually anticipated. They felt insecure within their own identities. The synod representatives reacted with more or less rationalized defense mechanisms, for example:

- There simply isn't enough time.
- I don't really know anything about it—I'll just look out of place.
- It's better to spare the handicapped people this kind of visit.
- I admit that I don't really know how I should act—would you come along?
- I think I'd like to go there with you, but I've never seen anything like it. What do I have to do?

In contrast, the students took the offensive, using criticism. At first, they looked with disdain on the ghetto situation, asking, "How can they have established an entire city of handicapped people?" Later they criticized the exploitation of the Bethel residents: "How can you accept a salary yourself when the people who work there only receive 3 pennies for 10 folders and never accumulate more than 35 deutschmarks as spending money?" Finally, they visited the "Dankort," or collecting point for donations of clothes, stamps and books, etc., which are sorted for sale by the residents. The students reacted to this by leaving in silent protest.

At both events there were offers of help. During personal conversations, the synod representatives were recruited to make visits since all the Bethel residents had been waiting for "their" synod representatives for weeks. Those who were interested were then personally escorted on their first visit to one of the Bethel buildings, often directly after one of the meals or before or after the committee meetings. It was amazing that it was the disabled people, with their undisguised joy, who repeatedly succeeded in spontaneously going up to those without disabilities, the synod representatives. Owing to their uninhibited approach, they were able to release the guests from their shock and sometimes were even able to help them feel their delight so that all of a sudden they were doing something together—building, painting, playing, listening, or just being close to each other. Personal contact bridged fears and allowed the first relationships to grow.

Jörg Zink[2] describes this process quite vividly:

> It is a fact: fear stirs in us healthy people. We think that, just as "they" did, we could lose our health, our upright gait, our security and power of achievement, our freedom and, in the end, our self-respect.
>
> And there a primeval fear begins to stir, which rises from the depths. We close our eyes, ears, and finally our mouths and walk past. Shutting it out and repressing it is the only thing which continues to work.
>
> In so doing, however, an entire mountain range of inhumanness is pushed between healthy and handicapped people.

The students had much more time available to them. Characteristic of their project-oriented course of studies was the intermingling of actual experience and theoretical reflection. Consequently, the project seminar thrived on the intermeshing of practice and theory, analogous to the model of clinical pastoral education (CPE). Each day of courses comprised three tasks. The program began in the morning, with practical experience in the cooperation of students and disabled adults in the various areas of activity going on in the Bethel communities and workshops. Over lunchtime came the theoretical reflection about processes of interaction with the Bethel residents, which they had experienced themselves in the form of "verbatim"—reports of encounters. As they noted down their conversations, all of the participants attempted to classify their specific questions about their own behavior. In the afternoon, the material from these reports became the content for seminars in which the group members together sought theoretical explanations for their behavior in order to gain insight into possible alternatives. The most important conclusions were as follows:

● It is not the disabled people who are handicapped—after all, they build bridges by establishing relationships with us. We, the "healthy people," are the handicapped ones when it comes to forming relationships. We shy away from the gaps that separate us, we destroy the bridges or are simply unable to find them;

● It is not the people with disabilities who are exploited in their workshops, since there they experience what it means to work and to work together with other people. We, those who have no disability, are the victims of our own idea that achievement and profit lead to a sense of meaning in life. Since we submit to the pressures of economic goals, our behavior often remains meaningless;

● Disabled people are not the only ones who must be integrated into the human community. Those who are able and fit have this need too. We who are not handicapped on the surface must be liberated from our wrong goals and one-sided norms. We need the critical correction that disabled people can show us in order to find, together, new possibilities for living.

Even if the synod representatives did not write any self-assessment reports, we can gather from their behavior and their reactions that most of them recognized that, on the inside, they were unprepared, and for that reason were rather nervous. Both times the experience was the same:

> It is not that the disabled and crisis-stricken are our problem. *We,* who are not disabled and not yet crisis-stricken, are *their* problem.

Jürgen Moltmann[3] had already thought about this question in theological terms:

> Defensive reactions place the disabled people among us in the situation of lepers. They are isolated, overlooked, or tortured by pity. It is not that they are our problem. We are their problem.

Thus, both synod representatives and students learned that social integration is less a question of information than one of interaction, that is, the ability to deal with and be concerned with each other. Subsequently, it can be concluded that if people (without disabilities) would just learn to see themselves as the problem of the disabled, they could change their attitudes and their behavior. Gaps in relationships can be overcome step by step. Yet this does not take place on the basis of information. Instead it primarily comes about through joint action. This means that for all work within the congregation and for all types of human support of the handicapped at home:

> Interaction takes precedence *over* information. Experience must precede the desired knowledge.

On the basis of their experiences, the students describe this as follows:

> This project-oriented seminar taught me a lot of new things. [It had] a key function regarding my attitudes toward my fellow human beings, whether

they were "handicapped" or not, and it affected my attitudes toward myself and my faith. This week I learned to what extent the ability to communicate with one another can further the integration of the "handicapped" with those who are not handicapped, despite the fact that it was different than I had expected it to be.

I'd like to begin with an experience in Bethel which enabled us students to learn concretely about the integration of "handicapped people": During the final days of that week, my friend Julia and I worked in two buildings which were situated near each other, Great Bethel and Nebo. Our walk to the buildings was a special one because two other people participated in it. They were Bethel residents, both female patients from the buildings in which we were working. My patient's name was Maria, and she was 36 years old. . . . In a cafe, the people looked at us curiously, yet they soon turned back to their conversations. No one got up and left. We helped Maria and Ursula take off their coats and let them choose what kind of cake they wanted. While we waited for our order, we made ourselves comfortable at the table. Ursula and Maria sat opposite Julia and me. We were not sure whether we had done the right thing or not, but then the two of them surprised us. They stroked each other's arms with their hands and complimented one another on their clothes, using gestures and words. Maria asked Ursula sympathetically: "Why aren't you saying anything? Are you sad? . . . But it doesn't matter that you can't say anything. . . ."

This excursion also showed me how much we can learn from people with disabilities. For example, they teach us to be delighted by what seem to be little things and to respect what seems to be so obvious to us: another way of seeing the world, an alternative to achievement-oriented life [student 1, female].

The problematic nature of one's own handicap, of the disruption in social relationships or the inability to participate in relationships is vividly described by the students:

During this semester it has become more and more clear that the actual problem in my conflict with disabled people has to do with me. . . . I have the same problems with establishing contact with them as I have with people who have no disability. The only difference is that I am unable to hide them or touch them up in the presence of the former people [student 7, female].

As we found out in the group, the uncertainties were mostly produced by us. They were projected from us to the other persons (the handicapped) [student 11, female].

In summary, I would like to say that, for me, the experience of my own [communication] handicap was important. On top of that, it was important to see the different ways I can deal with it, namely by treating difficulties, barriers, inhibitions, and fears as topics in themselves [student 15, male]. . . .

The same topic is raised in an excerpt from the seminar work:

> The morning was designated as the practice phase and the afternoon was intended for reflection. Looking at the verbatim reports on encounters . . . it became more and more clear that we were dealing with problems which were the same as the ones we have with "people without handicaps." How could we create a group experience or a group feeling so that each person feels a sense of belonging . . . ?
>
> In one discussion, it happened that I felt so moved by the isolated situation of one patient that I was no longer able to hold back my own feelings within the group and finally spoke about it. . . . In so doing, the discussion of my actual problem began. . . . With this discussion, the foundation was laid for one of my best group experiences, by exposing my own feelings and experiencing openness. . . . Once the level of relationships has been clarified, mastering the subject matter becomes simple. In this way, it is possible for me to live with others instead of next to them, because without my feelings, any intellectual approach has the effect of a wall [student 3, female].

This capacity for forming relationships demonstrated by the disabled people was discovered by both the church representatives and the students. It was used by Pastor von Bodelschwingh[4] as his keenest weapon in the struggle against Hitler's representative, Dr. Brandt, as he took on the task of dealing with Bethel under the "Zero-Point Formula," which was being propagated at the time. In this discussion, the question was raised, "What is the sign that the zero point has been reached?" Dr. Brandt is said to have answered:

> It is this, that it is no longer possible to establish human community with the patient who is ill.

Whereupon Pastor von Bodelschwingh is said to have responded:

> Professor, the capacity for community is determined by *two* sides. It [also] depends on whether I am able to be a partner to my neighbor. I have not yet met anyone who was unable to be a member of a community.

It was Pastor Fritz von Bodelschwingh (the nephew of Bethel's founder), who reported this conversation, which has only been passed down orally; he also tells about "his own case" and concludes that it was "a harsh lesson for my life":

> As a theological candidate clad in the required blue overall, I was transferred to New Ebeneezer and entered Ward 7 for the first time in my life at 6:00

in the morning. The orderly on the ward, whose name was Hollan, threw back the cover on the first bed from the door and said, "You can begin giving our Fritz a bath right away!" What I saw just about sent me out the door: a completely deranged young man of 20, a bedsore-ridden bundle of skin and bones, whose knees were permanently drawn up to his armpits in a cramp. His knees were wrapped in cotton to prevent them from being rubbed raw any further. He was incapable of uttering a word and had to be fed and have his excrements cleaned up. He lay on a bed of peat which had been especially invented for this unclean sick man. In a brief moment, I saw for the first time in my life this "zero point" of human existence. The first time this horrible bundle was laid in my arms, naked, so that I could bathe it in the bathroom, I could have almost thrown it on the ground. When, after a quarter of an hour, the "thing," diapered and bandaged, lay under the bed cover, I thought: "You are not staying here another day!"

Yet then it happened that this horrible bundle began to move and raised its arm. Frightened, I looked for Hollan, the orderly. Up until this point, he had observed the way I dealt with the most severely ill person on the ward in silence. . . . But now he had to help me. Today I can still hear the tone of his voice, in which were mingled pity for me as a person and amazement at an academically trained theologian's lack of understanding. "Sir, can't you tell? Fritz wants to thank you!" But I hadn't seen Fritz as a human being at all. How this sick man must have suffered as he noticed that I hadn't seen him as a human being, but as a disgusting object. Yet he did not make me atone for my behavior. Instead, he tried to find a way to help me in my helplessness at encountering such a ruin of a person for the first time by thanking me. He, the sick and deranged man, was capable of being part of a community. I, the healthy person, was not, and it took his help for me to develop this capacity. We quickly became good friends.[5]

The disabled persons' capacity for forming relationships was also vividly described by the students:

At first, my situation was determined by my attitude that I had to give them something and was simultaneously accompanied by the fear that I could do something wrong or that I would not live up to the expectations of the staff. However, my situation was then influenced by the fact that in our group of students, we analyzed our experience while we were in the middle of it so that it was no longer theoretically, but practically that I then learned that the men in the Araphra building could also give something to me . . . [student 4, male].

We were even able to learn that the so-called handicapped people attempted to build a bridge to us because we ourselves were handicapped when it came to being able to deal with the disabilities of others, which they dealt with quite naturally. In this area, many patients are far ahead of us. We can only learn from them to accept the fact that they are different just as naturally as they do and to learn to deal with our own so-called weaknesses in order to turn them into strengths [student 8, male].

In this context, another danger on the part of "healthy people" can be referred to, namely the oft-quoted "helper syndrome."[6] This is described as "the inbuilt inability to express one's own feelings and needs, which is connected with an apparently omnipotent, impregnable facade in the area of social service." This topic also arose during the above-mentioned seminar in Bethel. One student who had cerebral palsy herself examined her own difficulties in establishing contact with the Bethel residents using her verbatim notes on the encounters. In so doing, she also recognized her own problems in relationships with nonhandicapped persons:

I need disabled people to forget my own disability, because they show me that they need me. It is exactly the same with people who are not handicapped. We can do a super job of working together in groups, since I can always contribute something from my own practical experience (my former job as a preschool teacher, or the fact that I went back to school to meet qualifications). They practically all like to come to me with their problems. But what does it mean if I don't contribute anything and if I don't play my role? Then it's meaningless, it's total emptiness [student 13, female]. . . .

Later, this student (Anna) again treated her observation of this emptiness in a personal conversation and said:

It occurred to me that when I am alone, I often watch television programs for hours on end. Then I can really cry because I don't have any role to play. Then I'm only myself—handicapped. Then I'm only Anna with her desires for warmth and to be a complete human being. After the tears I usually feel better. But I can only do that when I am alone. The others have no idea that I am also that person [student 13, female].

In the group at the conclusion of the seminar, she added:

Now I begin to realize that as a disabled person myself, I deal with the disabled just as I don't want to be treated, just the way others so often deal with me. Instead of being me, Anna, with her needs, I play a role (Anna pretending that _____), yet I have learned that I can change that. I can take my problems and stand alongside them instead of only seeming to easily offer my help "from above" [student 13, female].

So far we can agree with Schmidbauer's statement in Helpless Helpers:

> It seems to me that estimable human qualities in no way lose their value when one carefully examines how they came about.[7]

However, we must question his criticism of the conflicts of the helping professions in his analysis of the Christian religion and social ethics.

Schmidbauer contended that "the historical connection between Christianity and the industrial culture [seems to be] indisputable." In the helper syndrome, he identified the following as essential elements:

> The first is the concept of original sin. . . . The second perspective is that Christianity clearly ranks altruistic values ahead of egotistical values. "Love your neighbor as yourself"! In so doing, the obligation to the golden rule continues to exist. It enters into a peculiar relationship with the doctrine of original sin and of the original evil of one's self and of others. Love for one's neighbor is, so to speak, achieved through self-hatred.[8]

On the basis of this assumption, Schmidbauer reached a premature conclusion in his argumentation:

> We can even assume that the social services of our society could no longer function if there were not always people available who, as a result of the mechanisms of the helper syndrome, are willing to devote themselves until they are burnt out. Selflessness and self-sacrifice continue to be values which are represented by a Christian-oriented set of ethics. The "as yourself" which follows the "love your neighbor" is often not heard clearly enough.[9]

Schmidbauer is certainly correct when he said that for a long time theology has been one-sided in stressing only the "love your neighbor" in the interpretation of Matthew 19:19. However, he overlooked the golden rule of the Sermon on the Mount (Matt. 7:12): "So in everything, do to others what you would have them do to you." In theological history, this verse has taken on more and more significance, especially at times of transition when it was important to overcome rigid traditions under altered living conditions and when new kinds of behavior were introduced, as in the time of the Reformation. The standard of the golden rule is often not preached clearly enough in the church today. Yet the message of the Sermon on the Mount does not overlook the role of our own needs for love and help in the way we act toward our neighbor.

Schmidbauer tones down the crucial dimension of the freedom of a Christian. We see this as a self-determined choice on the part of the believers. They contrast with Schmidbauer's "helpless helpers" who suffer from the syndrome of "helping others as a defense against fears, inner emptiness, and against their own wishes and needs."[10] Believers instead define themselves as "liberated helpers," people who help other people as a practical response to God's action. It is precisely because they have felt affirmed and accepted by God that they are moved to share these experiences with others. According to our previous considerations and on the basis of the stories, this is the Christian's *critical-sympathetic response.* Admittedly, each has the potential both for freedom and for imprisonment in compulsions and his or her own experiences. In Bethel, the students encountered both the joy of being "liberated helpers" and the needs of "helpless helpers."

On the basis of our experience, we are decidedly of the opinion that in our congregations we could find a large number of helpers who are capable of freedom. Yet we know too little about the crises that handicapped people go through. We have no idea to what extent we add to their burdens just through our everyday behavior, nor are we aware that human companionship can lessen their suffering in crises. Too often the opportunities for rehabilitation and social services that are available today are limited to specific office hours. This inquiry is intended to examine the way we live together in our neighborhoods, in the working world and in our congregations. As a result of the over-emphasis on achievement and material possessions, our life together is characterized by a lack of fellowship and by our inability to form relationships, a fact we do not recognize. This inability is enhanced in the case of our relationships with handicapped people. In their isolation it hits them with a particular impact. Using the spiral phases of crisis management, we were able to see that people can learn to give support if they want to. The essential problem lies in the inability to learn.

One may well ask where the social handicaps of nondisabled people came from. At the 17th German Protestant Church Assembly of 1977 in Berlin, Tobias Brocher[11] claimed: "The sickness of healthy people is equal to the wellness of sick people." He used a societal interpretation to explain his theory:

> The people who appear to be healthy have created an illness which has a devastating effect on our society. They have set up false ideals for health

and achievement which, it seems, can no longer be fulfilled. Those who appear to be ill and who refuse to go along with this degree of achievement are unable to convince the majority, who are used to the traditional standards, that less, with a higher quality, would actually be more.

Brocher described the illness of so-called healthy people as despondency, shame, doubt, inferiority complexes or obstinate defiance, and overcompensating megalomania. In contrast, he called for openness, honesty, and the liberation from fear. Brocher urged people to speak openly about themselves, not only for the interest of others, but also so others could identify with them and learn from their frankness. Brocher said that sick or handicapped people were unquestionably able to achieve this as a demand, a challenge, and as a corrective in that they allowed themselves to experience dependency on others.

Fischer[12] and others searched for human interpretations. By revealingly reversing the negative term "surplus existences," he spoke of the nonhandicapped as people who also become a burden for those around them owing to their health:

> People who, without hesitation, see their right to health and strength as a given are not satisfied until they seem to be so healthy that they need neither God nor other people. On the other hand, fearful and cautious, they are so afraid of losing their strength, their capabilities, and their time that they neglect to care for those who are in trouble and in need of help at times when they could do so. . . .
>
> The majority of these are "surplus existences" who indolently refuse to accept public or private responsibility and do not want to make any sacrifices or to share in bearing burdens and suffering.
>
> They, not the handicapped, are society's real burden. They paralyze by giving the impression that they are strong and healthy.

This proposition brings us gradually to the necessary interpretation of our inability to form relationships. Yet it requires more detailed consideration of the connections between the ability to maintain and form human relationships and the capacity to suffer, which will be dealt with in Chapter 10.

Moltmann,[13] as a German theologian, characterized the Federal Republic of Germany as an apartheid society that favored people who are healthy and high performers as against those who are handicapped and weak:

> A closed, impregnable society with apathetic structures is evolving in place of an open, vulnerable society. Lively, open, vulnerable life is being set in cement.

> This is modern death—called apathy: life without suffering—life without passion. . . .

He contrasted the fear of death through nuclear war, or of any kind of environmentally produced death, with death brought about by "our own apathy," which is much more foreseeable.

Horst Eberhard Richter[14] has examined the psychological causes of this problem. He recognizes them in the fundamental "fear felt by people who conform to society's norms that leads them to shut others out and build barriers between themselves and nonconformists." He based this observation on his conclusion that society is dependent on the handicapped because of the stabilizing role played by the contrasting world of marginalized groups. As an explanation, Richter referred to the following emotional dynamics:

> . . . we are interested in illnesses and deformities because we feel healthy and intact in comparison. It may be easier for us to keep our fear of our threatened integrity and of the inevitability of death in check if we can continually—in small doses—concern ourselves with the fact that there are people on the other side who are marked by illness and incurability.

Brocher described the illness of healthy people as their false ideals for health and achievement. Similarly, according to Richter, we unconsciously split off the part of our own image that we fear the most. Included in this picture are diseases, handicaps, and taboo sexual desires. Whatever people "perceive outside of themselves need not be recognized within themselves." Seen in terms of its total societal function, the process of splitting-off and the projection associated with it have the characteristics of a "reproduction of age-old attempts to conquer fear with the help of a dualistic model: Your frailty, sickness, and old age permit me to be strong, healthy, and young."

Carl Friedrich von Weizsäcker[15] gave a philosophical explanation for the role of the disabled in the fear-conquering mechanisms and stabilizing attempts of people who are not disabled. He described this role as emotional repression which is determined by society. Weizsäcker countered the common accusation that society is hostile to the disabled with the question of a "relative legitimacy" and of society's right to repress their existence. His reasoning began as follows:

> We cannot help people if we do not love them. We cannot improve society if we are not fair to it. Otherwise, we change it without improving it and

make exactly the same mistakes which we want to combat. The legitimacy of repression means that people need repression.

He defined the elementary purpose of repression—as a psychic process—as the screening out of undesirable contents and described any awareness of one's ego and its language as an emotional achievement. In so doing, he also recognized the necessity of psychic mechanisms that decide what elements are the basis of a person's identity and what are not.

> In this way, repression of the same elements can be legitimate at first. But later, precisely because we mature, they can become the most dangerous form of lie, a lie to our own conscience.[16]

Dorothee Sölle describes this lie to one's own conscience as a human being's living death, the death of a person who survives to engage in meaningless production, and whose death and hell is the very lack of relationships, like "the biblical death 'on bread alone.' "[17]

> The death which truly threatens us, which surrounds us in the midst of life, is the death of having no relationships. . . . That is the hell which devours us in the midst of life and in the midst of our production process.[18]

The Consultation of the World Council of Churches in 1978 made a statement on the isolation of disabled people:

> Where there are no handicapped people, a congregation is handicapped. The unity of all people, irrespective of their impairments, is a sign that the world can be preserved from inhumanity. The presence of handicapped people keeps us aware that each person is a frail, endangered, deficient being who has been created and blessed by God. . . . We strongly emphasize that uniting people who are disabled and who are not disabled . . . is a challenge which we must attempt to meet.[19]

As the result of our reflection, we can ascertain that, on the one hand, the disabled or the sick are obviously dependent on those who are not. At the same time, disabled people are able to reject this dependency. On the other hand, we observe the invisible dependency of the disabled on people without disabilities, or who are healthy. This dependency may be suppressed their entire lives if they avoid the process of learning crisis management. Yet the cost of this is that they do not find their identity. As a result, they allow their capacity for emotional experience to weaken or to atrophy.

In order to counteract this "death" where relationships are absent, we must get to grips with the results of our analysis of all the stories of suffering:

- People without disabilities are the problem of the disabled; it is not the disabled who are our problem.

- Society/the church needs the disabled in the same way that the disabled need society/our church.

This dual proposition prompts us to think through the task of human companionship once more. All of us in whose surroundings disabled people have appeared even marginally should ask ourselves whom we have overlooked thus far and what [negative] experiences we have caused them as a result of our behavior. The fact that we have failed to notice the continual suffering of people with disabilities and have failed to provide human companionship means that we have sacrificed opportunities to liberate ourselves from the constraints of false values. At the same time, we have missed the chance to discover and try out our own abilities. In our crises, we need partners who have lived out forms of humanness that we have repressed, who can accept limits and wait, who persevere where there seems to be no way out and in so doing develop abilities that make it possible to be human together.

However, people who work professionally with the disabled—social workers, special education teachers, occupational therapists, psychologists, doctors, trained lay assistants, and ministers—are also prompted to examine their behavior by the comments made by disabled people in their stories. The method of "helping people to help themselves" which is used in social occupations today still fails to communicate the awareness that in support to handicapped people—when it is understood correctly—the roles of teacher and pupil are constantly exchanged. Professionals can also experience "help to help themselves" from the people they work with if they are aware of their own weaknesses. We continue to lack the essential dimension of human support: the capacity to be in a relationship with others. This, in turn, calls for a further question, that of the meaning of suffering in human life. Life in partnership will only be realized when people regain their capacity to suffer.

Part Three: Theological Background

10

A New Theology of Suffering

Reflections on Suffering and the Ability to Endure Affliction

Before support-givers can be truly effective, they must have dealt with their own crises and be aware of the typical developmental phases (spiral phases) that people move through. It is assumed that they have consciously worked through these phases, and that in so doing, they have rediscovered their capacity to suffer.

This requirement is obviously of particular importance for those offering pastoral support to suffering people. If church professionals recognized and worked through the phases, both those afflicted by suffering and the support-givers themselves would benefit greatly. This is the only way their quality of life together can change.

Many of the examples that were presented in this book have demonstrated that in human companionship, theological questions constantly come into play. While it is not the task of this study to clarify theological questions, several theological perspectives have been raised. However, the purpose of presenting these perspectives was merely to show that developments are possible which can potentially provide people with more emotional support and relief. Nevertheless, the questions are only raised here; they cannot be answered at this point. In keeping with the main purpose of the study, it is not my intention to intervene in the domain of theological experts. Yet this cannot be avoided completely. Many statements take on color only when it is clear who the author had in mind when making them. Moreover, by making such clarifications, we can also learn how diverse the subject that is commonly called "theology" can be.

Thus, in this final chapter—as a digression, so to speak—the author, who is not a theologian, will attempt to present current theological perspectives. The point of this presentation is to acquaint both those who are affected by the problem, and those who have not yet come up against it with various possibilities for finding meaning in crisis, when the age-old question is asked, "What is suffering for?" With regard to both of the above-mentioned groups, I decided to dispense with a systematic treatment of the subject. Instead, on the basis of these groups' particular interests, I will attempt to make a presentation of examples of writings by Protestant and Roman Catholic theologians who have addressed the subject of suffering. From the Catholic perspective, Hans Küng's God and Suffering (*Gott und das Leid,* 1967) and Giesbert Greshake's The Price of Love (*Der Preis der Liebe,* 1978) were selected. From the Protestant viewpoint, *Suffering* (1973) by Dorothee Sölle and Klaus Müller's The Meaning of Suffering (*Vom Sinn des Leidens,* 1974) were chosen. Müller is a physicist, yet he sees his mission in life as dialog with theology.

The theological questions deal with "suffering per se." In contrast, the process of dealing with crisis poses the existential question of the capacity to suffer. It is only in this question that participation in the suffering of others is also considered. It is advisable not to lose sight of this fundamental question while looking at the following theological interpretations.

Hans Küng: God and Suffering, 1967

Among the great theologians of this century, Küng was one of the first to treat human suffering as the starting point for far-reaching systematic reflection. In a large-scale investigation, he outlined his interpretation of the question, "Suffering: why and for what purpose?" in five steps.[1]

In the first step, Küng did what the reader routinely expects of a theologian: he critically examined the traditional teaching of "the justification of God" (p. 7). He began with Leibnitz, who not only coined the now classical term "theodicy" (justification of God's goodness in the face of evil), but who simultaneously developed it into an extensive "cosmodicy" (1710). (At the time, Voltaire's *Candide* had already scoffed at the "best of all possible worlds.") Leibnitz examined metaphysical, physical, and moral evil. He disputed the contention that a world free of suffering would be a better one (p. 13). Küng found an explanation for this in an "unconquerable trust in God's goodness," which sustained Leibnitz and which led him "not only to justify God as one who is absolutely perfect and good, but at the same time to justify the world as the best of all possible worlds which God was able to create" (p. 12). Kant's work entitled "Concerning the Failure of All Philosophical Attempts at Theodicy" ("Uber das Misslingen aller philosophischen Versuche in der Theodizee") (1771) put forth enough cutting criticism. In addition, Küng posed the question, "Even if theodicy were conceivable, would its sharp logic also be existentially convincing, to the extent that it would persuade a person who was suffering?" Can it "give those who are despairing in their suffering the comfort and strength to stand it and carry it through? Or is it only capable of offering a suffering person an intellectual form of argumentation which would be something like giving the hungry and thirsty a lecture on hygiene and nutrition?" (pp. 17-18).

In the second step, Dostoyevsky's novel, *The Brothers Karamozov,* provided an example of undeserved suffering revealed in the chapter "Outrage" and, at the same time, as a terrible indictment of the church.

In a third step, Küng developed the question of "faith" (p. 19) in the face of undeserved suffering, using that unique document in world literature, the book of Job. Küng's proposition on this subject was that "within trusting faith, suffering cannot be 'explained,' yet—and this is the important thing—it can be 'overcome!' " (p. 25). Küng impressively portrayed Job's friends who "practiced theodicy" and whose logic of justice, with its theoretical arguments on the meaning of suffering, had the effect of renewed attacks on Job and drove him even further into "dangerous self-defense" and rebellion (p. 26). God gave Job an answer. For Küng, it was now most important to demonstrate that God did not answer with a "theory," but rather with his "revelation": "then the Lord answered Job out of the whirlwind: . . ." (Job 38:1-5). According to Küng, God did not reveal himself "as the equal partner who can be held liable, but as the creator, whose unfathomable glory is pure wisdom and goodness" (p. 34). Face to face with his living God, Job's rebellion grew dumb:

". . . I am unworthy—how can I reply to you? I put my hand over my mouth" (Job 40:31-35). For the sake of this God, Job was able to affirm the world with all its enigmas and all its evil and suffering. And he was able to recognize that he wanted to put God in the wrong by defending himself so that he, the human being, could be right (p. 35).

With this interpretation, Küng followed an exposition of the character of Job that is controversial even in the Old Testament history of this story. Assuming that the Job story (apart from the traditional drama) ends with 40:4 or 42:6, which corresponds to it, Job's silence can be interpreted as the resignation of the human being to a tyrannical God. One cannot argue with this kind of mighty force who boasted about creating monstrous beasts. The human being broke off communication. Did this break in communication make God the party who suffered? Did Dorothee Sölle perhaps have this in mind when she said, "Job is stronger than God"? (pp. 135ff.).[2] The conclusion, which was added later, that Job received everything again twofold, in my eyes, continued to intensify the tyrannical character of this God even more. God had won the bet with Satan, and Job cashed in on it. Are human suffering and human life worth so little to God that compensation in abundance can make one forget what has happened in the past?

According to Küng, wanting at all cost to be in the right is not just a mistake, but sinful. Job was not spared from arguing with himself. Although he was not tortured by particular sins and errors—which of course he never committed—he had to get clear in his mind what it was that was wrong with his basic attitude. "What is the 'solution' to this problem of suffering?" Küng answered briefly, "The risk of faith which is without guarantees, but which is liberating" (p. 42). We can see ourselves in Job. Behind him, the suffering servant of God who bore his own suffering, the "figure of that other Suffering Servant" appeared, who bore the suffering of the world and definitively conquered suffering, sin, and death" (p. 43). In Jesus Christ, the Old Testament prophecy was fulfilled.

In a booklet that has all but been forgotten today (*Hiob der Existentialist,* Heidelberg, 1952), Hans Ehrenberg spoke about "our age being ripe for Job" and brought the Book of Job to life in five pithy dialogs.[3] When, for example, he had Job ask, "Why does God, the real God (meaning not 'the omnipotent God' or 'the absolute God'), abandon his own son? Why does he command Abraham, the father of the promise, to sacrifice the promised son who is his own? God becomes the accused as his son draws his last breath: 'It is finished!' No one accuses the true God. Yet the real God is willing to bear the guilt and he bore it!'" (p. 16). Or, in another example, "If God had not tolerated the indictment against him, Job would have become an atheist and a nihilist" (p. 36). Here one painfully notices how little new information is available in recent Job interpretations and how often they have been written at the cost of our ignorance. Since Hans Ehrenberg, who scrupulously mentioned older exegetists (albeit critically after 1945), much of what has been written on Job has been repetition. Is there something here that should be kept quiet, because Ehrenberg played off the bare existence of faith against the type of theologizing that dresses up life and suffering? Hans Ehrenberg, who had already broken with the philosophical idealism of the university in 1925 and had begun to work as a pastor, met with little response in official theology. Before 1945, he lived as a political outcast and on the basis of this experience began a new "theological existence" in West Germany.[4]

In a fourth step on the "justification of the human being" (p. 44), Küng's proposition was as follows: "This is true theodicy: the justification of God through God himself by justifying the human being who is far from God!" This brings to mind Karl Barth (*Church Dogmatics* IV, 1, §61, particularly the splendid section on pp. 559-568). Of course, Küng did not claim to be original when he added that, in this act of justification, the "false theodicy by human beings who know by themselves and their own power yields before "anthropodicy" of God himself, who in his great mercy freely justifies powerless and sinful human beings and, in so doing, justifies himself too as a just and gracious God" (p. 55). For this reason, we can say, "I can rebel against the God who presides *over* all suffering in undisturbed bliss or apathetic transcendence, yet not against the God who reveals his own compassion *in* Christ's suffering" (p. 55). Küng showed that the gospel of Christ began where the story of Job ended. He demonstrated that while Job only revealed the "inconceivability" of the gracious God in whom he was supposed to place his faithful trust, this was surpassed by the grace of the "inconceivable God" shown us in Jesus Christ, and in his cross.

And "this grace which is revealed in Christ and which changes suffering into life makes possible a rational faith even if it always remains faith!" (p. 52).

In a fifth and final step, Küng outlined the idea of "freedom in suffering" (p. 58): "God's love does not preserve us from all suffering, but it preserves us in all suffering." With this, suffering and comfort have lost their sting, because a new future is opened up to the believer, who lives with Christ in the community of suffering and dying: "But whatever gain I had, I counted as loss for the sake of Christ. . . .Not that I have already obtained this or am already perfect; but I press on to make it my own, because Christ Jesus has made me his own" (Phil. 3:7, 12). In this way, Christ is essential in this "already" and "not yet," the dialectic "of suffering and of freedom from suffering," which simultaneously are parts of Christian existence (p. 59). In contrast, Küng decisively rejected an imitation of the cross which seeks suffering, since suffering and pain are an attack on a person's life. Thus, the imitation of Jesus' suffering does not mean "imitating Jesus' suffering, nor does it mean emulating the cross of Christ. Christ's suffering is, so to speak, not so much the ideal as the existential element of Christian existence" (p. 60). This is because, for the believer, the last days of new life have already begun with the crucified and risen Christ. Thus, within the process of dying in the present, the believer is already able to make the paradoxical statement: "I have been crucified with Christ; it is no longer I who live, but Christ who lives in me" (Gal. 2:20). Hence Küng's idea of the transformation of suffering: "Of course, suffering remains an evil. Yet it is no longer an unconditional evil that, as in Buddhism, is suspended by the denial of the will to live. Unconditional evil is merely the separation from God and his love" (p. 68).

Küng's statement that Christ's suffering is not so much the ideal as the existential element of Christian existence (p. 60) can be explained by K. Barth's *Church Dogmatics IV,* 2, pp. 598-613 (The Dignity of the Cross). Here, the cross of Christ and the cross of the Christian are explicitly identified as having an indirect relationship (see especially pp. 599ff. and 601ff.); in the same work is the corresponding interpretation of Galatians 2:20.[5]

It requires considerable effort to pass from the suffering of the disabled individual to "Christ's suffering." It may well be that faith alone is capable of doing this. The gap between reflection and experience is filled by "witnesses," who in their solidarity express the unthinkable and take upon themselves what they have not personally experienced. They even say, God is both distant *and* near to us. Those who are companions to sufferers are loving witnesses! How else can the bridges be built between the accursed fate of the individual and the execution of God by us all—unless it is done by the sufferers themselves?

The semantic problem, namely, that most theologians use the expression "suffering" to designate any kind of affliction as well as for "Christ's suffering at God's hand," may initially be logically vexing. Yet, in the end, it shows that even the tangible ills found "in faith" (e.g., a very real illness) can be neither "explained" nor "rendered meaningless." Remaining at this level only forces me continuously to argue with God. This is another reason why society needs people with disabilities: they compel us to deal with the question of God's righteousness. And here we must all answer in the same way: God suffers immeasurably from us, mostly from the healthy. And it is precisely to this situation that the afflicted individual bears witness, more than does the "healthy person" who has been spared all these trials and tribulations.

Küng responded to the final question, "Does suffering have any meaning?" as follows: "Endless suffering is meaningless 'in itself.' God offers us meaning through Christ's death and new life. It is an offer which is intended to be accepted in faith despite everything that shows it to be absurd." God is also present in darkness. Suffering is not a sign that God is absent. Rather, suffering can be seen in a completely different light, as the cross and the path to God. Küng concluded, "This was claimed by Leibnitz and vaguely perceived by Dostoyevsky. It was confirmed by Job and lived by Paul through the power of Christ: suffering is also embraced by 'God' and is taken up by him. Suffering can also become the place where we encounter God however 'God-forsaken' it may seem. Christians know of no way *around* suffering, but they know of a way *through* it!" (pp. 68-69).

Doesn't Küng also speak far too glibly (even apologetically) of suffering in the name of Jesus Christ or is he merely trying to defend it? May we push aside faith in a "hidden God" so quickly? After all, suffering people bitterly experience how little God the creator does about misery. How can one seriously offer consolation? H. Häring, in A. J. Buch/H. Fries (eds.), *The Question of God as the Question of*

Humankind (*Die Frage nach Gott als Frage nach dem Menschen,* 1981, p. 83), said, "God is not for violence. He is for love. He remains loyal to those who are suffering." "In the struggle against suffering, God has no power, but he has the last word."

Dorothee Sölle: *Suffering,* 1973

In this book, the thoughts on suffering are based on the biblical message that describes God as the "lover of life." Dorothee Sölle[6] bore witness to the fact that Jesus of Nazareth lived this infinite affirmation because he accepted and drew to him people who were despised and rejected and who were denied or who were forced by others to deny themselves. She concluded from this that all suffering, be it physical, emotional, individual or collective, continues to be a challenge that assigns us the task of doing away with it. However, this necessary and often one-sidedly emphasized aspect should not render us blind to a task that is just as important: learning from suffering (cf. W. Michaelis, *Theological Dictionary of the New Testament* 5:905ff.).

In line with theological tradition, Sölle assumed that this thought was already present among the ancient Greeks. She referred to Aeschylus, *Agamemnon,* verse 176ff. (p. 124, note 3). However, this translation was refuted by H. Neitzel (*Gymnasium* 87, 1980, pp. 283-293). He contended that Aeschylus' intention was as follows: Zeus commands that the path to reasoning is by means of the punishment of suffering (death). Zeus orders the way of thinking. However, it is not necessary to go to the trouble of looking for particular authors to quote. The saying "we learn from our mistakes" is familiar in many cultures. Whoever repeats this may do so without attaching any special theology to it. The maxim shares one characteristic with many other proverbs: it is only partially right. "Whoever digs a pit for someone else" by no means inevitably "falls into it himself," as the German proverb claims.

In the Christian tradition, suffering and learning have always been connected with the demand that one take up "one's own" (not just any) cross. Experiencing this suffering and the process of bringing about the capacity to suffer opens up the depth dimension of life in the first place. We are supposed to view life as meaningful in its totality and to see our work to change what needs changing as happiness. According to Sölle, the unwavering nature of this pursuit of happiness will "surround" and "recast" suffering.

Sölle posed two questions: "What are the causes of suffering, and how can these conditions be eliminated?" This modern sociocritical question, which is directed "outwards," can only be meaningfully posed when the traditional question, which refers to the individual and is directed "inwards," is not repressed: "What is the meaning of suffering and under what conditions can it make us more human?" (p. 5).

Dorothee Sölle first sharply criticized "Christian masochism," which glorifies the kind of suffering that can be abolished. She contends that such Christian interpretations say that suffering serves to break our pride, prove our powerlessness, and exploit our dependency, and that suffering is punishment and a trial, a means of chastening and discipline. These explanations tell us that the ultimate purpose of suffering is to lead us back to God "who only becomes great when he makes us small" (p. 19).

For D. Sölle, the problem is not so much the existential interpretation that people give to their pain as in "the later theological systematization, which has no use for suffering that hasn't been named and pigeonholed. . . . Theologians have an intolerable passion for explaining and speaking when silence would be more appropriate" (pp. 19-20). She illustrates the counterpart of a sadistic God as a type of ultimate consequence of this masochistic way of thinking. The logic of this way of interpreting suffering is actually not easy to refute: "1. God is the almighty ruler of the world, and he sends all suffering; 2. God acts justly, not capriciously; 3. all suffering is punishment for sin" (p. 24). Each attempt to view suffering as being directly or indirectly caused by God entails the risk of thinking of God as sadistic. Sölle says that the permanent justification of the modern objection to this God is the suffering of the innocent, adding that "in comparison with the enormity of human suffering, all are 'innocent' " (p. 25).

D. Sölle's chapter, "A Critique of Christian Masochism" (pp. 9-32), begins with a document of suffering and evolves into an effective showdown first with Christian sermons and tracts (on this point see also Daiber, K. F., Suffering as a Theme of Preaching (*Leiden als Thema der Predigt,* Munich, 1978), and secondly with contemporary theology of the cross. Here, J. Moltmann with his work, *The Crucified God* (*Der gekreuzigte Gott,* Munich, 1972), appeared to be an advocate of theological sadism (pp. 26-27). R. Strunk recently attempted to rectify Sölle's criticism of Moltmann. He contended that D. Sölle based her considerations on an authoritarian father image and that in many points she actually agreed with her opponents, at least in the basic intention that we should assume that suffering is part of God instead of attributing to him a type of condescending compassion. In addition, Strunk said that Sölle ascribed things to Moltmann that he had never said. Strunk expressed his criticism within the framework of a review of M. Welker's article about Jürgen Moltmann's book, *The Crucified God* (Munich, 1979) in Protestant Theology (*Evangelische Theologie* 41, 1981, pp. 90).[7]

I do not wish to burden readers with these kinds of controversies. However, they should be aware of how actively and even pugnaciously Protestant theologians are debating the relationship of God and suffering.

Furthermore, Sölle raised the accusation of a "post-Christian apathy," which presumably is more appropriate for the present (p. 33). Her proposition was as follows: "Desiring painlessness for oneself means desiring one's own death." She reminded us that apathy literally means "nonsuffering" and, accordingly, inability to suffer, and that it is already seen as a societal condition in which striving to avoid suffering controls people to such an extent that avoiding human relationships and contacts altogether becomes a goal. Logically, then, when with experiences of suffering, the *pathai* (misfortunes that happen to a person) of life, are repressed, the passion for life in general also disappears. Sölle claimed that when this happens, the joys of life lose their strength and intensity (p. 36).

The path of true love never did run smoothly, as the poet said. Sölle quoted Küng: "Fear of violating the principle of apathy was stronger than fear of mutilating the image of Christ in the gospels" (p. 43).

Of course, the problem of apathy should be treated very seriously.[8] Jüngel and Ebeling took up this question in their discussion of "death of God" theology, which in itself came about through wrestling with the question of theodicy.[9] The God who does not suffer, and who is the counterpart of a personality devoid of emotion, has been dethroned. Apathy can be found on both sides.

According to Sölle, the fact that members of our society accept pain as fate plainly contradicts the thrust of the Christian understanding of suffering, which rejects the idea of fate holding people remorselessly in its grip. "The transformation of pain, in which people move from passivity and flight into acceptance, could signify for the suffering such a 'strength,' found in pain" (p. 44). However, this type of theological thought only verges on the truth when it takes on a political form. The worst form of apathy is not the personal desire to live as free of pain as possible, but political apathy. The example of Vietnam demonstrated "that Auschwitz is not yet over," because for many Vietnam wasn't an issue (pp. 45-46).

Following this criticism, Sölle pointed out the relationship between "suffering and language" (p. 61). She said that the way out of the isolation of suffering is by way of communication in the form of an appeal to solidarity for change. "Active behavior replaces purely reactive behavior. The conquest of powerlessness . . . leads to changing even the structures" (pp. 72-73). This conquest also includes the hopelessness of certain forms of suffering that can be endured as long as the pain is articulated, provided that people share their lives—and that means their suffering—in the fellowship of a group. The meaning of liturgy is rediscovered. In its set formulations people can once again get in touch with their fears, pain, and happiness, in order not to become apathetic about them (p. 74). Prayer proves to be an all-encompassing act "by which people transcend the mute God of an apathetically endured reality and go over to the speaking God of a reality experienced with feeling in pain and happiness. It was this God with whom Jesus spoke in Gethsemane" (p. 78). For today's people, Jesus' dignity was revealed in his fear of death. Precisely because the threat to one's own life touches on one's relationship with God and jeopardizes one's original trust, Jesus' experience in Gethsemane pointed beyond destruction. It was the experience of consent: "Your will be done." "The cup of suffering becomes the cup of strengthening" (p. 86).

Following a detailed treatment of how suffering can be made bearable, Sölle concluded about "the truth of acceptance" that: "The strength of this position is its relationship to reality, even to wretched conditions. Every acceptance of suffering is an acceptance of that which exists. The denial of every form of suffering can result in a flight from reality in which contact with reality becomes ever thinner, ever more fragmentary. It is impossible to remove oneself totally from suffering, unless one removes oneself from life itself, no longer enters into relationships, makes oneself invulnerable" (p. 88). "Death is the total lack of relationships with other people" (Jüngel, *Death: The Riddle and the Mystery,* 1975).[10] It is no longer a matter of the old question of theodicy, whether God wants to punish those who suffer, or whether he has forgotten them, or whether he nevertheless, or even especially, loves them. It is no longer the child's question, "Do you love even me?" Adults ask, "How can people put their love for God into practice?" (p. 95). With this, D. Sölle's basic assumption recurred: "The God who is the lover of life does not desire the suffering of people, not even as a pedagogical device, but instead their happiness" (p. 108). Sölle said that in terms of the Christian perspective, the affirmation of suffering is a part of God's "yes" and not, as it may seem at times, the one and only concern behind which affirmation of life completely disappears.

Sölle again used the example of Job to illustrate that "the acceptance of suffering" cannot be taken care of by bowing down to that which we cannot change because it is stronger than we are. Acceptance means a kind of overcoming out of which we emerge conquered and strengthened at the same time. "Exodus from suffering" is the greatest theme of the Bible. Sölle believed that "Job is stronger than God" (p. 112) because he trusted in the God who led his people out of their sufferings in Egypt. However, the God whom Job experienced was only another Pharaoh. Job is stronger than God because he did not expect his answer from "the one who causes suffering" but instead from "the one who suffers" (p. 119).

In "Suffering and Learning," Sölle included the following statement: "There is a history of resurrections, which has vicarious significance. A person's resurrection is no personal privilege for himself alone—he is called Jesus of Nazareth. It contains within itself hope for all, for everything. . . ." There is someone who says, "I die, but I shall live." There is someone who says, "I and the Father are one." This gives hope to the speechless and the hopeless. Sölle pointed out there is no heaven that can rectify Auschwitz. But God, who is not a greater Pharaoh, justified himself by suffering with and dying with his son on the cross, and she emphasized that God can have no other hands than ours (pp. 149-150). We cannot compare situations of suffering by asking about the number of victims and the way they were killed. Instead, "the only thing that can be compared is the person's relationship to the suffering laid upon him, his learning, his change." The justification for a Christian interpretation to Auschwitz can only be established "when it undergirds and clarifies what the story from Auschwitz contains" (pp. 146-147). Yet in order to do this, God needs people, us, in order to work on the perfection of his creation. For this reason, God also suffers with [his] people, so that the human being's salvation does not come to us either from outside or from above. It comes about as an internal process, in and with us.

In the last chapter, "The Religion of Slaves," we hear about those people who have suffered consciously, "people we know who in suffering have become better and not more bitter, those who have willingly taken suffering upon themselves for the sake of others" (p. 151). Sölle used the life story of Simone Weil, who was Jewish, to depict a path of solidarity in suffering along with others. Simone Weil experienced her "why question," the search for the meaning of suffering as a horror that submerged her entire soul. "During this absence [of God], there is nothing to love" (p. 155).

The "paradox" remains an indispensable thought form for Christian faith. "I see the injustice, the destruction, the senseless suffering— I believe the justice, the coming liberation, the love that occurs in the night of the cross" (p. 158). Two elements constitute this process: the cross and the resurrection.

In his discussion of the dogmatism of philosophers and theologians, in the treatise on critical reason (Tübingen, 1968), Hans Albert also denounced the term *paradox* as an attempt at immunization. (p. 114, note 27). Inasmuch as the intermeshing of the cross and resurrection is a topic of discussion (and D. Sölle does not always use the term so precisely), theologians have a hard time doing without it. However, they run the risk of using an inconceivable concept that belies their own claim to scholarship.

According to Sölle, Christians are people whose deaths are already behind them by virtue of Christ's cross and his resurrection. In the lament "I can't go on!"—death in the form of lack of relationships— the only thing that remains is the choice between the absurd "cross" of meaninglessness and the cross of Christ, the choice between the death that we "apathetically" accept as a natural process and death that we suffer as an expression of our faith. Resurrection is the ability of the soul to keep going in darkness and to believe in God. However, that means affirming life in its totality.

The paradox that God loves us even when nothing of his love is visible is, in Sölle's opinion, the subjective enabling of the future. Without this paradox, the future would only be of interest for the people who survive. "The Christian God is no little Chinese god of fortune" (p. 166). Jesus identifies himself with those who suffer. In order to conquer death, he has become mortal like all others. Embarking on Jesus' path means adhering to the paradox. Using the example of pastoral care, Sölle demonstrated that this paradox is valid for the individual in the strict sense as well. One person can well suffer for another. Yet this individual cannot take on pain for the other person. However, one can stand alongside one's neighbor (pp. 166-167).

A. M. K. Müller: The Meaning of Suffering, (*Vom Sinn des Leidens*, 1974)/The Fall of the Dogma of the Guilty Party (*Der Sturz des dogmas vom Täter*, 1974)

Müller's basic thesis[11] was as follows: Suffering is productive energy. Behind this is the challenge for us to renounce the false premise of our worldview that says change comes about only by action, and that suffering is only passive. From this premise we think that we have to do everything possible to eliminate suffering through action, e.g., to make it go away by reinterpreting it, or by condemning the people who caused it or at least to alleviate the pain, by making the guilty party suffer. The aim of all action is to make suffering manageable by making it something objective.

Müller raised an alternative to this. He contended that suffering should be freed from the false polarity of active and passive. The dogma of the guilty party must be overthrown and, in its place, the "innocent" must live through their trials. This is to say that "the meaning of suffering is revealed only when the priority is given, not to action and manageability, but to interaction, which always means unmanageability" (p. 311, cf. D. Sölle, op. cit., p. 11). Interaction as the mixture of personal and structural interplay can become productive for vital perception if "solidarity" is lived, not merely as the educational objective of a group (cf. H. E. Richter), but also practiced in living relationships within the smallest unit, namely, the individual, in meditation on God and on oneself (p. 312). Müller explained the meaning of suffering on the brink of a crisis of survival in three phases: from the life of the individual, to the collectively perceived upheavals in the history of learning, and to the whole crisis of humanity.

Müller used examples from law and medicine to illustrate the first step, which is suffering in one's personal life. The way in which suffering is pronounced on by judges and treated by physicians stems from a very definite pattern of thinking. The "victims" (the injured party or the ill) live through an "untransferable internal trial" while for the "actors" (judges or physicians) it is a "transferable external process" (cf. Sölle, p. 11 and pp. 146ff.). Müller's thesis was that one cannot suffer on another's behalf, i.e., suffering is nontransferable.

He said that suffering can only be fruitful within the suffering persons themselves. According to Jesus' testimony in the Sermon on the Mount, it is only in their very suffering that those who suffer can hope for healing through new insight. This is why they yearn for inner mastery, which from their perspective is inseparably connected to the question of the meaning of suffering (p. 313). By placing emphasis on this inner process, Müller focused on the same basic thought as that of D. Sölle. This type of healing process which is directed inwards, as in a doctor-patient relationship, always constitutes a challenge. It demands much from the former actor. It requires the doctors in charge to cast off some of their "transferred" doctor role and, in so doing, expects of them a unique, painful compassion. If doctors accept what the patients' illnesses impose on them, the patients experience a type of acceptance that can become the basis for accepting themselves and their own nontransferable maladies (pp. 314-315).

For this reason, Jesus' suffering was unique because he perceived the suffering process differently, namely, consistently as an "internal" matter (p. 316). His witness showed that suffering does not become a productive and transformative power until it ceases to cause more suffering by striking back. It begins to bring about a transformation in the sufferers themselves, because their suffering remains nontransferable. Suffering can open up the perspective to us that "only those who endure suffering as suffering and not as some type of intellectual reinterpretation, only those who experience shock in it, enter the dimension of understanding in which the meaninglessness of suffering is suddenly transformed into a new future." The immediacy of this experience can no longer be questioned conceptually (p. 317). Müller said that this is why Soviet physicist Andrey Sakharov admitted, when unable to prevent a routine nuclear test explosion that cost human lives, "The feeling of powerlessness and the horror which gripped me on that day will be engraved on my memory for the rest of my life. It has changed me in many ways on my journey and shaped my present view of life" (p. 317).

In the second step of his consideration of the meaning of suffering at the threshold of a crisis of survival, Müller turned to the upheavals of collective understanding in science. Here, suffering also appears in the form of a crisislike process (p. 318). With reference to Kuhn, who used case studies to demonstrate that we must differentiate between the lengthier periods of "normal science" and the short upheavals of "scientific revolution," he quoted C. F. von Weizsäcker, whose arguments support those of Kuhn: "In general, a scientific revolution is preceded by a crisis of the prevailing paradigm. However, the prevailing paradigm is never overthrown by an apparently falsifying experience alone. . . . A paradigm is overthrown by a new paradigm" (p. 319). Müller intended to prove that the key experience is the crisis here too: "The apparently certain 'exterior' in the crisis which precedes the formation of a new paradigm is, as it were, dragged into the 'interior' of great uncertainty and is transformed there in an unimagined way. This mixture of interior and exterior in a crisis in the field of science is often experienced by active researchers as a period of turbulent but real impotence. However, at the same time, such a crisis is 'the precondition for all profoundly creative processes' " (p. 319).

According to Müller, it follows that part of discovering the meaning of suffering is that we become aware of the opportunities available to us even in such threatening times of upheaval (p. 320). The meaning of suffering, which remains disguised in normal times, can be revealed in crisis. A crisis can expose the fact "that human beings shun the inescapability of time which comes from the future. They tend to define who they are by focusing on a permanence and by striving to negate the essential temporality of their own existence." For Müller, this is also the motivation for establishing theories. "Theory captures time, as it were, 'prepares' it and with this act of 'deep-freezing' renders it permanently docile" (p. 321). In contrast, Müller discovered that, because of the abundance of time, there is always in the existence of the sufferer even a void (an absence) of concepts—indeed, even of thought. "Suffering leads to an emptiness which concretely enables a way of thinking which is more oriented to the hereafter and thereby opens a new type of thinking—on another, unexpected plane of perception" (p. 321). Müller said that in order for this type of productivity to occur, former thought patterns of all persons involved in a crisis must be crucified.

In the third step, suffering is considered within the total crisis. According to Müller, we are now, for the first time, being confronted with a total crisis affecting the survival of humanity. "What is at stake is the future possibility of objective observation of relationships in society and in nature, in which plateaus are portrayed as progress" (p. 322). Here he discovered a further possible meaning for suffering. "Could the meaning of suffering be to liberate us from the tendency toward the external relationship of objectification in a lengthy historical process?" (p. 323). The promise of an alternative gives hope to "those who are fundamentally 'free' of the will to power." The Sermon on the Mount calls them the "meek." Their potential for a possible future of human relationships lies in their perceptive way of bearing affliction." According to this, the meaning of suffering coincides with the power of open time, however, only at the cost of "abandoning the final plateau of knowledge that is free of suffering" (p. 324).

Giesbert Greshake: The Price of Love: A Meditation on Suffering (*Der Preis der Liebe: Besinnung über das Leid*, 1978)[12]

Whoever loves must suffer. Greshake's main thesis is revealed by the very title of his work. However, for this reason, suffering is also only comprehensible and conceivable to those who love. The author stated in his foreword that theological reflection may be as fluent and consistent as one pleases. It is only in the practice of faith, hope, and love that it proves its worth.

Greshake examined two questions in four sections. The first, theological and abstract, reads, "Suffering and the Question of God: An Outdated Problem?" (Chapter 1). He answered the questions in a section entitled, "Creation and Suffering" (2). The second question is existential and concrete: "A Cost Which Is Far Too High?" (3). Its answer lies in "Overcoming Suffering" (4).

In his treatment of "Suffering and the Question of God," Greshake confirmed beyond doubt that the human being's fundamental question, "Suffering—why?" continually revives the old question of theodicy. Yet, following Küng and Zahrnt,[13] he believes that the question of theodicy has little market value today. The rediscovery of the book of Job in past decades has relentlessly discredited all attempts to explain suffering in the world. According to Greshake, it was Dorothee Sölle who most radically condemned the conventional discussions of theodicy, thus providing the theological response to the abominations of the Nazi regime, a response that he had generally found to be lacking, as had sociologist Peter L. Berger, for example (p. 13).

It does not seem to be advisable to discuss the sheer pros and cons of "theodicy." I think that if we understand the term in the broad sense (What does God have to do with suffering and evil?), it fits D. Sölle's position just as well as that of her opponents. If we use the term to denote "God as the cause of suffering," we would surely incite theological resistance because of the "philosophical" starting point in terms of causation rather than of God's own personal words (Karl Barth). Thus, a "yes" or "no" to theodicy in itself decides very little as long as the particular theology that determines its context remains vague.

If there is no theodicy, what is there? What alternatives does present-day theology offer? The exclusively Christological solution has become predominant, i.e., the embedding of all suffering in that of God, in the life and death of Jesus, in whom God "placed suffering under the promise of unimaginable glory." However, is that not once again, or still, an almost cynical consolation (pp. 24-25)? Greshake made his own attempt to tie together the various traditional trains of thought and, at the same time, tried to adapt them to our present fundamental attitude: "We must not put up with suffering, we have to fight it" (p. 26).

Most likely, Greshake would be incapable of composing a sentence like this: "Any attempt to look upon suffering as caused directly or indirectly by God stands in danger of regarding him as sadistic" (Sölle, op. cit., p. 26). Consistently, he defended himself against D. Sölle's attacks on theism (p. 13). Indeed, he altogether rejected a "negative attitude toward theodicy" (pp. 14-19). Despite his general agreement with Küng, Greshake inserted "a few question marks" (p. 20), particularly on the subject of separating reflection from experience. Greshake claimed, and this is certainly true, that "thinking" should not be strictly separated from "experience." Theological reflection, he said, although most likely also an element of faith, can expose plausibilities, and as theory can create the framework for practical solutions (p. 22).

Yet Greshake's own outline, "Creation and Suffering," still, or again, demonstrates traces of an attempt to reconstruct theodicy with traditional elements. D. Sölle's verdict against the three axioms, God's omnipotence, God's righteousness, and "All suffering is punishment for sin" (op. cit., pp. 24-25), could well apply to Greshake, too. In essence, he distinguished between two types of suffering: first, the suffering that we humans inflict upon ourselves, I on myself, I on others, and others on me. Second, the suffering that we encounter from the given structures of reality, theologically speaking, "from creation" (p. 24). At the bottom of this is most likely the simplification of the three kinds of evil that Leibnitz once spoke about (metaphysical, physical, moral). It is evidently a matter of the relatively simple division into a subjective and objective sphere of suffering.

Human beings themselves are responsible for the first kind of suffering, suffering caused by human hand. It results from our own sin and that of our fellow human beings and humankind as a whole (p. 39). It will not do to demand that God, as the omnipotent creator of human freedom, simultaneously prevent suffering. That would mean construing the term "divine omnipotence" as unlimited power, instead of referring to a will that has made what it wants clear enough. Greshake's criticism was aimed at scholastic dogmatism and that which followed, which demanded all kinds of things of the term "omnipotence," including that God should be able to create a triangular circle, a wooden iron, and the like (p. 28). However, in reality, God's omnipotence—this was recognized by early theologians—has its limits in its freedom from contradiction. As this is the case, it does not make sense to say that God should be able to use his omnipotence to bring about creaturely freedom and prevent suffering at the same time. Greshake's thesis was as follows: "If God desires freedom for creation, the potential for suffering is automatically implied" (p. 29). He asked whether it might not be possible that a surfeit of suffering, involving our own pain in body and soul, is the only thing that makes us aware of the meaning of guilt, showing us its face and to what extent we entangle ourselves and others in it (p. 38).

Much of this recalls Karl Barth. His instructive discussion in *Church Dogmatics II, 1*, pp. 524-538, could perhaps be of help concerning the theology of God's omnipotence. Of particular interest is the question of seeing freedom from contradiction as the limit of divine omnipotence (ibid. pp. 534f.), in contrast to scholastic and older Protestant dogmatists. "God cannot do everything without distinction. He can only do what is possible for Him and therefore genuinely possible. This does not imply any limitation of His omnipotence. Rather, it defines his omnipotence as His and therefore true omnipotence. It is omnipotence, the true omnipotence over all and in all, in the very fact that He cannot do 'everything,' that the possibility of the impossible, the power of impotence, is alien to Him and excluded from his essence and His activity. . . . We have, indeed, to keep an inflexible grip on the truth that God is omnipotent in the fact that He and He alone and finally (because He is who He is) controls and decides what is possible and impossible for Himself and therefore at all. Whatever confirms Him is possible for Himself and therefore generally, and in the created world" (p. 535).

Thus, while the first kind of suffering is the responsibility of human beings, that is, as the other side of creaturely existence, the second type, "structural suffering," cannot be derived from human freedom and sin since it is found in the very nature of the world. Therefore, it is already part of creation itself. Early theology attributed this "physical suffering" to sin, so that all "objective" suffering appears to be punishment for guilt (pp. 39-40). Of course, for us today, that would mean a hardly tolerable objectification of sin. For Greshake, the problems lie in overcoming structural suffering in theological terms. He could allow a "purely eschatological answer" only as a "prima facie consideration." In its place, he sought the "inner meaning" of a world which produces structural suffering (pp. 39-40). Indeed, Greshake took up one of Teilhard de Chardin's thoughts: suffering is an essential "by-product" of evolution. In extrahuman development freedom has always had its price. Freedom advances when it is put to the test, or through strokes of luck. Working at it and investing one's energies also help. Life itself goes on in trial and error, so to speak, and it happens often enough that many failures precede a single success. The initial stages of matter show structural defects or a disturbed physical order. Pain in sensitive flesh is something else. At a yet higher point, there is malevolence or anguish of the spirit, which has powers of self-exploration and choice. "At all levels of evolution, always and everywhere, in us and around us, evil grows and is constantly forming anew!" (p. 45).

Thus, Greshake maintained, "Let's put it concretely from the start: The fact that something like cancer exists . . . is a necessary result of the fact that evolution foreshadows freedom. It is not determined, necessary, or fixed. Instead, it works through interplay, exploring different possibilities, and in coincidence." He substantiated the conclusiveness of his arguments with the following statement: "If, therefore, God desires human freedom as the condition for the possibility of love between him and his creation, and if human beings are essentially bound up in a world that corresponds to them, then the other side of freedom, as it were the negative of the print, is necessarily structural suffering" (p. 46).

Thus, freedom of human beings is intended by God as a condition of love, and since human beings are bound up in a world that corresponds to them, freedom necessarily has structural suffering as its negative reflector (p. 46). Therefore suffering cannot be played off against the good Creator. It is more the cost of freedom and the cost of love. There can be no love without suffering; such love is a contradiction in itself. A God who by virtue of his omnipotence would want to prevent suffering would thwart love.

Perhaps there are too many echoes here of the remains of earlier justifications of God. It is understandable that Greshake energetically proclaimed, "No, God absolutely does not wish suffering" (p. 51). Is, then, the price far too high? In the manner of his theological predecessors, Greshake brought up the classic example of Job, as well as Dostoyevsky's Alyosha, and like D. Sölle, assigned Simone Weil to the list of rebels. It seems as though Greshake presumed that more recent proposals are based on the acceptance of a God who is not sufficiently involved in the world or a definition of God that always views the Creator as being in danger when he enters into something which is beneath him (pp. 52-53).

One of the characteristics of the sinful world is that in the struggle against suffering born of sin, new suffering is produced; however, suffering that has been taken on voluntarily, suffering which is borne in solidarity with others, can transform sin and one's entanglement in it. In this way, this particular kind of suffering becomes suffering inspired by love, and suffering becomes God's service. According to Greshake, offering to suffer with others (Heb. 2:18) enables us to open up a path out of suffering. "The resurrection, the father's answer to his son's cross, is the beginning of the abolition of all suffering." For this reason, God paid "what was too high a price" for suffering for the sake of love. He did this so completely that every kind of human suffering can be harbored in God's love. Within the suffering that God does along with us, we find the strength to struggle against suffering, to bear up under it and give it meaning (p. 57).

On "Overcoming Suffering," Greshake maintains that the statement "suffering is abolished once and for all" should not only be understood eschatologically, so that it refers exclusively to the end as a final point. Rather, this statement also implies that perfection is already at work at this point and that it is being fulfilled bit by bit. Love as a process of suffering with others can already take small steps.

Greshake concluded by mentioning the following steps:

● Do away with suffering "through personal action, through societal reforms, and especially by suffering with others" (p. 61).

● Where suffering cannot be overcome, hold one's ground against destructive aggression and against loneliness which leads to giving up. In this way, suffering can be productively transformed (cf. Müller). On this subject, he referred to Paul's claims in 2 Corinthians 4:8 and 2 Corinthians 6:9.

● In one's personal life story, unavoidable suffering assumes a positive status when it is borne in love for God and in solidarity with the suffering of others. "People who have never suffered pain have never lived. . ." (E. Kübler-Ross). "What will become of a society in which certain forms of suffering are avoided gratuitously" (D. Sölle, p. 38).

● The answer to prayer, which is very hidden and apparent only to those whose eyes are focused on God's presence and action in faithful prayer. This can be transformed into a miracle that can disrupt all expectations and the routine patterns of behavior (pp. 69-70).

Thus, Greshake's final proposition was as follows: "God allows evil and suffering because the potential for this provides the necessary opposite to creaturely freedom and personal love. But God himself enters this world of suffering in order to transform and abolish suffering through love both in and through human beings, for the time being, bit by bit, but one day, completely" (pp. 70-71).[14]

Reflections and Questions for Theology

After working through these theological approaches to suffering, many Christians will have a bit of trouble with the fact that, in this chapter, traditional teachings on suffering (or ways of dealing with them) have been broken with. Indeed, according to many theological testimonies, it seems as though they must initially dispense with many familiar disclosures in the Bible. Congregational members may also read about this in E. Gerstenberger and W. Schrage, *Suffering* (1977). A note from the chapter entitled "The Will of God": Although the thought may not be particularly prominent in the New Testament, it all hinges on "God's surpassing will." If, however, he is to blame (for suffering), he ends up as a "sadist" or "hangman" (Sölle). Gerstenberger and Schrage attempt to get around this consequence. "The knowledge" remains "that according to God's will there should actually be no suffering and not every kind of suffering corresponds to his will" (pp. 204-207).[15]

It is not easy to reach agreements when, under the title "Suffering"—next to "confrontations"—which are no doubt loving—it must be admitted that "viewed as a whole," the New Testament "never actually dealt with suffering as such" (p. 210). In analyzing current portrayals of Christian theology, there is little to be found under the catchword *suffering*. Apparently each of us must accept for ourselves God's powerlessness in view of suffering that is caused by human hands, as he allows for it in the cross of Christ. He suffers ineffably from his humanity! Yet is this really true? Many may cry, "How can it bother God when he suffers?" God constantly acts as if he is in principle our superior. His suffering is not really convincing for them. (The more power he has, the easier it must be for him to deal with his suffering!) But what would happen if he were to experience unlimited suffering under you and me, from human beings and their behavior? Nothing but that? Would you consider faith as an expression of pity for God?

Suffering would then have a different meaning. That is, not suffering itself, but rather the despair at the loss of all relationships, arising because of suffering, or in this case, because of severe disability. Loneliness would be seen as absolute hopelessness. Yet God reveals in Christ that he encounters people in instances where they feel they have reached the limit. Even despair is an experience of faith! "My power is made perfect in weakness." This was Paul's experience of Christ's presence in the context of his suffering (2 Corinthians 12:9). In faith, those who have been abandoned experience God's presence and, strangely enough, this also comes about through the presence of people who persevere with them. The stories in this book bear witness to the fact that the significant experience in crisis is the interaction of God's care with inadequate human support.

As a layperson who does not possess the theological knowledge of the scholars included in this chapter, I am fascinated by these deep and extensive discussions of human suffering, reflecting their own experiences of suffering or suffering with others. Yet I am struck by one shortcoming. I find no reference to this unique, personal experience of the interaction between God's care and human support which the stories speak about.

Several questions occur to me:

● Is it possible to develop a "theology of suffering" without including both of these dimensions of relationship as highly significant?

● Has God's gift to humanity, the capacity for relationships, been adequately dealt with in theology?

● Does theology reflect the kinds of ambivalent human energies which are constantly working to stunt this capacity?

Human relationships are not only endangered by the tendencies of our time to overrate material values, work, and achievement, tendencies which also snare Christians. They are also threatened by the creative power of thought which comes from all branches of learning.

● Is it not the task of theology, as the partner of other disciplines, to bring to light the unique, personal dimension of the capacity for relationships, without being afraid of losing its scholarliness?

In education, we are beginning to recognize how impractical a lot of our approaches are, since we over-emphasize theory. However, finding ways around this problem is difficult. This capacity for relationships which has been lost, not only in academic work but in our lives together, can grow and become stronger when we suffer ourselves or along with others. We can recognize an intensity of life in relationship with others in people like those we encountered in the stories of disabled and crisis-stricken people and the people near to them. Such a degree of intensity is rarely achieved by people who are "healthy" and "able to cope." (This is often because they are not aware of what they lack.)

In the search for ways to change our threatened world and to support all kinds of people who face crises, an uncharted way of opening up the future is described in Matthew 25:34-40. It is not the exceptional acts, but the simple offers of help that bring about these changes, in the awareness that both people who suffer and those who provide support have needs.

The insight of sufferers is that there is no end to learning. The "spirals" of experiences occur repeatedly in the struggle against temptation from the outside and self-destructive powers on the inside, even when one succeeds in accepting one's own fate. We have the tendency to deny this insight. As a layperson, I wonder how such a perspective can be theologically communicated in discussions on suffering. So far, I have only been able to find a very old-fashioned statement, which I would still like to quote:

> God himself is not ashamed to teach it [or "such things" (i.e. the struggle against destructive forces in and around us. Author's note.)] daily, for he knows of nothing better to teach, and he always keeps on teaching this one thing without varying it with anything new or different. All the saints know of nothing better or different to learn, though they cannot learn it to perfection. Are we not most marvelous fellows, therefore, if we imagine, after reading or hearing it once, that we know it all and need not read or study it any more? . . . Actually, he is busy teaching it from the beginning of the world to the end, and all prophets and saints have been busy learning it and have always remained pupils, and must continue to do so. (Luther's Large Catechism, *Book of Concord*, p. 361)[16]

It seems to me that, even in theology, there is a prevalent consciousness that "we can do everything and need nothing else." Luther adds, "and most likely [we] need . . . to begin to learn."

Luther, in his *Small Catechism,* summed up what one needs to learn in a lifetime in a simple sentence:

> "To fear, love, and trust God above all else." [17]

Using the sources of Luther's theology, Gerta Scharffenorth's study of the relationship of men and women[18] has rediscovered the Reformation's insight into the meaning of human relations and the capacity for relationships. The author referred to the loss suffered by theology when this dimension of human existence is not taken into consideration. This recognition, which is anthropologically significant and can be concluded from the stories, was influential in Reformation thought. The reformers hoped for and worked toward building supportive relationships among Christians in congregations.

There is a suspicion that keeps nagging at me: I am wondering if the failures on the part of potential support-givers, and the resultant experiences of abandonment that the afflicted have, are rooted in an inadequate theology. Has theology overlooked the fundamental significance of the human capacity for relationships?

11

Summary: Not Knowing the Answer, but Finding One's Own Way

"There is no way to peace,
peace is the way."
Martin Luther King, Jr.

"I am the way,
the truth and the life."
Jesus

This study attempted to focus on faith and pastoral care from another point of view, namely, from the perspective of those who are directly affected by suffering. I attempted to do this by empirically "stock-taking" and in theoretically reflecting on the subject.

Consequently, in the first chapter, the study first summarized tendencies that were inferred from over 500 life stories. These tendencies can be presented as three central, fundamental experiences that suffering people have:

• *First experience:* They feel that they are usually forced into passivity as objects of mission and are rarely treated as real people who are in a relationship with God. They feel that they are not taken seriously in pastoral care.

● *Second experience:* They experience the proclamation of the gospel as an admonition that they should see their affliction or crisis as a kind of privilege that can lead to great benefit. The consolation they are supposed to feel rarely comes from a critical examination of the crisis.

● *Third experience:* People who give pastoral support tend to be seen as people who have been assigned official roles within the church rather than as people who are personally concerned and who are prepared to suffer with them as partners.

On the basis of these observations, the study has put forth the *first proposition: Despite negative experiences with the church, suffering persons, and people near them in time of crisis, hold fast to their experiences of faith.*

The second chapter treated the nearly lost dimension of human support, which, when offered to those coping with crisis, can meet needs. For that purpose, the "process of learning to cope with crisis" was presented as a model. I developed the theory of eight spiral phases. In the presentation of this model, I drew on the results of the analysis of over 500 stories, the findings having already been published. According to this result, only one-third of those who were afflicted by suffering reached the *target* stage of accepting their suffering (spiral phase 6) and achieving social integration (8), because they lacked human support. In contrast, the two-thirds of the sufferers who had to go it alone prematurely interrupted the learning process in the *initial* or *transit* stages. In so doing, they were condemned to social isolation.

The *second proposition* arose from the reflection on the question of the meaning of faith and human support in dealing with crisis: *In the process of learning to cope with crisis, Christian faith can take up* aggression *(3), which has been recognized as cathartic in the form of complaining and lamenting to God.*

This means that, on the one hand, Christian faith enables the crisis-stricken to "obediently" accept their suffering as God-given, affirming it and not questioning it. This is the believer's so-called *naive-apathetic reaction.*

On the other hand, Christian faith can liberate afflicted people and allow them to release their aggression (3) against their crisis or suffering. Initially, it grants them room to learn to bear their suffering together with God in dialog with him and to develop the capacity for an affirming acceptance (6). This is the so-called *critical-sympathetic response* by the suffering Christian.

For both it can be said that their Christian faith can take up aggression in the process of learning to cope with crisis. Therefore, Christians do not feel that they are at the mercy of their crisis. Instead, they have someone they can talk to, someone they can address and someone who will listen to them. They find that they are bound up in their relationship with God as persons whom God has accepted, even and perhaps especially in their aggressive laments (3). This also occurs at the point where they bargain with God (4) and finally, in the darkness of their depression (5).

The third chapter described the full learning process of crisis management with the example of one of the over 500 life stories studied—that of Pearl S. Buck. The fourth to eighth chapters illustrated the significance of faith and human support using selected autobiographies. Different types of suffering were included: acquired polio (physical disability), acquired depression (emotional disability), acquired blindness (impairment of the senses), acquired and congenital severe retardation (mental handicap) and acquired cancer (chronic life disturbance). In addition, those chapters treated various attitudes toward faith—both the naive-apathetic and critical-sympathetic responses—and finally, types of support that are appropriate, inadequate, or completely missing on the part of people who are officially assigned to provide support and people who personally suffer alongside others.

The result reconfirms the results of my research, which in 1980 were presented under the title The Social Integration of the Handicapped *(Soziale Integration Behinderter),* Volume 1: Biographical Experience and Scientific Theory *(Biographische Erfahrung und wissenschaftliche Theorie)* and Volume 2: Coping with Crisis as Continuing Education *(Weiterbildung als Krisenverarbeitung,* third revised and expanded edition, Bad Heilbrunn, 1987, with full bibliographies cf. p. 235 and pp. 431ff.).

● Our first basic assumption is that all suffering persons, regardless of the cause of crisis—i.e., whether disabled or not—must work through the spiral phases of the process of learning to cope with crisis in order to achieve social integration. All of the stories unanimously bear witness to this. However, in this study, the crisis-stricken speak for so-called nondisabled people: Pearl S. Buck, Silvia and Albert Görres and Ruth Müller-Garnn as the parents of mentally retarded children and Laurel Lee as a woman suffering from cancer. Representing the disabled are Luise Habel, who is physically disabled; Ingrid Weber-Gast, who is emotionally disturbed; and Jacques Lusseyran, who is blind.

- Our second basic assumption is that Christian faith is a power that makes aggression (3) as catharsis possible and that enables one to accept crisis (6). This was also confirmed by almost all the authors. Here, two different attitudes toward faith arise: Ruth Müller-Garnn lived with the *naive-apathetic reaction* of faith as unconditional obedient acceptance of the suffering that God had given her to bear. She saw that it could even nullify latent doubt in faithful allegiance and devoted acceptance of agony. However, like Job in the Old Testament, the majority of the writers struggled through the *critical-sympathetic response,* although this struggle was undertaken at various levels of intensity. Typical here are Luise Habel, Ingrid and Stephan Weber-Gast, Jacques Lusseyran, Silvia and Albert Görres, and Laurel Lee.

- Our third basic assumption, that aggression as catharsis plays a key role in the process of learning to cope with crisis, was reconfirmed by the case of Luise Habel's mother: She predictably ended up not accepting her situation of "life with a disabled child" because catharsis through aggression was not worked through. She broke off the learning process in the *transit* stage and committed suicide. This was because she directed her aggression inward, against herself, before fully working it through (compare our results: Two-thirds of more than 500 writers committed suicide. Without exception, all writers expressed their desire to die.)

- Our fourth basic assumption is that human and pastoral support which is absent or insufficient leads to an interruption of the process of learning to cope with crisis in the *transit* stage, and thus to nonacceptance in social isolation. We assume that the reverse is also true, that available and appropriate support brings about acceptance in the *target* stage of social integration. This assumption extends through all the stories like a recurring theme. As an example, the story of Luise Habel demonstrated both injurious and constructive pastoral care. Ingrid and Stephan Weber-Gast experienced marriage counseling. Jacques Lusseyran described the support on the part of his parents and later on the part of the blacksmith Jérémie in the Buchenwald concentration camp as his "reality of acceptance" which grew out of his experiences with suffering. This acceptance enabled him to become a helpful supporter to many other people. Laurel Lee described the power of her Christian faith in the face of abandonment. Both Ruth Müller-Garnn and Silvia and Albert Görres suffered from the absence of any kind of pastoral or human support.

All of the writers confirm the fact that they primarily drew support from their experiences with faith, although assistance on the part of pastoral care was frequently absent or went amiss. Here it must be noted that the biographical material frequently defies systematic categorization. Besides, it is extremely difficult to pin down, and put at one's disposal, the subjects of pastoral care and faith. Christian life remains a risk and a mystery!

The observation of deficiencies in pastoral care was what prompted me to dedicate the ninth chapter to raising questions on the personalities of pastoral support-givers. Using inductive reports on experiences dealing with encounters between disabled people and those without disabilities, the evidence showed that the main problem of people who have not yet suffered in this way is a disruption in their relationships with those who have. They had trouble relating to disabled individuals.

This led to the *third proposition: The disabled and crisis-stricken are not* our *problem. Instead,* we *who are not disabled and not yet crisis-stricken are* their *problem.*

In addition, various positions within scientific disciplines were cited, among others, Schmidbauers's "helper syndrome," Brocher's theory of the illness of healthy people, and Fischer's reversal of the problem in the form of the surplus existence of those who are not disabled. Also treated were Horst-Eberhard Richter's theory of defense mechanisms against fear, Moltmann's apartheid society which is comprised of high performers, and finally, C. F. von Weizsäcker's theory of the relative legitimacy of societal defense mechanisms. After examining these and other interpretations of human behavior, societal and human interpretation necessarily follow.

The results led to the *fourth proposition: The church/society needs those who are afflicted by suffering just as those who suffer need the church/society.*

In the tenth chapter, the study presented theological approaches from Protestant and Roman Catholic backgrounds. This was undertaken as a tangent in order to determine possible answers to the question of

the origin and meaning of suffering. The theologians unanimously interpreted "remaining on the path of trusting in God" as a life-long
process in which faith must be taken up and ventured upon each day
anew. However, they differed in the interpretations they gave to the
realities of Christian existence. In all of the descriptions of "moving
through the phases," we missed descriptions of the intermeshing of
God's care with *human* support, that is, the consideration of the capacity
for relationships with others as a gift of God.

Hans Küng spoke of "anthropodicy" as true theodicy, in which
God's justification is determined by God himself in justifying the human
being who is far away from God. Küng said that by accepting this
interpretation, we can become closer to God in "conditional suffering"
and be removed from "unconditional suffering" which separates us
from God. This is a very abstract statement, however, and far removed
from real-life experience.

Dorothee Sölle advocated the relating of suffering to learning,
which is part of Christian tradition. She recognized this as the process
of giving words to suffering, so that out of muteness comes action via
language (cry, lament). This caused her to radically reject Christian
masochism and post-Christian apathy. She directed her appeal to fellow
sufferers as those who seek to shape life along with others.

A. M. K. Müller discovered suffering as productive energy. He
advocated overthrowing the dogma of the guilty party, i.e., overthrowing
so-called "transferable" suffering through external processes. Instead,
he stressed "transferable" internal processes in which suffering alone
is accepted as the crisis and the afflicted are transformed. This implies
that in the abyss the sufferers are enabled to think of the hereafter,
which leads to a new kind of thinking on another plateau of understanding. In this way, for Müller, a chance of survival is theoretically opened
up regarding the crisis of humanity.

Giesbert Greshake explained suffering as both the price of freedom and the price of love. He said that according to this reasoning,
both types of suffering, i.e., "suffering caused by human hands" and
"structural suffering" can be explained as by-products of the evolution
of humanity. This, however, means that suffering is ultimately rooted
in human guilt.

Our finding is that the questions about the "whys and where-
fores" of suffering must remain unanswered because suffering evades

explanation and objective handling. However, it can be recognized that asking "what it is for and where it leads" can enable flashes of insight in the encounter between the suffering and God. Most often these come in the context of common experiences with support-givers, though on condition that they be willing to continue learning throughout their lifetimes.

In carrying out our study, it became clear that support-givers become capable of suffering alongside others. In certain phases of dealing with crisis—primarily in *aggression, negotiation,* and *depression*—they are able to partially or wholly dispense with the usual types of pastoral care, such as quoting comforting Bible verses and theological arguments. These types of assistance in the *transit* stage not only offer little help, but in fact tend to block the process. However, the unique thing is that the presence of pastors and care-givers, their warmth and their refusal to disguise their own helplessness and questions by playing conventional roles, give those who suffer exactly what they need. In what appears to be powerlessness and in silent *solidarity,* they convey the message that God sustains those who struggle and rail against him and does not let go of them. In this way, through support-givers who provide pastoral care—this can be any one of us—sufferers sense that someone shares their lot and this takes them out of their hopeless isolation. Both of them feel accepted by God, who shares darkness with human beings.

Pastoral support is difficult because it can only be given as back-up—as accompaniment to the soloist. Both must play their part, however, as they depend on each other. This means:

● *Listening,* walking *alongside* others and not ahead of or behind them;

● *Sensing* the moments when the means of assistance jam up the process, when they provide encouragement, and when they hurt;

● *Trusting* that God will lend a hand and help when no one else knows a way out;

● *Hoping and believing* that in weakness, both persons concerned can gain new strength.

Notes

In each of the notes, the German entry appears first, followed by its English version, if one exists. In these cases the author's name is not repeated in the English reference. The German entry has the page number, the English doesn't. Where the page number in the German version was unknown, only the English version was noted.

Chapter 1

1. Ökumenischer Rat der Kirchen, ÖRK (ed.), *Bericht aus Nairobi 1975* (Frankfurt, 1976), pp. 23-28. World Council of Churches, ed., *Report from Nairobi 1975* (Geneva, 1976).

2. Ökumenischer Rat der Kirchen, ÖRK (ed.), *"Gathered for life"—Berichte aus Vancouver* (Frankfurt, 1984); idem, "Wir brauchen einander," ed. Geiko Müller-Fahrenholz (Frankfurt, 1979), p. 9.
   World Council of Churches, ed., *"Gathered for life": Reports from Vancouver* (Geneva, 1984); idem, "Partners in Life: The Handicapped and the Church," Faith and Order Paper No. 89 (Geneva, 1979).

3. Lutherischer Weltbund, LWB, *In Christus Hoffnung für die Welt: Report 1984* (Geneva, Stuttgart, 1985), pp. 214ff.
   Lutheran World Federation, *In Christ: Hope for the World/Report 1984* (Geneva, 1985).

4. Luise Habel, *Herrgott, schaff die Treppen ab!* (Stuttgart, Berlin, 1978), pp. 167-170.

5. Andreas Hämer, *Rehabilitation von unten: Der Platz der Körperbehinderten im Aufgabenfeld der Kirche* (Mainz, 1978), p. 11.

6. Habel, *Herrgott*, pp. 65-66.

7. Heinz Zahrnt, *Warum ich glaube: Meine Sache mit Gott* (Munich, 1977), p. 320.

8. Christa Schlett, . . . *Kruppel sein dagegen sehr: Lebensbericht einer spastisch Gelähmten* (Wuppertal-Barmen, 1970), pp. 72-73.

9. Denise Legrix, *Und doch als Mensch geboren* (Freiburg, 1963; Berlin, 1977), p. 57. *Born Like That* (London: Souvenir, 1962).

10. André Miquel, *Warum musst du gehen?* (Freiburg, 1971), p. 88. *Le fils interrompu* (Paris: Flammarion, 1971).

11. Ingrid Weber-Gast, *Weil du nicht geflohen bist vor meiner Angst* (Mainz, 1978), p. 34.

12. Hämer, *Rehabilitation*, p. 12.
13. Christy Brown, *Mein linker Fuss*, 8th ed. (Berlin, 1978), p. 102; idem, *Ein Fass voll Leben*, 2d ed. (Bern, Munich, and Vienna, 1975).
    My Left Foot (New York: Simon & Schuster, 1955); idem, *Down All the Days* (New York: Stein & Day, 1970).
14. Hämer, *Rehabilitation*, p. 52.
15. Weber-Gast, *Weil du nicht geflohen bist*, p. 34.
16. Sylvia Görres, *Leben mit einem behinderten Kind* (Zurich, Cologne, 1974), pp. 129-130.
17. Edith Meisinger, *Über die Schwelle: Aufzeichnungen einer spastisch Gelähmten* (Berlin, 1957), pp. 74ff.

Chapter 2

1. Diakonisches Werk der Evangelischen Kirche in Deutschland (Diaconic Service of the Evangelical Church in Germany), EKD, ed., "Hilfe für Behinderte: Zweites Schwerpunktprogramm der Diakonie," *Diakonie: Jahrbuch 1975* (Stuttgart, 1975). The same organization has published 13 brochures, among them: on psychological illnesses, *Psychisch Kranke brauchen Verständnis, Förderung, Annahme und Begleitung* (Stuttgart, 1976); on mental retardation/sensory disabilities, *Sinnesbehinderte brauchen des anderen Auge, Ohr und Hand als Brücke zum Leben* (Stuttgart, 1977); on physical disabilities, *Behinderte Menschen unterwegs aus dem Abseits zur aktiven Partnerschaft* (Stuttgart, 1977); on mental/emotional illness, *"Gemeinsam leben" mit geistigbehinderten Menschen muss durch Zuwendung, Ermutigung und Begleitung verwirklicht werden* (Stuttgart, 1978); on life-disturbances, *Evangelische Familien und Lebensberatung hilft Menschen in Krisen und Beziehungsstörungen ihr Leben neu zu entdecken* (Stuttgart, 1979). See also, in E. Wormann et al, *Mitbestimmung von Problemgruppen in der Gesellschaftpolitik*, "Eltern von behinderten und nicht-behinderten Kindern ('Bildungsurlaub')," Information from the Sozialamt (social service office) of the Evangelical Church in Westfalen, No. 26 (Schwerte, 1979). Finally, see Diakonisches Werk der Evangelischen Kirche in Deutschland, ed., *Initiativen für Behinderte und Nichtbehinderte: "Nehmt einander an, wie Christus uns angenommen hat"* (informational material, helps for work, media, among other things), produced by Public-Relations-Aktion, Referat Öffentlichkeitsarbeit (Stuttgart, 1981).
2. Erika Schuchardt, "Biographische Erfahrung und wissenschaftliche Theorie," in *Soziale Integration Behinderter*, Vol. 1, with alphabetical, classified, annotated bibliography of biographies from 1900 to 1986 (Bad Heilbrunn, 1980; 3d ed., rev. and enl., 1987).
3. As Elisabeth Kübler-Ross (in *Interviews mit Sterbenden*, 1979) explored the question, How can I learn to die? we are here concerned with the question, How can I learn to live, given limitations that seem to make life not worth living any more?
4. See also Jill Purce's fascinating study of the spiral, *Die Spirale: Symbol der Seelenreise*. Munich: Kösel, 1988. Originally published in English: *The Mystic Spiral: Journey of the Soul*. Art and Imagination series. London: Thames and Hudson, 1974.

Chapter 4

1. Habel, *Herrgott, schaff die Treppen ab!* Stuttgart: Kreuz, 1978.

Chapter 5

1. Weber-Gast, *Weil du nicht geflohen bist vor meiner Angst.* 6th ed. Mainz: Matthias Grünewald, 1984.

Chapter 6

1. Jacques Lusseyran, *And There Was Light* (New York: Parabola, 1987); *idem, Le monde commence aujourd'hui* (Paris: La Table Ronde, 1959).

Chapter 7

1. Ruth Müller-Garnn, *. . . und halte dich an meiner Hand* (Würzburg: Echter, 1977); idem, *Das Morgenrot ist weit: Geschichte der Hoffnung* (Würzburg: Echter, 1980).
2. Silvia Görres, *Leben mit einem behinderten Kind.* (Munich: Piper, 1986).

Chapter 8

1. Laurel Lee, *Walking through the Fire* (New York: Bantam, 1977).

Chapter 9

1. Kirchenamt der Evangelischün Kirche in Deutschland, EKD, ed., *Leben und Erziehen wozu? Eine Dokumentation über Entschliessungen der Synode der EKD 1978* (Gütersloh, 1979).
2. Jörg Zink, Foreword, in Habel, *Herrgott,* p. 9.
3. Jürgen Moltmann, *Neuer Lebensstil: Schritte zur Gemeinde* (Munich, 1977), p. 22. *The Passion for Life: A Messianic Lifestyle* (Philadelphia: Fortress, 1978).
4. Fritz von Bodelschwingh, "Gespräch mit Dr. Brandt, dem Abgeordneten Hitlers," in *Bote von Bethel,* special edition 66 (Bielefeld, 1964), pp. 9ff. Compare also P. Göbel and H. E. Thormann, *Verlegt—vernichtet—vergessen . . . ? Leidenswege von Menschen aus Hephata im Dritten Reich: Eine Dokumentation,* edited by Hephata Hessisches Diakoniezentrum, 2d ed. (Schwalmstadt/Treysa: Plag-Druck, 1986).
5. Fritz von Bondelschwingh (nephew of the above-named pastor), in Bodelschwingh, Gespräche.
6. Wolfgang Schmidbauer, *Die hilflosen Helfer: Über die seelische Problematik der helfenden Berufe* (Reinbek bei Hamburg, 1977), p. 12.
7. Schmidbauer, *Die hilflosen Helfer,* p. 10.
8. Ibid., pp. 42, 43, 44.
9. Ibid., pp. 90, 91.
10. Ibid., p. 219.
11. T. Brocher, "Vortrag auf dem 17. Deutschen Evangelischen Kirchentag" (Lecture at the 17th German Evangelical Church Assembly) 8-12 June 1977, reprinted in *Kirchentag: Dokumentarband* (Stuttgart, 1978).
12. M. Fischer, "Das Geheimnis des Menschen: Theologische Überlegungen zur Zielsetzung der Behindertenhilfe," in *Diakonie: Jahrbuch 1975* (Stuttgart, 1975), p. 75.
13. Moltmann, *Neuer Lebensstil,* pp. 12, 13. *Passion for Life.*
14. Horst Eberhard Richter, *Lernziel Solidarität* (Hamburg, 1974), pp. 222, 223.
15. Carl Friedrich von Weizsäcker, "Der Behinderte in unserer Gesellschaft." Lecture given at the Bayerische Landesschule für Blinde (Bavarian State School for the Blind)

on the occasion of the 150th anniversary of its establishment, October, 1976, reprinted in *Der Garten des Menschlichen: Beiträge zur geschichtlichen Anthropologie,* 3d ed. (Munich, Vienna, 1977), p. 107.

The Ambivalence of Progress: Essays on Historical Anthropology (New York: Paragon House, 1988).

16. Ibid., p. 112.

17. Dorothee Sölle, *Die Hinreise* (Stuttgart, 1975), p. 9.
Death by Bread Alone: Texts and Reflections on Religious Experience (Philadelphia: Fortress, 1978).

18. Ibid., pp. 10ff.

19. World Council of Churches, *Leben und Zeugnis der Behinderten in der christlichen Gemeinde: Memorandum einer Konsultation 1978,* in *Documentation epd., Evangelischer Pressedienst,* No. 36a, 1978. See also World Council of Churches, *Partners in Life (Wir brauchen einander).*

Chapter 10

1. Hans Küng, *Gott und das Leid,* 5th ed. (Einsiedeln, 1974).

2. Compare Ernst Sellin, *Einleitung in das Alte Testament,* 10th ed. (Heidelberg, 1965), § 50, pp. 352-365.
Introduction to the Old Testament (Minneapolis: Augsburg, 1975).

3. This also appeared in 1952 in the 3d edition of C.G. Jung's *Antwort auf Hiob* (Zurich).
Answer to Job (Princeton, NJ: Princeton University, 1973).

4. Did Ernst Bloch's *Atheismus im Christentum* (Frankfurt 1968), pp. 148-167, about Job, *Atheism in Christianity* (New York: Herder and Herder, 1972), really have to raise such stormy reactions in Tübingen and elsewhere, since he was familiar with the tradition of thought there? Ehrenberg dealt with H. Gollwitzer's sympathetic critique *Krummes Holz—aufrechter Gang* (Munich, 1970), pp. 244-250, esp. pp. 247-250), within a wider framework, it seems to me, long before Bloch's book appeared.

5. What Barth wrote in 1955 appears to be quite different from D. Bonhoeffer's chapter "Die Nachfolge und das Kreuz," in *Nachfolge* (Munich, 1937) pp. 39-46, *The Cost of Discipleship* (New York: Macmillan, 1965). When one used to speak of "suffering," one generally spoke of "suffering for Jesus' sake," or words to that effect, and as far as that goes, of the "cross" that the Christian takes upon him or herself—which is mentioned consistently in the New Testament.

6. Dorothee Sölle, *Suffering* (Philadelphia: Fortress Press, 1984).

7. This discussion volume also gathers together more "dogmatic" points of view, which presume that Moltmann is on his way to a speculative theodicy (D. L. Migliore, p. 42), or which at least see him as concerned with theodicy as a central question. (H. H. Miskotte, pp. 76-89).

8. Those who would like more precise information about the so-called apathy-axiom will find it, among other places, in Eberhard Jüngel, *Gott als Geheimnis der Welt,* 3d ed. (Tübingen, 1979), pp. 508 and 511 (*God as the Mystery of the World* [Grand Rapids, MI: Eerdmanns, 1983]. Jüngel's thorough discussion of the Death-of-God theology enables us laypeople to arm ourselves to some degree against sometimes too fashion-prone judgments in this area. I would also observe that Jüngel, pp. 69ff, takes up the theodicy question and leads from it into the question, Where is God?

9. G. Ebeling, *Dogmatik des christlichen Glaubens,* Vol. 2 (Tübingen, 1979), pp. 202-205, also argues against the "vor wenigen Jahren modisch gewordene und wohl schon

wieder aus der Mode kommende Rede vom Tode Gottes" (p. 203). Actually, given that early-church Christology had already spoken of the death of God, a fixation on modern atheism('s concern about this) would seem to indicate too little attention to past history. In view of this, Ebeling's extensive §19, entitled "Der Tod Gottes" (pp. 128-255), deals first with "Das Sterben des Menschen" (pp. 132-149), and second (B), as the main section (1), with "Die Versöhnung von Gott und Mensch im Sterben Jesu" (pp. 149-255). Measured against Jüngel or Ebeling, this theme (which came up in the U.S. in 1961) is handled almost flippantly by Zahrnt under the heading, "Der Tod Gottes—ein logischer Widerspruch," in *Gott kann nicht sterben*, 3d ed. (Munich, 1970), pp. 52-60 *What Kind of God? A Question of Faith*. (Minneapolis: Augsburg, 1972).

Ebeling's pages about the theodicy problem *Dogmatik*, Vol. 3 (Tübingen, 1979), pp. 511-519), within the framework of the chapter about "Die Gerechtigkeit Gottes," (pp. 509-528) are recommended, if more information is desired. "Die Selbsttrechtfertigung Gottes" (Karl Barth!) "ist die Rechtfertigung des Menschen durch Gott. Das ist die entscheidende Antwort auf die Frage nach der Theodizee. Die Hiobfrage ist damit nicht verdrängt, sondern in das Christusgeschehen hineingenommen, so dass jeder Leidende glauben darf, sein Leiden und Sterben sei in dem Leiden und Sterben Christi mit aufgehoben." This does not by any means mean a justification of evil, which remains much more decidedly an inexplicable obscurity (pp. 518ff). Surely, a philosophical theodicy can offer little help to the suffering person, "weil sie ihn nicht auf sein Sein vor Gott ihm anzusprechen vermag," while theological talk of God carries with it solidarity with the suffering person and places the person's question Why? at center stage. It also means, however, that the word *theodicy* always recalls in a hidden way the real God, whose power sees itself as identical with his love, "im Glauben," despite all the doubts about this identity that are nourished by suffering.

To conclude this point: W. Sparn, ed., *Leiden—Erfahrung und Denken. Materialien zum Theodizeeproblem*. Theol. Bücherei, Vol. 67 (Munich, 1980), provides all the necessary material, in an appendix "Hinweise zur Revision des Theodizeeproblems" at present (pp. 247-274), along with a comprehensive bibliography. I found there sentences like "auch wenn die Klage des angefochtenen Glaubens vor Gott zum Lob Gottes fortschreiten kann, so ist doch kein erfahrbares Leiden erklärt und aufgelöst. Nietzsche wie Luther haben, wenngleich aus ganz verschiedenen Gründen, recht behalten. Sinngebung ist als 'Theodizee' nicht mehr möglich" (p. 274). I lack both space and competence to follow up these most recent clues; they can, however, at least serve as suggestions, or, briefly quoted, as correctives to some of the ideas referred to here in piecemeal fashion. In his appendix Sparn also pulls together, with admirable conciseness, current theological solutions (Barth, Ehlert, Gogarten, Tillich [pp. 248-252]). Philosophy, psychology, sociology follow, and— last but not least—"theological tasks" (pp. 264-272), described against the backdrop of the "post-theistic situation."

10. Eberhard Jüngel, *Death: The Riddle and the Mystery* (Philadelphia: Westminster, 1975).
11. A. M. K. Müller, "Der Sturz des Dogmas vom Täter," *Lutherische Monatshefte* 13 (1974), pp. 468-474; idem, "Vom Sinn des Leides," in *Die vielen Namen Gottes: Festschrift für Gerd Heinz-Mohr* (Stuttgart, 1974); idem, *Wende der Wahrnehmung: Erwägungen zur Grundlagenkrise in Physik, Medizin, Pädagogik und Theologie* (Munich, 1978).
12. Giesbert Greshake, *Der Preis der Liebe: Besinnung über das Leid* (Freiburg, 1978).

13. Heinz Zahrnt, Leiden: "Wie kann Gott das auslassen?" In *Warum ich glaube: Meine Sache mit Gott* (Munich, 1977).
14. Overlapping Greshake's theories are the "Prologomena zu einer theologischen Bewältigung des Leides (pp. 257-266), which are developed by F. Wolfinger in "Leiden als theologisches Problem: Versuch einer Problemskizze," *Catholica* 32 (1978), pp. 242-266.
15. E. S. Gerstenberger and Wolfgang Schrage, *Suffering* (Nashville: Abingdon, 1980).
16. Martin Luther, "Vorrede zum Grossen Katechismus," in *Luther deutsch,* ed. Kurt Aland, Vol. 3 (Stuttgart, 1961), pp. 14ff.
   The Large Catechism of Martin Luther (Philadelphia: Fortress, 1959).
17. Luther's lead-in sentence in the explanation of the first commandment, abbreviated from the following commandments in the Small Catechism.
18. Gerta Scharffenorth, "Die Beziehung von Mann und Frau bei Luther im Rahmen seines Kirchenverständnisses," in Gerta Scharffenorth and Klaus Thraede, *"Freunde in Christus werden . . ." Die Beziehung von Mann und Frau als Frage an Theologie und Kirche,* Kennzeichen Series, Vol 1 (Gelnhausen/Berlin, 1977), pp. 186-295.

References

Altheit, P. Biographieforschung in der Erwachsenenbildung (Part I). In H. Siebert and J. Weinberg, *Literatur- und Forschungsreport Weiterbildung,* Münster 13/1984, pp. 40ff. and (Part II) 14/1984, pp. 31ff.

Altner, G. *Die Überlebenskrise in der Gegenwart.* Darmstadt, 1987.

Arbeitsgruppe Bielefelder Soziologen. *Kommunikative Sozialforschung.* Munich, 1976.

Baacke, D., and Schulze, T., eds. *Aus Geschichten lernen. Zur Einübung pädagogischen Verstehens.* Munich, 1979.

Bach, U. *Boden unter den Füssen hat keiner: Plädoyer für eine solidarische Diakonie.* Göttingen, 1980.

Bach, U. *Dem Traum entsagen, mehr als ein Mensch zu sein. Auf dem Wege zu einer diakonischen Kirche.* Vluyn: Neukirchener Verlag, 1986.

Barth, Karl. *Church Dogmatics,* Vol. 1 I-IV 4. New York: Harper Torchbooks, 1962.

Berger, Peter L. *A Rumor of Angels: Modern Society and the Rediscovery of the Supernatural.* Garden City, NY: Doubleday, 1970.

Berger, Peter L. *Zur Dialektik von Religion und Gesellschaft.* Frankfurt, 1973. American edition, 1967.

Berger, Peter L., and Luckmann, Thomas. *The Social Construction of Reality.* Garden City, NY: Doubleday, 1967.

Bloch, Ernst. *Atheism in Christianity.* New York: Herder & Herder, 1972.

Bodelschwingh, Fritz von. Gespräch mit Dr. Brandt, dem Abgeordneten Hitlers. In *Bote von Bethel,* Special Edition 66, Archiv Bethel. Bielefeld, 1964.

Böhme, W., ed. Ist Gott grausam? Eine Stellungnahme zu Tilmann Mosers 'Gottesvergiftung.' *Tagungsbericht der Evangelischen Akademie Bad Herrenalb,* no date.

Bollnow, O. F. *Existenzphilosophie und Pädagogik.* Stuttgart, 1962.

Bonhoeffer, Dietrich. *Letters and Papers from Prison.* Edited by E. Bethge. New York: Macmillan, 1972. (see also London: SCM Press, 1984)

Bonhoeffer, Dietrich. *The Cost of Discipleship,* New York: Macmillan, 1965.

Brenning, J., et al. *Leid und Krankheit im Spiegel religiöser Traktatliteratur.* Hamburg, 1972.

Brocher, T.: Lecture at the 17th Deutschen Evangelischen Kirchentag, 8-12 June, 1977. In *Kirchentag: Dokumentarband.* Stuttgart, 1978.

Capra, Fritjof. *The Tao of Physics,* New York: Bantam, 1984.

Cloerkes, G. *Einstellung und Verhalten gegenüber Behinderten. Eine kritische Bestandaufnahme internationaler Forschung.* 3d ed. Berlin, 1985.

Concilium. Frauen in der Männerkirche? In *Concilium* 4/1980.

Daiber, K. F. Leiden als Thema der Predigt. Dokumentation und Auswertung einer Predigtreihe: *Leiden des Menschen—Leiden Gottes.* Munich, 1978.

Deutsches Allgemeines Sonntagsblatt, DAS, No. 44, October 22, 1978.

Diakonisches Werk der Ev. Kirche in Deutschland, EKD, ed. "Hilfe für Behinderte. Zweites Schwerpunktprogramm der Diakonie." *Diakonie: Jahrbuch 1975.* Stuttgart, 1975.

Diakonisches Werk der Ev. Kirche in Deutschland, EKD, ed. Thirteen brochures, among them: on psychic illness, 1976; on mental retardation, 1977; on physical disabilities, 1977; on emotional disabilities, 1978; on life disturbances, 1979. *Diakonische Initiativen für Behinderte und Nichtbehinderte, 'Nicht nur 1981.'* Stuttgart, 1982.

Dreitzel, H. P. *Die gesellschaftlichen Leiden und das Leiden an der Gesellschaft? Vorstudien zu einer Pathologie des Rollenverhaltens.* Stuttgart, 1968.

Duquoc, J., et al. Das Kreuz Christi und das Leid der Menschen. In *Concilium* 12/1976.

Ebeling, G. *Dogmatik des christlichen Glaubens.* Vols. 1-3. Tübingen, 1979.

Ehlert, W. *Der christliche Glaube. Grundlinien der lutherischen Dogmatik.* Hamburg, 1940.

Ehrenberg, H. *Hiob der Existentialist.* Heidelberg, 1952.

Erikson, Erik H. *Identity and the Life Cycle.* New York: Norton, 1980.

Filipp, S. H., ed. *Kritische Lebensereignisse.* Munich, 1981.

Fischer, M. Das Geheimnis des Menschen. Theologische Überlegungen zur Zielsetzung der Behindertenhilfe. In *Diakonie Jahrbuch 1975.* Stuttgart, 1975.

Freire, Paulo. *Pedagogy of the Oppressed.* New York: Continuum, 1985.

Fromm, Erich. *To Have or to Be?* New York: Harper & Row, 1976.

Gadamer, Hans Georg. *Truth and Method.* New York: Continuum, 1988.

Gerstenberger, E. S., and Schrage, Wolfgang. *Suffering.* Nashville: Abingdon, 1980.

Gogarten, F. *Der Mensch zwischen Gott und Welt.* Stuttgart, 1956.

Gollwitzer, H. *Krummes Holz—aufrechter Gang: Zur Frage nach dem Sinn des Lebens.* 8th ed. Munich, 1979.

Gornick, H. A. Begegnung am Rhein: Die amerikanische Bestsellerautorin Laurel Lee in der Bundesrepublik. "Zauberhafte Dinge im Tod." In *Deutsches Allgemeines Sonntagsblatt, DAS,* No. 36, 3 September 1978.

Greshake, G. *Der Preis der Liebe: Besinnung über das Leid.* Frieburg, 1978.

Habermas, Jürgen, and Luhmann, N. *Theorie der Gesellschaft oder Sozialtechnologie— Was leistet die Systemforschung?* Frankfurt, 1971.

Hämer, Andreas. *Rehabilitation von unten. Der Platz der Körperbehinderten im Aufgabenfeld der Kirche.* Mainz, 1978.

Henningsen, J. *Autobiographie und Erziehungswissenschaft.* Essen, 1981.

Hentig, H. von. *Aufgeräumte Erfahrungen. Texte zur eigenen Person.* Berlin: Ullstein, 1985.

Hephata Hessisches Diakoniezentrum (ed.); Göbel, P., and Thormann, H. E. *Verlegt— vernichtet—vergessen . . . ? Leidenswege von Menschen aus Hephata im Dritten Reich. Eine Dokumentation.* 2d ed. Schwalmstadt/Trysa: Plag-Druck, 1986.

Hildenhagen, G. *Geschlossene Räume. Photographien.* Museum für Kunst und Gewerbe Hamburg. Exhibition from 4 October-9 November, 1983. Hamburg, 1983.

Hofer, Th., et al. *Wenn das Weizenkorn in die Erde fällt. Mit Kindern über Gott und Auferstehung reden.* Gütersloh: GTB, 1985.

Jens, W., ed. *Warum ich Christ bin.* Munich, 1979.

Jüngel, Eberhard. *Death: The Riddle and the Mystery*. Philadelphia: Westminster, 1975.
Jüngel, Eberhard. *God as the Mystery of the World*. Grand Rapids, MI: Eerdmanns, 1983.
Jung, C. G. *Answer to Job*. Princeton, NJ: Princeton University Press, 1973.
Kaiser, Otto. *Introduction to the Old Testament*. Minneapolis: Augsburg 1975.
Kaufmann, H.B. *Begleitung in Lebenskrisen als Herausforderung des christlichen Glaubens*. In *Jede Krise ist ein neuer Anfang: Aus Lebensgeschichten lernen*, edited by E. Schuchardt. 3d ed. Düsseldorf: Comenius Institut, 1984.
Keller-Hüschemenger, M. *Die Kirche und das Leiden. Versuch einer systematischen Besinnung über ein Menschlichkeitsproblem vom Worte Gottes und der Kirche her*. Munich, 1954.
Kirchenamt der Ev. Kirche in Deutschland, EKD, ed. *Leben und Erziehen wozu? Eine Dokumentation über Entschliesssungen der Synode der EKD 1978*, Gütersloh, 1979, and in *Bildung und Erziehung. Die Denkschriften der Ev. Kirche in Deutschland*, Vol. 4/1. Gütersloh: GTB, 1987.
Klee, E. *"Euthanasie" im NS-Staat. Die "Vernichtung lebensunwerten Lebens."* Frankfurt, 1983.
Knoll, J. H. *Lebenslauf, Lebenszyklen und Erwachsenenbildung*. In *Internationales Jahrbuch der Erwachsenenbildung*. Cologne, 1980.
Kodalle, K. M. *Überwindung antagonistischer Realität?* In 1/1980, *Frankfurter Hefte*.
Kohli, M. *Biographie und soziale Wirklichkeit*. Stuttgart, 1984.
Krämer, H. M. *Eine Sprache des Leidens. Zur Lyrik von Paul Celan*. Munich, 1979.
Kübler-Ross, E. *Interviews mit Sterbenden*. Berlin, 1971.
Kübler-Ross, E. *Kommerzialisierte Leiden für verborgene Leiden*. In *Concilium* 12/1976.
Küng, Hans *Gott und das Leid*. 5th ed. Einsiedeln, Zurich, 1974.
Kushner, H. *When Bad Things Happen to Good People*. New York: Avon, 1983.
Leontev, A. N. *Problems of Mental Development*. Washington, D.C.: U.S. Joint Publications Research Service, 1964.
Loch, W. *Lebenslauf und Erziehung*. Essen, 1979.
Lohse, E. *Märtyrer und Gottesknecht. Untersuchungen zur urchristlichen Verkündigung vom Sühnetode Jesu Christi*. Göttingen, 1955.
Luhmann, N. *Sinn als Grundbegriff der Soziologie*. In *Theorie der Gesellschaft oder Sozialtechnologie—Was leistet die Systemforschung?* edited by J. Habermas and N. Luhmann. Frankfurt, 1971.
Luhmann, N. *Funktion der Religion*. Frankfurt, 1977.
Luther, Martin. *Luther's Large Catechism*. Trans. J. N. Lenker. Minneapolis: Augsburg Publishing House, 1967.
Luther, Martin. *The Small Catechism*. Minneapolis: Augsburg Publishing House, 1979.
Marti, K. *Zärtlichkeit und Schmerz*. Neuwied, Darmstadt, 1979.
Maurer, F., ed. *Lebensgeschichte und Identität. Beiträge zur Anthropologie*. Frankfurt, 1981.
Mead, George Herbert. *Mind, Self and Society from the Standpoint of a Social Behaviorist*. Chicago: University of Chicago, 1970.
Mitscherlich, Alexander and Margaret. *The Inability to Mourn*. New York: Grove, 1984.
Mitscherlich, M. *Erinnerungsarbeit: Zur Psychoanalyse der Unfähigkeit zu trauern*. Frankfurt, 1987.
Moltmann, Jürgen. *The Crucified God: The Cross of Christ as the Foundation and Criticism of Christian Theology*. New York: Harper & Row, 1974.
Moltmann, Jürgen. *The Passion for Life: A Messianic Lifestyle*. Philadelphia: Fortress, 1978.
Moser, T. *Gottesvergiftung*. Frankfurt, 1976.

Müller, A. M. K. *Die präparierte Zeit. Der Mensch in der Krise seiner eigenen Zielsetzungen.* Stuttgart, 1972.

Müller, A. M. K. Der Sturz des Dogmas vom Täter. In *Lutherischer Monatshefte,* 13th Annual, 1974.

Müller, A. M. K. Vom Sinn des Leidens angesichts der totalen Krise. In *Die vielen Namen Gottes: Festschrift für Gerd Heinz-Mohr.* Stuttgart, 1974.

Müller, A. M. K. *Wende der Wahrnehmung: Erwägungen zur Grundlagendkrise in Physik, Medizin, Pädagogik und Theologie.* Munich, 1978.

Nipkow, K. E. *Erwachsenwerden ohne Gott? Gotteserfahrung im Lebenslauf.* Munich, 1987.

Paul, S. *Begegnungen: Zur Geschichte persönlicher Dokumente in Ethnologie, Soziologie, Psychologie.* 2 vols. Hohenschäftlarn. 1979.

Peccei, A., ed. *Zukunftschance Lernen. Club of Rome. Bericht über die achtziger Jahre.* Gütersloh, 1980.

Peck, M. Scott. *The Road Less Traveled: A New Psychology of Love, Traditional Values and Spiritual Growth.* New York: Simon and Schuster, 1978.

Purce, Jill. *The Mystic Spiral: Journey of the Soul.* Art and Imagination series. London: Thames and Hudson, 1974.

Richter, H.E. *Lernziel Solidarität.* Hamburg, 1974.

Richter, H.E. *Der Gotteskomplex: Die Geburt und die Krise des Glaubens an die Allmacht des Menschen.* 2d part: *Die Krankheit, nicht leiden zu können.* Reinbek bei Hamburg, 1979.

Richter, H. E. *Sich der Krise stellen: Reden, Aufsätze, Interviews.* Reinbek bei Hamburg, 1981.

Rosenmayr, L. *Biographie und Geschichtswissenschaft: Wiener Beiträge zur Geschichte der Neuzeit.* Vol. 5. Vienna, 1979.

Rosenzweig, R. *Solidarität mit den Leidenden im Judentum.* Berlin, New York, 1978.

Rumpeltes, Chr. *Arbeitslos: Betroffene erzählen.* Reinbek bei Hamburg, 1982.

Scharffenorth, Gerta, and Thraede, Klaus. *"Freunde in Christus werden": Die Beziehung von Mann und Frau als Frage an Theologie und Kirche.* Kennzeichen Series, Vol. 1. Gelnhausen/Berlin, 1977.

Schiffers, N. *Fragen der Physik an die Theologie: Die Säkularisierung der Wissenschaft und das Heilsverlangen nach Freiheit.* Düsseldorf, 1968.

Schmidbauer, Wolfgang. *Die hilflosen Helfer: Über die seelische Problematik der helfenden Berufe.* Reinbek bei Hamburg, 1977.

Schmitz, E. Erwachsenenbildung als lebensweltbezogener Erkenntnisprozess. In *Erwachsenenbildung,* by E. Schmitz and H. Tietgens. Stuttgart, 1984.

Schuchardt, Erika. Biographische Erfahrung und wissenschaftliche Theorie. *Soziale Integration Behinderter,* Vol. 1. With annotated bibliography of biographies 1900 to 1986. Series: *Theorie und Praxis der Erwachsenenbildung.* 3d ed., enl. Bad Heilbrunn, 1987.

Schuchardt, Erika. Weiterbildung als Krisenverarbeitung. *Soziale Integration Behinderter,* Vol. 2. With annotated bibliography of crisis-treatment 1900 to 1986. Series: *Theorie und Praxis der Erwachsenenbildung.* 3d ed., enl. Bad Heilbrunn, 1987.

Schuchardt, Erika. Internationale Dekade der Behinderten 1982-1993. In *International Yearbook of Adult Education,* edited by J. H. Knoll. Cologne, 1984.

Schuchardt, Erika. *Women and Disability.* JUNIC/NGO Series on Women and Development. Geneva, 1984.

Schuchardt, Erika. *Fernstudium für evangelische Religionslehrer.* Studienbrief 7, Deutsches Institut für Fernstudien. Tübingen, 1984.

Schuchardt, Erika. Weiterbildung mit behinderten und nichtbehinderten Menschen. *Handbuch der Erwachsenenbildung*, Vol. 7. In *Didaktik der Erwachsenenbildung*, edited by F. Pöggeler; H. D. Raapke; and W. Schulenberg. Stuttgart, 1985.

Schuchardt, Erika. Menschen mit Behinderungen—Mitmenschen wie wir. In *Unterrichtseinheiten für die sekundärstufe I und II. Im Auftrag des Bundesministers für Jugend, Familie, Frauen, und Gesundheit*, edited by Bundeszentrale für gesundheitliche Aufklärung. Stuttgart: Klett, 1989.

Schuchardt, Erika. *Warum gerade ich . . . ? Leiden und Glaube: Pädagogische Schritte mit Betroffenen und Begleitenden*. 4th ed., enl. Offenbach, 1987.

Schuchardt, Erika. *Jede Krise ist ein neuer Anfang. Aus Lebensgeschichten lernen*. With contributions by H.-B. Kaufmann, M. Winkelheide, et al (those affected in our time comment on the call for biographies). 3d ed. Dusseldorf: Comenius Institute, 1987.

Schuchardt, Erika. *Krise als Lernchance: Analyse von Lebensgeschichten*. With an Introduction by H. Siebert (scientific research resulting from the call for biographies). Düsseldorf: Comenius Institute, 1985.

Schuchardt, Erika. Wechselseitiges Lernen—Wissenschaftliches Kolloquium Weiterbildung. In *Dokumentation des BMBW-Kolloquiums und der Ausstellung. Schriftenreine des Bundesministers* für Bildung und Wissenschaft. Vol. 58. Bonn, 1988.

Schuchardt, Erika. *Schritte aufeinander zu. Soziale Integration durch Weiterbildung: Zur Situation Behinderter in der Bundesrepublik Deutschland*. Forschungsauftrag des Bundesministers für Bildung und Wissenschaft. With contributions by U. Bleidick and G. Greza. Bad Heilbrunn, 1987.

Schuchardt, Erika. *Darüber habe ich eigentlich noch nie nachgedacht . . . ! Kritische Ereignisse in 500 Kinder- und Jugend-Büchern*. With classified and annotated bibliography. Hamburg, forthcoming.

Schuchardt, Erika. *Geschwister kann man sich nicht aussuchen. Wir gehören doch zusammen*. Hamburg, forthcoming.

Schultz, W. Die Deutung des Leids im Humanismus und im Christentum. In *Theologie und Wirklichkeit*, edited by G. H. Pust. Kiel, 1969.

Schulze, H. ed. *Der leidende Mensch*. Neukirchen-Vluyn, 1974.

Sellin, Ernst. *Introduction to the Old Testament*. London: SPCK, 1976.

Siebert, H. *Erwachsenenbildung als Bildungshilfe*. Bad Heilbrunn, 1983.

Sölle, Dorothee. *Death by Bread Alone: Texts and Reflections on Religious Experience*. Philadelphia: Fortress, 1978.

Sölle, Dorothee. *Suffering*. Philadelphia: Fortress, 1984.

Sparn, W., ed. *Leiden—Erfahrung und Denken: Materialien zum Theodizeeproblem*. (Appendix: Suggestions for a revision of the theodicy problem, together with a comprehensive bibliography.) Theologische Bücherei, Vol 67. Munich, 1980.

Sporken, Paul. *Begleitung in schwierigen Lebenssituationene: Ein Leitfaden für Helfer*. Freiburg, 1984.

Thomas, K. *Selbstanalyse: Die heilende Biographie, ihre Abfassung und ihre Auswirkung*. Stuttgart, 1976.

Tietgens, H. *Die Erwachsenenbildung*. Munich, 1981.

Tillich, Paul. *Systematic Theology*. 3 vols. Chicago: University of Chicago, 1975.

Tischler, G. Leiden an der Allmacht Gottes. In *Information* 82/1981, published by Evangelische Zentralstelle für Weltanschauungsfragen (EZW).

Vaillant, George E. *Adaptation to Life*. Boston: Little, Brown, 1977.

Weil, Simone. *Waiting for God*. New York: Harper & Row, 1973.

Weizsäcker, Carl F. von. Der Behinderte in unserer Gesellschaft. Lecture given at the Bayerische Landesschule für Blinde, on the 150th anniversary of its establishment.

In *Der Garten des Menschlichen: Beiträge zur geschichtlichen Anthropologie.* 3d ed. Munich, Vienna, 1977. See *The Ambivalence of Progress: Essays on Historical Anthropology.* New York: Paragon House, 1988.

Weizsäcker, Carl F. von. In Christ—Hope for the World. Report on the question of peace. 7th Assembly of the Lutheran World Federation in Budapest, 22 July–5 August, 1984. In *Documentation of the 7th Assembly of the Lutheran World Federation in Budapest.* Geneva, 1985.

Weizsäcker, Carl F. von. *The Politics of Peril: Economics, Society, and the Prevention of War.* New York: Seabury, 1978.

Welker, M., ed. *Diskussion über Jürgen Moltmanns Buch "Der gekreuzigte Gott."* Munich, 1979.

Wiese, Benno von. *Die deutsche Tragödie von Lessing bis Hebbel.* 2d ed., enl. Hamburg, 1952.

Wilson, T. P. Theorien der Interaktion und Modelle soziologischer Erklärung. In *Alltagswissen, Interaktion und gesellschaftliche Wirklichkeit.* Vols. 1 and 2, edited by Arbeitsgruppe Bielefelder Soziologen. Reinbek bei Hamburg, 1973.

Wolfinger, F. Prolegomena zu einer theologischen Bewältigung des Leidens. In Leiden als theologisches Problem: Versuch einer Problemskizze. In *Catholica* 32/1978.

World Council of Churches. *Leben und Zeugnis der Behinderten in der christlichen Gemeinde. Memorandum einer Konsultation 1978.* In *Dokumentation epd., evangelischer Pressedienst* No. 36a, 1978.

World Council of Churches. *Partners: A World Council of Churches Contribution for the International Year of Disabled Persons.* Geneva: World Council of Churches, 1981.

World Council of Churches. *Partners in Life: The Handicapped and the Church.* Faith and Order Paper No. 89. Geneva, 1979.

Zahrnt, Heinz. *What Kind of God? A Question of Faith.* Minneapolis: Augsburg, 1972.

Zahrnt, Heinz. Leiden—wie kann Gott das zulassen? In *Warum ich glaube: Meine Sache mit Gott.* Munich, 1977.

Zink, Jorg. Foreword in *Herrgott, schaff die Treppen ab!* by Luise Habel. Stuttgart, Berlin, 1978.

Alphabetical Bibliography

Biographies and Autobiographies about Coping with Crisis Written between 1900 and 1989

(Writers and disabilities or disruption in their lives; compare illustrations and survey figures 1-4 on pages 26 and 27.)

Ahrens, Hildegard. *Ist es Schicksal?* Bad Rothenfelde: Rompf Druck (self-published), no date.

Aly, Monika and Götz; and Tumler, Molind. *Kopfkorrektur oder der Zwang gesund zu sein: Ein behindertes Kind zwischen Therapie und Alltag.* Berlin: Rotbuch, 1981.

Ambrosio, Richard d'. *Der stumme Mund.* 3d ed. Bern, Munich, Vienna: Scherz, 1973.

Anders, Renate. *Grenzübertritt.* Frankfurt: Fischer, 1984.

Arcy, Paula d'. *Song for Sarah.* Wheaton, IL: Harold Shaw, 1979.

Armes, Jay J. and Nolan, Frederick. *Jay J. Armes, Investigator.* New York: Avon, 1977.

Arndt, Ralf. *Spiegelbilder: Eine Antwort an die Kinder vom Bahnhof Zoo.* 5th ed. Asslar: Schulte & Gerth, 1983.

Atkinson, Sandy A., and Markel, Jan. *Somebody Loves Me!* Wheaton, IL: Tyndale House, 1979.

Atwood, Margaret E. *The Edible Woman.* New York: Popular Library, 1976.

Atwood, Margaret E. *Bodily Harm.* New York: Bantam, 1982.

Aucoutuier, Bernard, and Lapièrre, André. *Bruno.* Munich: Reinhardt, 1982. Original French title: *Bruno: Psychomotricité et thérapie.*

Augustin, Ernst. *Raumlicht: Der Fall Evelyne B.* Frankfurt: Suhrkamp, 1976.

Axline, Virginia M. *Dibs: In Search of Self.* Harmondsworth: Penguin, 1981.

Axt, Renate. *Und wenn du weinst, hört man es nicht.* Bergisch Gladbach: Bastei-Lübbe, 1986.

Bach, Heinz. *Die heimlichen Bitten des Peter M.* Berlin: Marhold, 1985.

Bach, Katharina. *Geklagt wird nicht und geheult erst nachts.* Münster: Tende Druck (self-published), 1981.

Bach, Ulrich. *Boden unter den Füssen hat keiner.* Göttingen: Vandenhoeck & Ruprecht, 1986.

Bach, Ulrich. *Kraft in leeren Händen.* Freiburg im Breisgau: Herder, 1986.

Bach, Ulrich. *Vollmarsteiner Rasiertexte: Notizen eines Rollstuhfahrers.* Gladbeck: Schriftenmissions-Verlag, no date.

Bacher, Ingrid. *Das Paar.* Hamburg: Hoffmann & Campe, 1981.

Baily, Faith C. *These, Too, Were Unshackled: Fifteen Dramatic Stories from the Pacific Garden Mission.* Grand Rapids, MI: Zondervan, 1962.

Bappert, Lieselotte. *Der Knoten: Vertrauen und Verantwortung im Arzt-Patienten-Verhältnis am Beispiel Brustkrebs.* Reinbek bei Hamburg: Rowohlt, 1979.

Barnes, Mary. *Two Accounts of a Journey through Madness.* New York: Ballantine, 1973.

Bartholomäus. *Ich möchte an der Hand eines Menschen sterben.* Mainz: Matthias Grünewald, 1981.

Bauer, Ernst W. *Ein Stuhl zwischen den Stühlen.* Munich: Sociomedico-Verlag, 1974.

Bayer, Ingeborg. *Trip ins Ungewisse.* 4th ed. Munich: Deutscher Taschenbuch, 1982.

Beauvoir, Simone de. *Adieux: A Farewell to Sartre.* New York: Pantheon, 1984.

Beck, Dieter. *Krankheit als Selbstheilung.* Frankfurt: Suhrkamp, 1986.

Becker, Klaus Peter. *Ich habe meinen Krebs besiegt.* Unterhaching: Luitpold Lang, 1982.

Bellvré, Katharina. *Durch den Tunnel der Angst.* Heidelberg: Verlag für Medizin Dr. Ewald Fischer, 1985.

Berg, Thomas. *Aufs Spiel gesetzt.* Königstein/Ts: Athenäum, 1984.

Bernhard, Thomas. *Die Kälte.* Munich: Deutscher Taschenbuch, 1984.

Bettelheim, Bruno. *Truants from Life: The Rehabilitation of Emotionally Disturbed Children.* New York: Free Press, 1964.

Bettelheim, Bruno, and Karlin, Daniel. *Liebe als Therapie.* Munich: Piper, 1986.

Beuys, Barbara. *Am Anfang war nur Verzweiflung.* Reinbek bei Hamburg: Rowohlt, 1984.

Billisch, R. Franz. *Süchtig: Aufstieg und Fall des Fotomodells Doris W.* Rastatt: Moewig, 1986.

Bjarnof, Karl. *Das gute Licht.* Gütersloh: Bertelsmann, 1958. Original Danish edition published by Güldendahl, Copenhagen.

BK Erzählung. *Befreit von der Sucht.* Wuppertal, Bern: Blaukreuz, 1981.

Blanton, Smiley. *Diary of My Analysis with Sigmund Freud.* New York: Hawthorn, 1971.

Blatchford, Claire H. *All Alone (Except for My Dog Friday).* Elgin, IL: Chariot, 1983.

Blauensteiner-Stephan, Yvonne. *Das stille Jahr.* Vienna: Kurt Kleber, 1946.

Bleimann, Annemarie. *Leben ist die Alternative.* Munich: Tomus, 1985.

Blieweis, Theodor. *Wer ein Warum zu leben hat, erträgt fast jedes Wie! Beispiele von Persönlichkeiten in Krankheit und Leid.* Vienna, Linz, Passau: Veritas, 1979.

Bodelschwingh, F. von. *Vom Leben und Sterben vier seeliger Kinder.* 32d ed. Bielefeld-Bethel, (first edition published circa 1869).

Bodenheimer, Ronald A. *Doris: Die Entwicklung einer Beziehungsstörung und die Geschichte ihrer Behebung bei einem entstellten taubstummen Mädchen.* Basel, Stuttgart: Schwabe, 1968.

Bok, Sissela. *Lying: Moral Choice in Public and Private Life.* London, New York: Quartet, 1980.

Bolland, John, and Sandler, Joseph. *The Hampstead Psychoanalytic Index: A Study of the Psychoanalytic Case Material of a Two-Year-Old Child.* New York: International University Press, 1966.

Boston, Sarah. *Will, My Son: The Life and Death of a Mongol Child.* London: Pluto, 1981.

Breinersdorfer, Fred. *Notwehr.* Reinbek bei Hamburg: Rowohlt, 1986.

Brender, Irmela. *In Wirklichkeit ist alles ziemlich gut.* Munich: Knaur, 1986.

Brodhage, Barbara. *Caroline, lass dir an meiner Gnade genügen.* Moers: Brendow, 1981.

Bronnen, Barbara. *Die Überzählige.* Munich: Droemer-Knaur, 1986.

Brown, Christy. *My Left Foot.* New York: Simon & Schuster, 1955.

Brown, Christy. *Down All the Days.* New York: Stein & Day, 1970.

Brunnengräber, Richard. *Christiane: An Leukämie erkrankt und geheilt.* Munich: Meyster, 1984.

Bruns, Ingeborg. *Das wiedergeschenkte Leben: Tagebuch über die Leukämieerkrankung eines Kindes.* Frankfurt: Fischer, 1987.

Bryant, Lee. *The Magic Bottle.* Philadelphia: A. J. Holman, 1978.

Buch, Andrea, et al. *An den Rand gedrängt: Was Behinderte daran hindert, normal zu leben.* Reinbek bei Hamburg: Rowohlt, 1980.

Buck, Pearl S. *A Bridge for Passing.* New York: Pocket, 1963.

Buck, Pearl S. *The Child Who Never Grew.* New York: J. Day, 1950.

Buck, Pearl S. *My Several Worlds.* New York: Pocket, 1960.

Bulgakov, Mikhail. *Aufzeichnungen eines Toten.* Neuwied: Luchterhand, 1986.

Burch, Jennings Michael. *They Cage Animals at Night.* New York: New American Library, 1985.

Burnham, Elizabeth Dean. *When Your Friend Is Dying.* Lincoln, VA: Chosen, 1982.

Burroughs, William S. *Junky.* New York: Ace, 1973.

Burton, Josephine. *Crippled Victory.* New York: Sheed & Ward, 1956.

Cameron, Jean. *For All That Has Been: Time to Live and Time to Die.* New York: Macmillan, 1982.

Capote, Truman, and Grobel, Lawrence. *Conversations with Capote.* New York: New American Library, 1986.

Cardinal, Marie. *The Words to Say It: An Autobiographical Novel.* Cambridge, MA: Van Vactor & Goodheart, 1984.

Carette, Jeanine. *Te mettre au monde.* Paris, 1973.

Carlson, Earl R. *Born That Way.* New York: J. Day, 1941.

Carson, Mary. *Ginny: A True Story.* New York: Popular Library, 1971.

Carsten, Catarina. *Wie Thomas zum zweiten Mal sprechen lernte.* Vienna: Herder, 1985.

Cermak, Ida. *Ich klage nicht.* Zurich: Diogenes, 1983.

Christoph, Franz. *Krüppelschläge: Gegen die Gewalt der Menschlichkeit.* Reinbek bei Hamburg: Rowohlt, 1983.

Claypool, John. *Tracks of a Fellow Struggler: How to Handle Grief.* Waco, TX. Word, 1982.

Cleland, Max. *Strong at the Broken Places: A Personal Story.* Lincoln, VA: Chosen, 1980.

Clement, Barbara. *Ein Kind wird gesund . . . Der Weg einer psychologischen Behandlung.* "Psychologisch gesehen" 41. Ed. by Hildegund Fischl-Carl. Fellbach: Bonz, 1982.

Cohnen, Elfriede. *Ein Leben wie andere.* Heilbronn: Eugen Salzer, 1979.

Conrad, Klaus. *Dauerndes Glück: Chris.* Frankfurt: Fischer, 1980.

Conti, Adalgisa. *Manicomio 1914.* Milan: G. Mazzotta, 1978.

Cooke, Susan. *Ragged Owlet.* London: Arrow, 1979.

Cousins, Norman. *Anatomy of an Illness as Perceived by the Patient: Reflections on Healing and Regeneration.* New York: Bantam, 1979.

Craig, Mary. *Blessings.* New York: Bantam, 1980.

Cunéo, Anne. *Une cuillerée de bleu.* Zurich: Limat, 1982.

Deiss, Elfriede. *Diamant wächst im Dunkel.* 5th ed. Stuttgart: Christliches Verlagshaus, 1984.

Diderot, Denis. *Lettre sur les aveugles pour ceux qui voient.* Geneva: Droz, 1970.

Dieke, G. *Todeszeichen.* Neuwied: Luchterhand, 1981.

Diggelmann, Walter Matthias. *Schatten: Tagebuch einer Krankheit.* Frankfurt: Fischer, 1981.

Diggelmann, Walter Matthias. *Tage von süsslicher Wärme.* Zurich, Cologne: Benziger, 1982.

Dirks, Walter. *Der singende Stotterer.* Munich: Kösel, 1983.

Döll, Hermann K. A. *Philosoph in Haar: Tagebuch über mein Vierteljahr in einer Irrenanstalt.* 2d ed. Frankfurt: Syndikat Autoren- and Verlagsgesellschaft, 1981.

Dolto, Françoise. *Dominique: Analysis of an Adolescent.* New York: Outerbridge & Lazard, 1973.

Deutscher Paritätischer Wohlfahrtsverband (DPWV), ed. *Unser Alltag: behinderte Menschen, ihre Eltern und Familienangehörige berichten.* Frankfurt, 1981.

Drescher, Peter. *Birkenhof.* East Berlin: Evangelische Verlagsanstalt, 1981.

Drescher, Peter. *Montag fange ich wieder an.* 2d ed. East Berlin: Evangelische Verlagsanstalt, 1981.

Düren, T.; Hauser, H.; and Neugebauer, H., eds. *. . . aber sie können nicht sehen.* Cologne: Rheinland, 1977.

Düren, T.; Hauser, H.; and Neugebauer, H., eds. *. . . aber sie geben nicht auf.* Cologne: Rheinland, 1983.

Düren, T., and Strehle, W. *Die besten Jahre.* Cologne: Rheinland, 1979.

Duval, Aimée. *One More Tomorrow.* New York: Berkley, 1984.

Eareckson, Joni. *Joni.* Grand Rapids, MI: Zondervan, 1981.

Eareckson, Joni. *A Step Further.* Grand Rapids, MI: Zondervan, 1983.

Eareckson-Tada, Joni. *Choices Changes.* Grand Rapids, MI: Zondervan, 1986.

Ebner, Ferdinand. *Schriften in 3 Bänden.* Munich: Kösel, 1963.

Eckstaedt, Anita, and Klüwer, Rolf, eds. *Zeit allein heilt keine Wunden: Psychoanalytische Erstgespräche mit Kindern und Eltern.* 2d. ed. Frankfurt: Suhrkamp, 1980.

Eggli, Ursula. *Herz im Korsett: Tagebuch einer Behinderten.* 5th ed. Gümlingen, Bern: Zytglogge, 1979.

Eggli, Ursula. *Die Zärtlichkeit des Sonntagsbratens.* Bern: Eigenverlag, Wangenstr. 27, CH 3018 (self-published), 1986.

Eickstedt, Schieche von, ed. *Ist Aufopferung eine Lösung? Mütter behinderter Kinder berichten.* Berlin: Frauenbuchvertrieb, 1981.

Ekstein, Rudolf. *The Challenge: Despair and Hope in the Conquest of Inner Space.* New York: Brunner/Mazel, 1971.

Eramo, Luce d'. *Finché la testa vive.* Milan: Rizzoli, 1964.

Erlensberger, Maria. *Der Hunger nach Wahnsinn.* Reinbek bei Hamburg: Rowohlt, 1983.

Ewinkel, Hermes, et al. *Geschlecht: Behindert, bes. Merkmal: Frau.* 2d ed. Munich: AG Spak Publikationen, 1986.

Fabré, Jacqueline. *Die Kinder, die nicht sterben wollten: Bericht aus einer Leukämie-Kinderklinik.* Düsseldorf: Econ, 1982.

Falisse, Gaston and Marie-Françoise. *Nos enfants handicapés.* Paris: Editions universitaires, 1962.

Feid, Anatol F . . . Ingo. *Wenn du zurückschaust, wirst du sterben: Protokoll einer Phase im Kampf gegen das Heroin.* Mainz: Matthias Grünewald, 1981.

Feldenkrais, Moshé. *The Case of Nora: Bodily Awareness as Healing Therapy.* New York: Harper & Row, 1977.

Fell, Alison. *Every Move You Make.* London: Virago, 1984.

Ferguson, Sarah. *A Guard Within.* New York: Penguin, 1976.

Ferguson, Sarah. *To the Place of Shells.* New York: St. Martin's, 1975.

Fingerhut, R., and Manske, C. *Ich war behindert an Hand der Lehrer und Ärzte.* Reinbek bei Hamburg: Rowohlt, 1984.

Fischer, Bernhard. *Mein Geheimnis gehört mir.* Stuttgart: Freies Geistesleben, 1974.

Formaz, Casimir. *A l'ecole du Christ souffrant: journal de malade.* Paris: Editions du Cerf, 1975.

Franck, Barbara. *Trotzdem leben: Reportagen über die Angst*. Hamburg: Hoffmann & Campe, 1983.

Frank, P. Helmut. *Kinder ohne Perspektive*. Rastatt: Moewig, 1986.

Frédéric, Hélène, and Malinsky, Martine. *Martin*. Boston: Routledge & Kegan Paul, 1981.

Frederiksson, Dorrit. *Lennart dog ung*. Stockholm, 1973.

Frédet, Francine. *Mais, Madame, vous êtes la mère*. Paris: Le Centurion, 1979.

Frisch, Helga. *Tagebuch einer Pastorin*. Frankfurt: Fischer, 1981.

Fritze-Eggimann, Ruth. *Du bist mir anvertraut*. Evangelische Frauenarbeit in der Pfalz (self-published), no date.

Fritze-Eggimann, Ruth. *Ich habe viele Freunde*. Evangelische Frauenarbeit in der Pfalz (self-published), 1972.

Fuchs, Rosemarie. *Stationen der Hoffnung*. Stuttgart: Kreuz, 1984.

Fühmann, Franz, and Riemann, Dietmar. *Was für eine Insel in was für einem Meer: Leben mit geistig Behinderten*. Rostock: Hinstorff, 1985.

Fulda, Edeltraud. *. . . und ich werde genesen sein*. Vienna: Zsolnay, 1983.

G., Katharina [pseud.]. *Die Geschichte der Katharina G.: Aus dem Tagebuch einer Strafgefangenen*. Asslar: Schulte & Gerth, 1984.

Gabel, Claudia and Wolfgang. *Hindernisse oder Wir sind keine Sorgenkinder*. Zurich: Benziger, 1981.

Gabel, W. *Fix und fertig*. Weinheim: Beltz & Gelberg, 1978.

Gagelmann, Hartmut. *Kai lacht wieder: Ein autistisches Kind durchbricht seine Zwänge*. Munich: Droemer-Knaur, 1986.

Gauchat, Dorothy. *All God's Children*. New York: Ballantine, 1985.

Geisler, Helga. *Danke, das kann ich selbst: Wie ich meine Behinderung besiegte*. 2d ed. Stuttgart: Otto Bauer, 1984.

Georg, Hans. *Ich suchte das Glück*. Wuppertal: Blaukreuz, 1982.

Geppert, Roswitha. *Die Last, die du nicht trägst*. 7th ed. Halle: Mitteldeutscher Verlag, 1986.

Gerlinghoff, Monika. *Magersüchtig*. Munich: Piper, 1985.

Giudice, Liliane. *Die Kraft der Schwachen: Über das Kranksein*. Berlin: Kreuz, 1979.

Goetz, Rainald. *Irre*. Frankfurt: Suhrkamp, 1986.

Gohn, Ludwig. *Ein Weg zum Glück*. Rotterdam: van Witsen, 1957.

Goldmann-Posch, Ursula. *Tagebuch einer Depression*. Munich: Kindler, 1985.

Golinski, Edith. *Der Blick nach innen*. 2d ed. Kiel, 1971.

Gollner, Anna. *Christine*. Vienna: Jungbrunnen, 1982.

Gordon, Barbara. *I'm Dancing as Fast as I Can*. New York: Bantam, 1981.

Görres, Albert. *Kennt die Psychologie den Menschen? Fragen zwischen Psychotherapie, Anthropologie und Christentum*. Munich: Piper, 1978.

Görres, Silvia. *Leben mit einem behinderten Kind*. 2d ed. Munich: Piper, 1986.

Gösling-Geske, Rauthende. *Blüten und Abgründe*. Isernhagen (self-published), 1982.

Gotkin, Janet and Paul. *Too Much Anger, Too Many Tears: A Personal Triumph over Psychiatry*. New York: Quadrangle, 1975.

Gots, Anton. *Das "Ja" zum Kreuz*. 8th ed. Vienna, Linz & Passau: Veritas, 1984.

Graf, Andrea. *Die Suppenkasperin*. Frankfurt: Fischer, 1985.

Graham, Judy. *Multiple Sclerosis: A Self-Help Guide to Its Management*. Rochester, VT: Thorsons, 1987.

Green, Hannah [pseud.]. *I Never Promised You a Rose Garden*. New York: New American Library, 1964.

Greenberg, Joanne. *In This Sign*. New York: Avon, 1972.

Guibert, Hervé. *Des aveugles*. Paris: Gallimard, 1985.

Guillion, Jacques. *Cet enfant qui se drogue, c'est le mien*. Paris: Editions du Seuil, 1978.

Haas, Gisela. *Ich bin ja so allein: Kranke—krebskranke—Kinder zeichnen und sprechen über ihre Ängste*. Ravensburg: Otto Maier, 1981.

Habel, Luise. *Herrgott, schaff die Treppen ab! Erfahrungen einer Behinderten*. Stuttgart: Kreuz, 1978.

Habel, Luise. *Ich bring' Dir einen Arm voll Leben*. Munich: Kösel, 1984.

Habel, Luise. *Ich muss nicht immer stark sein*. Munich: Kösel, 1985.

Habel, Luise. *Umarmen möcht' ich dich: Briefe an einen Therapeuten*. Frankfurt: Fischer, 1986.

Haebler, W. *Mein Dorf zwischen den Wäldern*. Karlsruhe: Hans Thoma, 1965.

Haebler, W. . . . *Wir haben einen Hund, einen Vater und eine Mutter*. Karlsruhe: Hans Thoma, 1967.

Häusler, Ingrid. *Kein Kind zum Vorzeigen? Bericht über eine Behinderung*. Reinbek bei Hamburg: Rowohlt, 1979.

Hahn, Reinhardt. *Das letzte erste Glas*. Halle, Leipzig: Mitteldeutscher Verlag, 1986.

Hahn, Mechthild. *Lebenskrise Krebs*. Hannover: Schlütersche Verlagsanstalt, 1981.

Hambrecht, Martin. *Das Leben neu beginnen: Wenn Therapie zur Lebensschule wird*. Munich: Kösel, 1983.

Hampe, Johann Christoph. *To Die Is Gain: The Experiencing of One's Own Death*. Atlanta: John Knox, 1979.

Harpwood, Diane. *Tea and Tranquillisers: The Diary of a Happy Housewife*. London: Virago, 1981.

Hauch, Gerta. *Der Aufschrei: Warum?* Eupen: Grenz Echo, 1984.

Hauke, Felicitas. *Steine im Weg: Ein Lebensbericht*. Freiburg: Herder, 1981.

Haun, Ernst. *Jugenderinnerungen eines blinden Mannes*. Stuttgart, 1918.

Hayakawa, S. I. *Our Son Mark*. San Francisco State College, San Francisco, CA, 1969. [author's mss.]

Hayden, Torey L. *Murphy's Boy*. New York: Avon, 1983.

Hayden, Torey L. *One Child*. New York: Avon, 1981.

Hayden, Torey L. *Somebody Else's Kids*. New York: Putnam, 1981.

Hénault, Marcelle. *Mon fils Emmanuel*. Tours: Mame, 1973.

Hermann, K., and Rieck, H. *Christiane F.: Wir Kinder vom Bahnhof Zoo*. Hamburg: Gruner & Jahr, 1978.

Herrera, Hayden. *Frida: A Biography of Frida Kahlo*. New York: Harper & Row, 1983.

Herrmann, Nina. *Go Out in Joy!* New York: Pocket, 1978.

Hertzog, G., and Barnea-Braunstein, R. *"Beroschim."* Munich: Reinhardt, 1980. Original Hebrew title: *"Beroschim."*

Hesse, Jürgen, and Schrader, Hans Christian. *Auf einmal nicht mehr weiter wissen*. Frankfurt: Fischer, 1987.

Heyst, Ilse van. *Das Schlimmste war die Angst: Geschichte einer Krebserkrankung und ihrer Heilung*. Frankfurt: Fischer, 1982.

Hill, Archie. *Closed World of Love*. New York: Avon, 1976.

Hobrecht, Jürgen. *Du Kannst mir nicht in die Augen sehen*. Berlin: März 2001, 1981.

Hock, Kurt. *Die Heimkehr*. Freiburg: Herder, 1983.

Hocken, Sheila. *Emma and I*. New York: New American Library, 1979.

Hofbauer, Friedl. *Federball*. Freiburg: Herder, 1981.

Hofmann, Albert. *LSD, My Problem Child*. Los Angeles: J. P. Tarcher, 1983.

Hong, Edna. *Bright Valley of Love*. Minneapolis: Augsburg, 1979.

Horn, Sabine. *Ein Leben im Rollstuhl*. 2d ed. Hannover: Fehldruck, 1984.

Horn, Sabine. *Begegnungen einer Rollstuhlfahrerin mit ihrer Umwelt.* Hannover: Falk, 1986.

Hourdin, Georges. *Le Malheur innocent.* Paris: Stock, 1976.

Hudson, Rock, and Davidson, Sarah. *Rock Hudson: His Story.* New York: Avon, 1987.

Hundley, Joan M. *The Small Outsider.* New York: Ballantine, 1973.

Hunt, Nigel. *The World of Nigel Hunt: The Diary of a Mongoloid Youth.* Norwich, CT: Asset Recycling, 1982.

Hurter, C. *Und ein bisschen glücklich sein.* Haan: Oncken, 1981.

Immendorf, Ruth. *Ich sage ja: Körperbehinderte in der Bewältigung ihres Lebens.* East Berlin: Evangelische Verlagsanstalt, 1983.

Ireland, David. *Letters to an Unborn Child.* New York: Harper & Row, 1974.

Isaksson, Ulla. *The Blessed Ones.* Washington, D.C.: R. B. Luce, 1970.

Jackson, Marjorie. *The Boy David.* London: British Broadcasting Corporation, 1985.

Jan, Edmund; Marlies, Eva; and "Doctor S." *End-täuschung: Dokumente einer Trennung.* Frankfurt: Extrabuch, 1983.

Jankowich, St. von. *Ich war klinisch tot: Der Tod—Mein schönstes Erlebnis.* Munich, 1984.

Joachim, Doris. J. *Entzug: Oder die Angst vor der Angst.* Frankfurt: Frauenliteraturvertrieb, 1982.

Joesten, Renate. *Stark wie der Tod ist die Liebe: Bericht von einem Abschied.* Stuttgart: Kreuz, 1985.

Johannes, Ingrid. *Das siebente Brennesselhemd.* Berlin: Verlag Neues Leben, 1986.

Johansen, Margaret. *Damenes vals.* Oslo: Tiden, 1978.

Johansen, Margaret. *Du kan da ikke bare gå—.* Oslo: Tiden, 1981.

Johansen, Otto. *Ridderspranget: Erling Stordahl og hans verden.* Oslo: Gyldendal Norsk, 1972.

Jun, Gerda. *Kinder, die anders sind.* 4th ed. East Berlin: VEB Verlag Volk & Gesundheit, 1986.

Jurgensen, Geneviève. *La folie des autres.* Paris: R. Laffont, 1973.

Kadenbach, Hans. *Requiem für Sabrina.* Halle, Leipzig: Mitteldeutscher Verlag, 1986.

Karasek, Horst. *Blutwäsche.* Neuwied: Luchterhand, 1986.

Kardiner, Abram. *My Analysis with Freud: Reminiscences.* New York: Norton, 1977.

Kast, Verena. *"Trauern."* Stuttgart: Kreuz, 1982.

Kaufman, Barry N. *Son-rise.* New York: Warner, 1977.

Kavan, Anna. *Who Are You?* London: Peter Owen, 1975.

Keller, Helen. *Midstream: My Later Life.* New York: Greenwood, 1968.

Keller, Helen. *The Story of My Life.* Rahway, NJ: Watermill, 1980.

Keller, Helen. *Teacher: Anne Sullivan Macy.* Westport, CT: Greenwood, 1985.

Kellner, Jakob. *Zwiesprache mit Ziwjah: Das Werden einer neuen Identität.* Freiburg: Lambertus, 1972.

Kelly, Petra K., ed. *Viel Liebe gegen Schmerzen.* Reinbek bei Hamburg: Rowohlt, 1986.

Kenzaburo, Oe. *Eine persönliche Erfahrung.* Frankfurt: Suhrkamp, 1972. Original Japanese title: *Kojinteki na Taiken.*

Kerremans, Helen. *Abschied von Angst.* Bergisch Gladbach: Bastei-Lübbe, 1987.

Kessling, Volker. *Tagebuch eines Erziehers.* 4th ed. Berlin: Verlag Neues Leben, 1985.

Killilea, Marie. *Karen.* New York: Dell, 1983.

Kipphardt, Heiner. *März: Autobiographischer Roman eines Arztes über Schizophrenie.* Munich: Bertelsmann, 1976.

Klee, Falk-Ingo. *Jasmin K. (3 Jahre): Diagnose: Krebs.* Rastatt: Moewig, 1986.

Klein, Norma. *Sunshine.* New York: Avon, 1982.

Kneller, Pamela. *Das Leben geht weiter: Der Weg einer Behinderten.* Wemding: Verlag für Grundlagenwissen Herbert Wirkner, 1981.

Knop, Jürgen. *Sie werden uns doch bemerken müssen . . . Geschichten aus einem behinderten Leben.* Hannover: SOAK, 1981.

Kobbe, Ursula. *Die Brücke ohne Geländer: Tagebuch einer Heilpädagogin.* 2d ed. Freiburg: Herder, 1974.

König, Hera. *Der tödliche Hunger: Erfahrungen einer Diabetikerin.* Frankfurt: Fischer, 1983.

Königsdorf, Helga. *Respektloser Umgang.* East Berlin: Aufbau, 1986.

Kratzmeier, Heinrich, ed. *Behinderte aus eigener und fremder Sicht.* Heidelberger sonderpädagogische Schriften, vol. 14. Rheinstetten: Schindele, 1980.

Krents, Harold. *To Race the Wind.* New York: Bantam, 1973.

Kreye, Ulrike. *. . . betroffen: Sonderschüler erzählen.* Wetter: Freundeskreis der Sonderschule Wetter, no date.

Kris. *Weil ich leben will.* 2d ed. Haan: Brockhaus, 1983.

Kronenberg, Martin, ed. *Behindertenschicksale.* Wolfenbüttel: Kallmeier, 1980.

Krüger, Barbara. *Mein Sohn Andi: Tagebuch einer Mutter.* Freiburg: Herder, 1979.

Kübler-Ross, Elisabeth. *Befreiung aus der Angst.* Stuttgart: Kreuz, 1983.

Kübler-Ross, Elisabeth. *On Children and Death.* New York: Collier, 1985.

Küster, Hermann. *Nachrufe.* Bern: Blaukreuz, 1977.

Kupferschmidt, Alfred. *In des Töpfers Hand.* Bern: Blaukreuz, 1968.

Kushner, Harold. *When Bad Things Happen to Good People.* New York: Avon, 1983.

Lagercrantz, Olof. *Mein erster Kreis.* Frankfurt: Insel, 1984. Originally published in Swedish.

Lair, Jacqueline, and Lechler, Walter H. *I Exist. I Need. I'm Entitled.* Garden City, NY: Doubleday, 1980.

Lair, Jess and Jacqueline. *Hey God, What Should I Do Now?* New York: Ballantine, 1982.

Lake, Alexander. *You Need Never Walk Alone.* Anderson, IN: Warner, 1973.

Lamla, Gertraud. *Muss ich auch wandern in finsterer Schlucht.* Freiburg: Herder, 1985.

Lane, Robert. *A Solitary Dance.* New York: New American Library, 1984.

Langsdorff, Maja. *Die heimliche Sucht, unheimlich zu essen.* Frankfurt: Fischer, 1985.

Lavant, Christine. *Kunst wie meine ist nur verstümmeltes Leben.* Salzburg: Otto Müller, 1978.

Lawrence, Marilyn. *The Anorexic Experience.* New York: P. Bedrick, 1987.

Lee, Laurel. *Walking through the Fire.* New York: Bantam, 1978.

Lefranc, Alain. *Le courage de vivre.* Paris: Editions du Cerf, 1975.

Lefranc, Alain. *Les malheureux.* Paris: Editions du Cerf, 1978.

Legrix, Denise. *Born Like That.* London: Souvenir, 1962.

Leisen, Trabert. *Selbsterfahrung.* Munich: AG Spak Publikationen, 1985.

Lenker, Christiane. *Krebs kann auch eine Chance sein.* Frankfurt: Fischer, 1984.

Lennhof, Friedrich Georg. *Problem-Kinder.* Munich: Reinhardt, 1967. Originally published in English.

Lenz, Siegfried. *Der Verlust.* Hamburg: Hoffmann & Campe, 1981.

Leroyer, Micheline. *Me: Mother of a Drug Addict.* Belfast: Christian Journals, 1981.

Leuprecht, Winfried. *Der Versuch, aufrecht zu stehen.* Stuttgart: Radius, 1980.

Lewis, C. S. *The Problem of Pain.* New York: Collier, 1986.

Liebscher, Fred. *Multiple Sklerose: Eine Krankheit, mit der man leben kann.* Heidelberg: K. F. Haug, 1982.

Liebscher, Siegfried. *Der Behinderte ist normal, "wenn man ihn normal behandelt."* Hamburg: Claudius, 1971.

Lindenberg, Nita. *Sich selber fremd.* Stuttgart: Urachhaus, 1981.

Lindenberg, Vladimir. *Schicksalsgefährte sein . . .* 3d ed. Munich, Basel: Reinhardt, 1970. Originally published in Russian.

Lindenberg, Vladimir. *Gespräche am Krankenbett.* Munich, Basel: Reinhardt, 1983. Originally published in Russian.

Lipke, Cordula. *Lauf, solange du kannst! Bericht über eine Krankheit.* Regensburg: Habbel, 1980.

Lister, Barbara. *Briefe an die heile Welt: Behinderte schreiben an "sogenannte" Nichtbehinderte.* Frankfurt: Eichborn, 1981.

Loewy, Alfred. *Blinde grosse Männer.* Zurich: Kommissionsverlag Rascher, 1935.

Lohner, Marlene. *Plötzlich allein.* Frankfurt: Fischer, 1984.

Loosen, Werner. *Neuanfang.* Bern, Wuppertal: Blaukreuz, 1982.

Lorde, Audre. *The Cancer Journals.* San Francisco: Spinsters/Aunt Lute, 1987.

Lucas, Christel. *Silke—ein blindes Kind: Anregungen für Elternhaus und Kindergarten.* Stuttgart: Kösel, 1979.

Ludwig-Klein, Elisabeth. *Krebs-Kinder-Tagebuch: Wagnis einer Hoffnung.* Stuttgart: Radius, 1980.

Lüdecke, Barbara. Eine Brücke zu Dir: Behinderte Jugendliche erzählen. Munich: Schneider, 1981.

Lukasz-Aden, Gudrun. *Tiefer kannst du nicht fallen.* Munich: Heyne, 1986.

Lund, Doris. *Eric.* New York: Dell, 1979.

Lundholm, Anja. *Zerreissprobe.* Munich: Goldmann, 1978.

Lusseyran, Jacques. *And There Was Light.* New York: Parabola, 1987.

Lusseyran, Jacques. *Le monde commence aujourd'hui.* Paris: La Table Ronde, 1959.

Maas, Hermann. *Der Seewolf.* Olten: Walter, 1984.

Maass, Siegfried. *Keine Flügel für Reggi.* 2d ed. East Berlin: Verlag Neues Leben, 1986.

MacCracken, Mary. *Lovey: A Very Special Child.* New York: New American Library, 1977.

MacLeod, Sheila. *The Art of Starvation: A Story of Anorexia and Survival.* Schocken, 1982.

Madeisky, Uschi, and Werner, Klaus. *Flucht in die Sucht: In Selbsthilfegruppen finden Eltern ein neues Verhältnis zu ihren Kindern.* Reinbek bei Hamburg: Rowohlt, 1983.

Maier-Gerber, Hartmut. *In der Hoffnung auf das Jenseits.* Munich: Kösel, 1985.

Mann, Iris. *Aus der Behinderung ins Leben: Sorgenkinder entfalten ihre Fähigkeit.* Reinbek bei Hamburg: Rowohlt, 1981.

Mannoni, Maud. *Un lieu pour vivre: les enfants de Bonneuil, leurs parents et l'équipe des "soignants."* Paris: Editions du Seuil, 1976.

Mansfeld, F. C. *Die Lichtbringer.* Vienna: Kurt Kleber, 1953.

Margolis, Karen. *Die Knochen zeigen.* Berlin: Rotbuch, 1985. Originally published in English.

Marshall, Alan. *I Can Jump Puddles.* Cleveland: World, 1957.

Martell, Inge. *Morgen-Grauen.* Berlin: Frauenbuchvertrieb, sisi, 1982.

Martini, Werner, and Schroif, Angelika. *Der Tod wird keine Grenze für uns sein: Wir begleiten Martin beim Sterben.* 2d ed. Mainz: Matthias Grünewald, 1981.

Marx, Annemarie. *Die heile Insel.* Hamburg: Rauhes Haus, 1975.

Maurina, Zenta. *Die weite Fahrt.* Memmingen: Maximilian Dietrich, 1951.

Maurina, Zenta. *Die eisernen Riegel zerbrechen.* Memmingen: Maximilian Dietrich, 1957.

Maurina, Zenta. *Denn das Wagnis ist schön: Geschichte eines Lebens.* 9th ed. Memmingen: Maximilian Dietrich, 1977.

McKnew, Donald H.; Cytryn, Leon; and Yahraes, Herbert C. *Why Isn't Johnny Crying? Coping with Depression in Children.* New York: Norton, 1985.

Mehringer, Andreas. *Verlassene Kinder.* Munich: Reinhardt, 1985.

Meidinger-Geise, Inge. *Ich schenke mir ein Jahr.* Freiburg: F. H. Kerle, 1982.

Mein Name ist Adam: Ein Anonymer Alkoholiker zieht Bilanz über sein Leben. Munich: Mosaik, 1980.

Meisinger, Edith. *Über die Schwelle: Aufzeichnungen einer spastisch Gelähmten.* 5th ed. East Berlin: Evangelische Verlagsanstalt, 1986.

Melton, David. *Todd.* Englewood Cliffs, NJ: Prentice-Hall, 1968.

Menninger, Dieter. *Belügt uns nicht!* Berlin, Stuttgart: Kreuz, 1978.

Mentz, Gerda and Siegfried. *Mit Andreas fing alles an: Wie Sport und Spiel das Leben eines geistig behinderten Kindes verändern können.* Göttingen: Sass & Co. (Self-published), 1982.

Merfert-Diete, Christa, and Soltau, Roswitha, eds. *Frauen und Sucht.* Reinbek bei Hamburg: Rowohlt, 1986.

Mesrine, Jacques. *L'instinct de mort.* Paris: J. C. Lattès, 1977.

Meulenbelt, Anja. *Alba.* Amsterdam: Van Gennep, 1984.

Meuser, Luise. *. . . denn die Freude hat das letzte Wort.* Kevelaer: Butzon & Bercker, 1985.

Meves, Christa. *Ich will mich ändern: Geschichte einer Genesung.* Freiburg: Herder, 1986.

Mey, Daniel. *Stahlbein.* Zurich: Pendo, 1986.

Meyer, Olga. *Das war Martin.* Bern, 1957.

Meyer, Willi, and Wydler, Gertrud. *Anja: Abenteuer einer Kindertherapie.* Olten: Walter, 1982.

Meyer-Auhausen, Otto. *Als das Dorf noch meine Welt war.* Oettingen: Fränk.-Schwäb. Heimatverlag, 1963.

Meyer-Auhausen, Otto. *Wenn auch das Licht erlosch.* Leipzig: Kochler & Amelang, 1936.

Meyer-Hörstgen, Hans. *Hirntod.* Frankfurt: Suhrkamp, 1985.

Minahan, John. *Mask.* New York: Berkley, 1985.

Minwegen, Hiltrud. *Mario: Von der Sucht zur Hoffnung. Eine Mutter sucht im Rom ihren drogensüchtigen Sohn.* Frankfurt: Fischer, 1983.

Miquel, André. *Le fils interrompu.* Paris: Flammarion, 1971.

Möckel, Klaus. *Hoffnung für Dan: Ein Bericht.* 4th ed. East Berlin: Verlag Neues Leben, 1986.

Moore, Walter. *Set Me Free.* London: Pickering & Inglis, 1980.

Moser, Annemarie E. *Vergitterte Zuflucht.* Graz: Styria, 1983.

Moser, T., ed. *Gespräche mit Eingeschlossenen.* Frankfurt: Suhrkamp, 1974.

Moser. T. *Romane als Krankheitsgeschichten.* Frankfurt: Suhrkamp, 1984.

Moser, Tilman. *Das erste Jahr.* Frankfurt: Suhrkamp, 1986.

Moster, Mary B. *Living with Cancer.* Wheaton, IL: Tyndale House, 1985.

Mühlbauer, Helmut. *Kollege Alkohol.* Munich: Kösel, 1986.

Müller-Garnn, Ruth. *Das Morgenrot ist weit: Geschichten der Hoffnung.* Würzburg: Echter, 1980.

Müller-Garnn, Ruth. *. . . und halte dich an meiner Hand: Die Geschichte eines Sorgenkindes.* Würzburg: Echter, 1977.

Müller-Garnn, Ruth. *Wie man durchs Leben stolpert: Die Geschichte, wie ich wurde.* Würzburg: Echter, 1982.

Muhr, Caroline. *Depressionen: Tagebuch einer Krankheit.* Frankfurt: Fischer, 1978.

Murphy, Robert. *Christianity Rubs Holes in My Religion.* Houston: Hunter Ministries, 1976.

Muthesius, Sibylle. *Flucht in die Wolken.* 4th ed. East Berlin: Buchverlag Der Morgen, 1984.

Narbesher, Maximilian. *Weg ins Licht.* St. Florian: Verlag Stiftsbuchhandlung, 1949.

Neidhart, Kristel. *Niemand soll mich so sehen.* Berlin: Rotbuch, 1983.

Nethery, Susan. *One Year and Counting: Breast Cancer, My World, and Me.* Grand Rapids, MI: Baker, 1978.

Noack, Hans-Georg. *Trip.* Ravensburg: Otto Maier, 1975. (Novel with factual information on drugs and youth.)

Noll, Peter. *Diktate über Sterben und Tod mit Totenrede von Max Frisch.* Munich: Piper, 1987.

Nouwen, Henri J. M. *Sterben um zu Leben.* Freiburg: Herder, 1983.

Noy, Gisela. *Zerstörungen.* Reinbek bei Hamburg: Rowohlt, 1986.

Nullmeyer, Heide. *Ich heisse Erika und bin Alkoholikerin: Betroffene und Angehörige erzählen.* Frankfurt: Fischer, 1983.

Oberthür, Irene. *Mein fremdes Gesicht.* 3d ed. East Berlin: Buchverlag Der Morgen, 1986.

Offenbach, Judith. *Sonja.* Frankfurt: Suhrkamp, 1983.

Opitz, Elisabeth. *Horch in das Dunkel.* Frankfurt: Fischer, 1981.

Ostrovski, Nikolai. *Wie der Stahl gehärtet wurde.* East Berlin: Verlag Neues Leben, 1986. Originally published in Russian.

Palmer, Lilli. *Um eine Nasenlänge.* Munich: Droemer-Knaur, 1984.

Panara, R. F.; Denis, T. B.; and McFarlane, J. H., eds. *Taubheit: Du Schicksal. Verband ehemaliger Studenten des Gallaudet-College zu Washington, D.C.* Essen: Gehörlosen-Verlag, 1976. Originally published in English.

Park, Clara C. *The Siege: The First Eight Years of an Autistic Child.* Boston: Little, Brown, 1982.

Parker, Merren, and Mauger, David. *Children with Cancer: A Handbook for Families and Helpers.* London: Cassell, 1979.

Pause, Walter. *Helen Keller: Das Leben triumphiert.* Gütersloh: G. Mohn, 1960.

Petzold, Heinz-Joachim. *Anerkennung statt Mitleid.* 2d ed. Rudolstadt: Greifenverlag, 1983.

Petzold, Heinz-Joachim. *Verstehen und fördern.* East Berlin: Evangelische Verlagsanstalt, 1984.

Philipe, Anne. *No Longer Than a Sigh.* New York: Atheneum, 1964.

Philipe, Anne. *Je l'écoute respirer.* Paris: Gallimard, 1984.

Philips, Carolyn E. *Michelle.* New York: New American Library, 1982.

Piechota, Ulrike. *Trauert nicht wie die, die keine Hoffnung haben.* Stuttgart: Radius, 1983.

Piechowski, Joachim. *Der Mann ohne Arme: Dokumentar-Roman über Carl Herrmann Unthans.* Hamburg: Matari, 1967.

Pilgrim, Volker Elis. *Die Elternaustreibung.* Düsseldorf: Claasen, 1984.

Pinney, Rachel. *Bobby: Breakthrough of a Special Child.* New York: McGraw-Hill, 1986.

Pla, Frieda le. *Blicke in eine verborgene Welt.* Duisburg: Deutsches Blindenhilfswerk, no date. Originally published in English.

Pray, Lawrence M., and Evan, Richard. *Journey of a Diabetic*. New York: Simon & Schuster, 1983.

Prekop, Irina. *Wir haben ein behindertes Kind: Eltern geistig behinderter Kinder berichten*. Stuttgart: Quell, 1979.

Prévost, Françoise. *Ma vie en plus*. Paris: Stock, 1975.

Prinzen, Helma. *. . . aber sonst geht's mir gut*. Munich: Knaur, 1986.

Prollius, Helga. *Die Angst liegt hinter mir: Frauen und Krebs*. 2d ed. Freiburg, Basel & Vienna: Herder, 1980.

Quincey, Thomas de. *The Confessions of an English Opium-Eater*. Harmondsworth: Penguin, 1986.

Ragsdale, Grady. *Steve McQueen, the Final Chapter*. Ventura, CA: Vision House, 1983.

Rauchfuss, Hildegard Maria. *Schlusstrich*. Halle, Leipzig: Mitteldeutscher Verlag, 1986.

Raymond, Jean. *L.* Paris: Editions du Seuil, 1982.

Redl, Fritz. *Children Who Hate: The Disorganization and Breakdown of Behavior Controls*. New York: Free Press, 1965.

Reed, David. *Anna*. New York: Bantam, 1979.

Reimann, Brigitte. *Die Geliebte, die verfluchte Hoffnung*. Neuwied: Luchterhand, 1986.

Reuss, Alexander. *Verlorenes Licht*. Heilbronn: Eugen Salzer, 1933.

Rey, Karl Guido. *Neuer Mensch auf schwachen Füssen: Erfahrungen eines Psychotherapeuten mit Gott*. 2d ed. Munich: Kösel, 1984.

Ring, Kenneth. *Heading toward Omega: In Search of the Meaning of the Near-Death Experience*. New York: Morrow, 1985.

Rodman, F. Robert. *Not Dying*. New York: Norton, 1988.

Rollin, Betty. *Last Wish*. Harmondsworth: Penguin, 1987.

Roman, Jo. *Exit House*. New York: Seaview, 1980.

Roth, Joseph. *Job: The Story of a Simple Man*. Woodstock, NY: Overlook, 1985.

Rother, Thomas. *Das plötzliche Verstummen des Wilhelm W.* Bern, Munich, & Vienna: Scherz, 1981.

Ruderisch, Gustav. *Ist der Weg auch weit . . .* Munich: Kindler, 1956.

Rupp, H. *Schlag die Hand nicht aus: Blindsein. Mit Blinden lernen*. Haan: Brockhaus, 1981.

Ruppert, Johanna. *Mehr als ich erwarten durfte: Auch Behinderte werden erwachsen*. Trier: Spee, 1979.

Ruppert, Johanna. *Warum gerade ich? Eine Mutter überwindet Resignation und Verzweiflung*. Trier: Spee, 1979.

Russel, Robert. *To Catch an Angel: Adventures in the World I Cannot See*. Leicester, England: Ulverscroft, 1965.

S., Nina. *Und der Jones ist immer pünktlich: Eine Fixerkarriere—ein authentischer Bericht*. Munich: Goldmann, 1983.

Saint-Dizier, Jean. *Ich bin geheilt*. 3d ed. Wuppertal: Blaukreuz, 1981.

Sandkorn, Anemone. *Das Signal oder die Entfernung des Knotens*. Frankfurt: Fischer, 1986.

Sarton, May. *A Reckoning*. So. Yarmouth, MA: J. Curley, 1985.

Schah-Mohammedi, Abbas. *Bis die Nacht vergeht: Erfahrungen und Erkenntnisse eines Blinden. Denkanstösse für Sehende*. Berlin: Hass & Co., 1981.

Schaumann, Ruth. *Das Arsenal*. Freiburg: Kerle, 1968.

Scheel, Karin. *Katrin: Ein Sorgenkind?* Gütersloh (self-published), 1979.

Scheresky, Jeanne. *Diagnosis, Cancer: Where Do We Go from Here?* Old Tappan, NJ: Revell, 1977.

Schiff, Harriet S. *The Bereaved Parent*. New York: Penguin, 1978.

Schine, Cathleen. *Alice in Bed*. New York: Berkley, 1984.

Schlag, Evelyn. *Die Kränkung*. Frankfurt: Fischer, 1987.

Schlett, Christa. *Babs: Eine Mutter entscheidet sich für ihr behindertes Kind*. Gütersloh: Siebenstern, 1978.

Schlett, Christa. *Ich will mitspielen. Behinderte: Falsches Mitleid und falsche Hilfe*. Wuppertal-Barmen: Jugenddienst Verlag, 1978.

Schlett, Christa. *. . . Krüppel sein dagegen sehr: Lebensbericht einer spastisch Gelähmten*. Frankfurt: Fischer, 1986.

Schmidt, Klaus-Jürgen G. *Mein Kind ist behindert: Ein Beitrag zum Verständnis*. Rheinstetten: Schindele, 1986.

Schmitt, Christian, ed. *Reise ans Ende der Angst*. Munich: Bertelsmann, 1983.

Schmitz, Marlies. *Kati lernt hören*. Berlin: Marhold, 1986.

Schöler, L.; Lindenmeyer, J.; and Schöler, H. *Das alles soll ich nicht mehr können? Sozialtraining für Rollstuhlabhängige*. Weinheim & Basel: Beltz, 1981.

Schreiner, Robert. *Wach auf, kleine Annette*. Zurich: Kreuz, 1984.

Schröder, Mathias. *Linda*. Munich: Langen-Müller, 1978.

Schroeder-Horstmann, Karin. *L(i)eben mit Handicap: Körperbehinderte geben Auskunft über ihre Sexualität*. Frankfurt, Berlin, Vienna: Ullstein, 1980.

Schuchardt, Erika, ed. *Jede Krise ist ein neuer Anfang: Aus Lebensgeschichten lernen*. 3d ed. With contributions by Hans-Bernhard Kaufmann, Marlies Winkelheide, et al. A publication of the Comenius Institut. Düsseldorf: Patmos, 1987.

Schuchardt, Erika. *Geschwister kann man sich nicht aussuchen: Wir gehören doch zusammen*. Hamburg, forthcoming.

Schuchardt, Erika. *Krise als Lernchance: Analyse von 331 Lebensgeschichten unserer Zeit*. With an introduction by Horst Siebert. A publication of the Comenius Institut. Düsseldorf: Patmos, 1985.

Schultz, Hans Jürgen, ed. *Letzte Tage: Sterbegeschichten aus zwei Jahrtausenden*. Stuttgart: Kreuz, 1983.

Schwartz, Lynne Sharon. *Disturbances in the Field*. New York: Bantam, 1985.

Schwartzenberg, Leon, and Viansson-Ponté, Pierre. *Changer la mort*. Paris: A. Michel, 1977.

Schwarz, Hildegard. *Mit Träumen leben: Einsichten*. Darmstadt: Verlag Darmstädter Blätter, 1981.

Schwarz, Jutta-Ute. *Gegenseitigkeit*. Neukirchen-Vluyn: Neukirchener Verlag, 1982.

Schweppenhäuser, Ekkehard. *Multiple Sklerose: Ein Weg zur Heilung. Eigene Erfahrungen mit einer schubförmigen MS*. 2d ed. Freiburg: Verlag Die Kommenden, 1982.

Scotson, Linda. *Doran: How a Mother's Love and a Child's Spirit Made a Medical Miracle*. New York: New American Library, 1986.

Sechehaye, Marguerite. *Journal d'une schizophrène: Auto-observation d'une schizophrène pendant le traitement psychothérapique*. Paris: Presses universitaires de France, 1969.

Segal, Marilyn M. *Run Away, Little Girl!* New York: Random House, 1966.

Segal, Patrick. *The Man Who Walked in His Head*. New York: Morrow, 1980.

Seibt, Rainer. *Ich möchte in Eurer Liebe baden! Eine Knast- und Heroin-Biographie*. Bensheim: Päd-extra Buchverlag, 1981.

Seidick, Kathryn. *. . . Or You Can Let Him Go*. New York: Dell, 1985.

Sharkey, Frances. *A Parting Gift*. New York: Bantam, 1984.

Shave, Marjorie. *Aus dem Leben eines geistig behinderten Kindes*. Hannover (self-published), 1961. Original English title: *The Story of a Backward Child*.

Shipp, Tom. *Kummer mit dem Alkohol: Begegnungen und Erfahrungen mit Alkoholkranken. Ein Gemeindepfarrer berichtet.* Wuppertal & Bern: Blaukreuz, 1980.

Signer, Martha. *Im Rollstuhl um die Welt: Eine Körperbehinderte berichtet über ihre Weltreise.* Rheinstetten: Schindele, 1970.

Simonton, Stephanie. *The Healing Family: The Simonton Approach for Families Facing Illness.* New York: Bantam, 1984.

Sinninger, Michel. . . . *aber die Liebe bleibt: Zeugnis einer Ehe.* Freiburg: Herder, 1980. Originally published in French.

Skorokhodova, Olga. *Jenseits der Nacht.* East Berlin: Verlag Kultur & Fortschritt, 1951.

Smithdas, Robert. *Mit Händen ergriffen.* Stuttgart: Engelhorn, 1960. Originally published in English.

Sontag, Susan. *Illness as Metaphor.* New York: Farrar, Strauss and Giroux, 1988.

Souter, John C. *The Pleasure Seller.* Wheaton, IL: Tyndale House, 1979.

Sporken, Paul, ed. *Was Sterbende brauchen.* Freiburg: Herder, 1982.

Steenbuch, Rikke. *Ich bin auch da: Lebensbericht einer Spastikerin.* Stuttgart, 1960. Original Norwegian title: *Jeg lever ogsa.*

Steiner, Erika, and Geissler, J. *Neurodermitis: Der geglückte Behandlungsversuch einer Mutter.* Stuttgart: Hippokrates, 1986.

Steller, Odile. *Un espoir infini.* Paris: Presses de la Renaissance, 1985.

Stephan, Lydia. *Du hättest so gern noch ein bisschen gelebt.* Frankfurt: Fischer, 1986.

Stier, Karin. *Ich wollte immer grösser sein: Geständnisse einer Ausgeflippten.* Asslar: Schulte & Gerth, 1984.

Stoeckel, Alfred. *Von Homer bis Helen Keller.* Bonn: Verlag des Deutschen Blindenverbandes, 1984.

Storz, Claudia. *Jessica mit Konstruktionsfehlern.* Zurich: Benziger, 1983.

Stüssi, Rosmarie. *Aufzeichnungen aus dem Leben mit einem blinden Kind.* Bern: Hans Huber, 1982.

Sullivan, Tom, and Gill, Derek. *If You Could See What I Hear.* New York: New American Library, 1976.

Sutherland, Stuart. *Breakdown.* St. Albans: Granada, 1977.

Tahara, Yoneko, and Palmer, Bernard. *Yoneko: Daughter of Happiness.* Chicago: Moody Press, 1976.

Taitl-Münzert, Irene. *Jeder hat ein Gesicht: Mit Behinderten leben.* Stuttgart: Radius, 1976.

Tangen, Ragnhild. *Michael.* Tring: Lion, 1983.

Tausch, Anne-Marie. *Gespräche gegen die Angst.* Reinbek bei Hamburg: Rowohlt, 1981.

Tausch, Anne-Marie and Reinhard. *Sanftes Sterben: Was der Tod für das Leben bedeutet.* Reinbek bei Hamburg: Rowohlt, 1985.

Tausch, Anne-Marie and Reinhard. *Wege zu uns.* Reinbek bei Hamburg: Rowohlt, 1983.

Teilhard de Chardin, Marguerite-Marie. *L'energie spirituelle de la souffrance: éscrits et souvenirs recueillis par Monique Givelet.* Paris: Editions du Seuil, 1951.

Terlan, G. *Zwölf Monate sind mehr als ein Jahr.* 2d ed. Wuppertal: Oncken, 1979.

Thieme, Gerda. *Dirk lernt Verstehen: Ein Bericht Hber weitere vier Lebensjahre.* Lüdenscheid: Gerda Crummenerl, 1974.

Thieme, Gerda. *Leben mit unserem autistischen Kind: Möglichkeiten und Grenzen einer Hilfe im Elternhaus. Ein Bericht über die ersten 12 Lebensjahre.* Lüdenscheid: Gerda Crummenerl, 1974.

Thom, Wilhelm and Elfriede. *Rückkehr ins Leben.* 5th ed. East Berlin: Verlag Neues Leben, 1986.

Tibbe, Trudi and Johann. *Leben an der Grenze des Todes.* 6th ed. Brecklum: Neukirchener, 1981.

Tibol, Raquel. *Frida Kahlo.* México: Ediciones de Cultura Popular, 1977.

Tobias, Karl-Heinz. *Damit ich wieder normal leben kann.* Recklinghausen: Psychiatrie Verlag, 1984.

Tobias, Rainer. *Die grossen und die kleinen Hände: Briefe an den Vater eines unheilbar kranken Kindes.* Munich: Kaiser, 1968.

Tobino, Mario. *Die Frauen von Magliano.* Zurich: Unionsverlag, 1986.

Tropp-Erblad, Ingrid. *Katt böjar pa S.* Stockholm, 1982.

Tuckermann, Albrecht. *Down-Kind Andreas: Der Weg eines Heimkindes.* Munich: Reinhardt, 1981.

Twersky, Jacob. *The Face of the Deep.* Cleveland: World, 1953.

Ude, Anneliese. *You Must Always Be Good.* Palo Alto, CA: Science and Behavior Books, 1977.

Ude-Pestel, Anneliese. *Ahmet—Geschichte einer Kindertherapie, ". . . weil ich nicht weiss, wohin ich gehöre."* 2d ed. Munich: Piper, 1983.

Vajda, Albert. *Lend Me an Eye.* New York: St. Martin's, 1975.

Valère, Valérie. *Le pavillon des enfants fous.* Paris: Editions Stock, 1978.

Viscardi, Henry. . . . *A Letter to Jimmy.* New York: Eriksson, 1962.

Völling, Kornelia. *Ich danke Dir Gott für Lydia.* Neukirchen-Vluyn: Schriftenmissionsverlag, 1984.

Vogel, Robert. *Zwischen hell und dunkel.* Vienna, 1982.

Vollmer-Jensen, Regina. *Wohin mit Katja?* Göttingen: Vandenhoeck & Ruprecht, 1972.

Vries-Kruyt, Truus de. *A Special Gift: The Story of Jan.* New York: P. H. Wyden, 1974.

Vuillemier, John Frederich. *Der letzte Tunnel.* Wiesbaden: Walter, 1970.

Wackernagel, Christof. *Bilder einer Ausstellung.* Reinbek bei Hamburg: Rowohlt, 1986.

Wagner, Gesine. *Im Feuer ist mein Leben verbrannt.* 2d ed. Gütersloh: GTB Siebenstern, 1986.

Wallace, Marjorie, and Robson, Michael. *On Giant's Shoulders: The Story of Terry Wiles.* London: Corgi, 1977.

Wallburg, Hans-Dieter. *Du, Herr, bist grösser . . .* Wuppertal, Bern: Blaukreuz, 1983.

Wallburg, Hans-Dieter. *Endlos schien die Nacht.* Wuppertal, Bern: Blaukreuz, 1983.

Wallisfurth, Maria. *Sie hat es mir erzählt.* Freiburg, Basel, & Vienna: Herder, 1979.

Walter, Otto F. *Der Stumme.* Reinbek bei Hamburg: Rowohlt, 1984.

Wander, Maxie. *Leben wär' eine prima Alternative: Tagebuchaufzeichnungen und Briefe (Part 1).* Wander, Fred, ed. *Die Geschichte einer Krebskrankheit (Part 2).* Darmstadt: Luchterhand, 1984.

Wanacek, Ottokar. *Licht im Dunkel.* Vienna, 1960.

Ward, Mildred M. *Liza.* Anderson, IN: Warner, 1976.

Weber, Marianne. *Lernprozess: Leben mit einem neuen Gesicht.* Frankfurt: Fischer, 1985.

Weber, Monika. *Die dunkle Seite meines Lebens: Überwindung einer Selbstzerstörung.* Frankfurt: Fischer, 1983.

Weber, Walter. *Jenseits der Nacht: Erfahrungen im Krankenhaus.* Stuttgart: Kreuz, 1981.

Weber-Gast, Ingrid. *Weil du nicht geflohen bist vor meiner Angst: Eine Ehepaar durchlebt die Depressionen des einen Partners.* 6th ed. Mainz: Matthias Grünewald, 1984.

Wecker, Konstantin. *Und die Seele nach aussen kehren. Ketzerbriefe eines Süchtigen. Uns ist kein Einzelnes bestimmt. Neun Elegien.* Reinbeck bei Hamburg: Rowohlt, 1983.

Wedler, Hans-L. *Gerettet?* Neuwied: Luchterhand, 1979.

Weidenhöfer, Margit. *Du führst mich hinaus ins Weite.* Frankfurt: Knecht, 1984.

Wendeler, Jürgen. *Autistische Jugendliche und Erwachsene*. Weinheim, Basel: Beltz, 1984.

Wengrow, N., and Efros, M. *Ein Mensch wie Du: Das Leben des Nikolai Ostrovski*. East Berlin: Verlag Kultur & Fortschritt, 1950. Original Russian title: *Zizn Nikolaja Ostrowskogo*.

Werner, Frank. *Herzland*. Munich: List, 1983.

Weyrich, Walter. *Wir haben gewusst, dass Du früher gehen würdest: Drei Jahre Zeit zum Sterben und Leben*. Zurich: Gotthelf, 1980.

Whitaker, Carl A., and Napier, Augustus. *The Family Crucible*. New York: Bantam, 1980.

Whitehouse, Elizabeth S. *There's Always More*. Valley Forge, PA: Judson, 1968.

Wiesenhütter, Eckart. *Blick nach drüben: Selbsterfahrungen im Sterben*. Gütersloh: Gütersloher Verlag, 1977.

Wiesner, Wolfgang. *Ich bin clean*. Munich: Heyne, 1987.

Wilson, Dorothy Clarke. *Take My Hands: The Remarkable Story of Dr. Mary Verghese*. New York: McGraw-Hill, 1963.

Winnicott, Donald W. *The Piggle: An Account of the Psychoanalytic Treatment of a Little Girl*. Madison, CT: International Universities Press, 1987.

Wochele, Rainer. *Der Absprung*. Reinbek bei Hamburg: Rowohlt, 1981.

Wölfing, M.-L. *Komm, gib mir deine Hand*. Düsseldorf, 1985.

Wola, Frank. *Sebastian, ich will es dir erklären*. Frankfurt: Fischer, 1985.

Woodson, Meg. *If I Die at Thirty*. Grand Rapids, MI: Zondervan, 1979.

Worgitzky, Charlotte. *Heute sterben immer nur die anderen*. East Berlin: Büchverlag Der Morgen, 1986.

Wright, David. *Deafness*. New York: Stein & Day, 1975.

Wulf, Hans, ed. *Kein Anlass zu kapitulieren*. Neukirchen-Vluyn: Neukirchener Verlag, 1976.

Wyss, Laure. *Ein schwebendes Verfahren*. Frankfurt: Fischer, 1983.

Yurtdas, Barbara. *Einen Mondmonat lang*. Munich: Frauenoffensive, 1985.

Zeun, Renate. *Betroffen: Bilder einer Krebserkrankung*. East Berlin: Verlag Volk & Gesundheit, 1986.

Zickgraf, Cordula. *I Am Learning to Live Because You Must Die: A Hospital Diary*. Philadelphia: Fortress, 1981.

Zierling, Elfriede. *Das Mass des Lebens*. East Berlin: Verlag Neues Lebens, 1984.

Ziesche, Marie. *Calasanz: Die letzte Freiheit*. Ludwigsburg: Süddeutsche Verlagsanstalt, 1982.

Zink, Jörg. *Vielleicht ist es noch nicht zu spät*. Stuttgart: Kreuz, 1983.

Zorca, Victor and Rosemary. *A Way to Die*. New York: Knopf, 1980.

Zorn, Fritz. *Mars*. New York: Knopf, 1982.

Classified Bibliography

Biographies and Autobiographies about Coping with Crisis Written between 1900 and 1989 with Short Annotations

This classification corresponds to the classification by disabilities or disruption in their lives in figures 1-4 on pages 26 and 27.

MENTAL RETARDATION

Affected individuals

PARENTS

a) Mothers

Boston, Sarah. *Will, My Son: The Life and Death of a Mongol Child*. London: Pluto, 1981.
 Account of a Down's syndrome child.
Buck, Pearl. *The Child Who Never Grew*. New York: J. Day, 1950.
 Mother and Nobel Prize winner, about her brain-damaged child.
Buck, Pearl. *My Several Worlds*. New York: Pocket, 1960.
 Autobiography.
Buck, Pearl. *A Bridge for Passing*. New York: Pocket, 1963.
 The Nobel Prize winner and mother of an emotionally/mentally handicapped child recounts how she overcame her loneliness.
Craig, Mary. *Blessings*. New York: Bantam, 1980.
 The English journalist must learn to grasp the truth: two of her children are severely emotionally/mentally disabled.
Fritze-Eggimann, Ruth. *Du bist mir anvertraut*. Evangelische Frauenarbeit in der Pfalz (self-published), no date.
Fritze-Eggimann, Ruth. *Ich habe viele Freunde*. Evangelische Frauenarbeit in der Pfalz (self-published), 1972.
Geppert, Roswitha. *Die Last, die du nicht trägst*. 7th ed. Halle: Mitteldeutscher Verlag, 1986.
 A mother writes about her son, who because of a metabolism disorder, phenylke-tonury, that is diagnosed too late, is severely emotionally/mentally disabled.
Gollner, Anna. *Christine*. Vienna: Jungbrunnen, 1982.
 The story of a girl with Down's syndrome.

174

Häusler, Ingrid. *Kein Kind zum Vorzeigen? Bericht über eine Behinderung.* Reinbek bei Hamburg: Rowohlt, 1979.

Hénault, Marcelle. *Mon fils Emmanuel.* Tours: Mame, 1973.

Lundholm, Anja. *Zerreissprobe.* Munich: Goldmann, 1978.
Parents who take responsibility for their emotionally and physically disabled child face a difficult crisis.

Meyer, Olga. *Das war Martin.* Bern, 1957.

Müller-Garnn, Ruth. *Das Morgenrot ist weit: Geschichten der Hoffnung.* Würzburg: Echter, 1980.

Müller-Garnn, Ruth. *. . . und halte dich an meiner Hand: Die Geschichte eines Sorgenkindes.* Würzburg: Echter, 1977.
The story of a mother's response to a child who suffered from meningitis.

Ruppert, Johanna. *Mehr als ich erwarten durfte: Auch Behinderte werden erwachsen.* Trier: Spee, 1979.

Ruppert, Johanna. *Warum gerade ich? Eine Mutter überwindet Resignation und Verzweiflung.* Trier, Spee, 1979. (1972 in original).
A mother overcomes resignation and despair. A daughter, Gabi, is born with Down's syndrome.

Scheel, Karin. *Katrin: Ein Sorgenkind?* Gütersloh (self-published), 1979.

Segal, Marilyn M. *Run Away, Little Girl!* New York: Random House, 1966.
The mother of a brain-damaged child describes her role as cotherapist.

Shave, Marjorie. *Aus dem Leben eines geistig behinderten Kindes.* Hannover (self-published), 1961. Original English title: *The Story of a Backward Child.*

Taitl-Münzert, Irene. *Jeder hat ein Gesicht: Mit Behinderten leben.* Stuttgart: Radius, 1976.
The account of a woman who is both the mother of an emotionally/mentally handicapped child and a special-education teacher.

Tangen, Ranghild. *Michael.* Tring: Lion, 1983.

Vollmer-Jensen, Regina. *Wohin mit Katja?* Göttingen: Vandenhoeck & Ruprecht, 1972.

b) Fathers

Görres, Albert. *Kennt die Psychologie den Menschen? Fragen zwischen Psychotherapie, Anthropologie und Christentum.* Munich: Piper, 1978.
Görres—father of two emotionally/mentally handicapped children, and scientist—poses the question of the point of suffering. Compare also the title under c) Parents together: Görres, Silvia and Albert. *Leben mit einem behinderten Kind.*

Hayakawa, S. I. *Our Son Mark.* San Francisco State College, 1969. [author's mss.]

Hourdin, Georges. *Le Matheur innocent.* Paris: Stock, 1976.
A French journalist writes about his Down's syndrome daughter.

Hunt, Nigel. *The World of Nigel Hunt: The Diary of a Mongoloid Youth.* Norwich, CT: Asset Recycling, 1982.

Kenzaburo, O. *Eine persönliche Erfahrung.* Frankfurt: Suhrkamp, 1972.
Original Japanese title: *Kojinteki na Taiken.*
The birth of a child with an incurable cerebral hernia confronts a father with a heavy sense of responsibility.

Melton, David. *Todd.* Englewood Cliffs, N.J.: Prentice-Hall, 1968.
An account of helping a brain-damaged child.

Miquel, André. *Le fils interrompu.* Paris: Flammarion, 1971.

Tobias, Rainer. *Die grossen und die kleinen Hände: Briefe an den Vater eines unheilbar kranken Kindes.* Munich: Kaiser, 1968.
> The author is the father of a brain-damaged child.

Vries-Kruyt, Truus de. *A Special Gift: The Story of Jan.* New York: P. H. Wyden, 1974.
> Originally published in Dutch.

c) Parents, together

Falisse, Gaston and Marie-Françoise. *Nos enfants handicapés.* Paris: Editions universitaires, 1962.

Görres, Silvia. *Leben mit einem behinderten Kind.* Munich, Piper, 1986.
> The parents of four children, among them two with congenital and acquired emotional/mental handicaps, tell their story.

Mentz, Gerda and Siegfried. *Mit Andreas fing alles an: Wie Sport und Spiel das Leben eines geistig behinderten Kindes verändern können.* Göttingen: Sass & Co. (self-published), 1982.

Partners

No entries

Professionals

a) Professional women

Buch, Andrea, et al. *An den Rand gedrängt: Was Behinderte daran hindert normal zu Leben.* Reinbek bei Hamburg: Rowohlt, 1980.

Hong, Edna. *Bright Valley of Love.* Minneapolis: Augsburg, 1979.
> A young boy finds life in Bethel.

Kobbe, Ursula. *Die Brücke ohne Geländer: Tagebuch einer Heilpädagogin* 2d ed. Freiburg: Herder, 1974.
> Diary of a teacher-therapist.

Mann, Iris. *Aus der Behinderung ins Leben: Sorgenkinder entfalten ihre Fähigkeit.* Reinbek bei Hamburg: Rowohlt, 1981.
> Problem children develop their abilities.

Prekop, Irina. *Wir haben ein behindertes Kind: Eltern geistig behinderter Kinder berichten.* Stuttgart: Quell, 1979.
> Parents of emotionally/mentally disabled children tell their stories.

b) Professional men

Bach, Heinz. *Die heimlichen Bitten des Peter M.* Berlin: Marhold, 1985.
> A fictitious dialog between the author and the son of a close colleague.

Fühmann, Franz, and Riemann, Dietmar. *Was für eine Insel in was für einem Meer: Leben mit geistig Behinderten.* Rostock: Hirnstorff, 1985.
> A photographic record.

Kessling, Volker. *Tagebuch eines Erziehers* 4th ed. Berlin: Verlag Neues Leben, 1985.
> On living with severely emotionally/mentally disabled children.

Petzold, Heinz-Joachim. *verstehen und fördern.* East Berlin: Evangelische Verlagsanstalt, 1984.
> Report on emotionally/mentally disabled persons.

Tuckermann, Albrecht. *Down-Kind Andreas: Der Weg eines Heimkindes.* Munich: Reinhardt, 1981.

Wulf, Hans, ed. *Kein Anlass zu kapitulieren.* Neukirchen-Vluyn: Neukirchener Verlag, 1976.

Doctors from Bethel, along with the head of the facility, attempt to give counsel.

c) Professionals, together

No entries

PHYSICAL DISABILITY

Affected individuals

a) Women

Bach, Katharina. *Geklagt wird nicht und geheult erst nachts.* Münster: Tende Druck (self-published), 1981.

Cohnen, Elfriede. *Ein Leben wie andere.* Heilbronn: Eugen Salzer, 1979.

Autobiographical novel. Amputation.

Eareckson, Joni. *A Step Further.* Grand Rapids, Mich.: Zondervan, 1978.

Eareckson, Joni. *Joni.* Grand Rapids, Mich.: Zondervan, 1981.

A young woman becomes a quadriplegic at the age of 17.

Eareckson-Tada, Joni. *Choices Changes.* Grand Rapids, Mich.: Zondervan, 1986. Marriage; work with the disabled; movie.

Eggli, Ursula. *Herz im Korsett: Tagebuch einer Behinderten.* 5th ed. Gümlingen, Bern: Zytglogge, 1979.

Diary of a disabled person with muscular paralysis.

Eggli, Ursula. *Die Zärtlichkeit des Sonntagsbratens.* Bern: Eigenverlag, Wangenstr. 27, CH 3018 (self-published), 1986.

Eramo, Luce de. *Finché la testa vive.* Milan: Rizzoli, 1964.

Autobiographical novel.

Geisler, Helga. *Danke, das kann ich selbst: Wie ich meine Behinderung besiegte.* 2d ed. Stuttgart: Otto Bauer, 1984.

Consequences of an accident.

Habel, Luise. *Hergott, schaff die Treppen ab! Erfahrungen einer Behinderten.* Stuttgart: Kreuz, 1978.

Habel, Luise. *Ich bring' Dir einen Arm voll Leben.* Munich: Kösel, 1984.

Habel, Luise. *Ich muss nicht immer stark sein.* Munich: Kösel, 1985.

Habel, Luise. *Umarmen möcht ich dich: Briefe an einen Therapeuten.* Frankfurt: Fischer, 1986.

Letters to a therapist.

Hauke, Felicitas. *Steine im Weg: Ein Lebensbericht.* Freiburg: Herder, 1981.

Horn, Sabine. *Begegnungen einer Rollstuhlfahrerin mit ihrer Umwelt.* Hannover: Falk, 1986.

Horn, Sabine. *Ein Leben im Rollstuhl.* 2d ed. Hannover: Fehldruck, 1984.

Kneller, Pamela. *Das Leben geht weiter: Der Weg einer Behinderten.* Wemding: Verlag für Grundlagenwissen Herbert Wirkner, 1981.

Documentary novel.

Legrix, Denise. *Born Like That.* London: Souvenir, 1962.
The destiny of a painter without arms and legs. Originally published in French.

Lister, Barbara. *Briefe an die heile Welt: Behinderte schreiben an sogenannte "Nicht-behinderte."* Frankfurt: Eichborn, 1981.
Disabled people write to so-called non-disabled people.

Lüdecke, Barbara. *Eine Brücke zu Dir: Behinderte Jugendliche erzählen.* Munich: Schneider, 1981.
Disabled young people tell their stories.

Maurina, Zenta. *Die weite Fahrt.* Memmingen: Maximilian Dietrich, 1951.

Maurina, Zenta. *Denn das Wagnis ist schön: Geschichte eines Lebens.* 9th ed. Memmingen: Maximilian Dietrich, 1977.

Maurina, Zenta. *Die eisernen Riegel zerbrechen.* Memmigen: Maximilian Dietrich, 1957.

Meidinger-Geise, Inge. *Ich schenke mir ein Jahr.* Freiburg: F. H. Kerle, 1982.
A complex arm fracture leads the author to reflect on her life.

Meisinger, Edith. *Über die Schwelle: Aufzeichnungen einer spastisch Gelähmten.* 5th ed. East Berlin: Evangelische Verlagsanstalt, 1986.
Notes of a woman with spastic paralysis.

Meuser, Luise. . . . *denn die Freude hat das letzte Wort.* Kevelaer: Butzon & Bercker, 1985.
Reflections by a woman with severe physical disabilities.

Offenbach, Judith. *Sonja.* Frankfurt: Suhrkamp, 1983.
This book is an account of grief. It tells the story of a non-disabled student and a woman in a wheelchair.

Schlett, Christa. *Babs: Eine Mutter entscheidet sich für ihr behindertes Kind.* Gütersloh: Siebenstern, 1978.

Schlett, Christa. *Ich will mitspielen-Behinderte: Falsches Mitleid und falsche Hilfe.* Wuppertal-Barmen: Jugenddienst, 1978.

Schlett, Christa. . . . *Krüppel sein dagegen sehr: Lebensbericht einer spastich Gelähmten.* Frankfurt: Fischer, 1986.
Life story of a woman with spastic paralysis.

Schroeder-Horstmann, Karin. *L(i)eben mit Handicap: Korperbehinderte geben Auskunft über ihre Sexualität.* Frankfurt, Berlin, Vienna: Ullstein, 1980.
Physically handicapped people talk about their sexuality.

Signer, Martha. *Im Rollstuhl um die Welt: Eine Körperbehinderte berichtet über ihre Weltreise.* Rheinstetten: Schindele, 1970.
A physically disabled woman tells about her trip around the world.

Steenbuch, Rikke. *Ich bin auch da: Lebensbericht einer Spastikerin.* Stuttgart, 1960.
Original Norwegian title: *Jeg lever ogsa.*
A spastic woman tells her life story.

Storz, Claudia. *Jessica mit Konstruktionsfehlern.* Zurich: Benziger, 1983.

Tahara, Yoneko and Palmer, Bernhard. *Yoneko: Daughter of Happiness.* Chicago: Moody Press, 1976.

Tibol, Raquel. *Frida Kahlo.* México: Ediciones de Cultura Popular, 1977.
A physically disabled Mexican artist tells her story. She is one of the first women in the history of art who focuses exclusively on female subjects. (Compare also the title under Professionals *a) Professional women:* Herrera, Hayden. *Frida Kahlo*). Originally published in Spanish.

b) Men

Armes, Jay J. and Nolan, Frederick. *Jay J. Armes, Investigator,* New York: Avon, 1977.
As a 12-year-old, the author loses both arms in experiments.

Aucoutuier, Bernard, and Lapière, André. *Bruno.* Munich: Reinhardt, 1982. Original French title: *Bruno: Psychomotricité et thérapie.*

Account of psychomotor therapy with a cerebrally damaged child.

Bach, Ulrich. *Boden unter den Füssen hat keiner.* Göttingen: Vandenhoeck & Ruprecht, 1986.

Bach, Ulrich. *Kraft in leeren Händen.* Freiburg: Herder, 1986.

Bach, Ulrich. *Vollmarsteiner Rasiertexte: Notizen eines Rollstuhlfahrers.* Gladbeck: Schriftenmissions-Verlag, no date.

Bauer, Ernst W. *Ein Stuhl zwischen den Stühlen.* Munich: Sociomedico-Verlag, 1974.

Brown, Christy. *My Left Foot.* New York: Simon & Schuster, 1955.

A completely unschooled 22-year-old man, who has spastic paralysis, discovers a way to express himself by writing with his left foot.

Brown, Christy. *Down All the Days.* New York: Stein & Day, 1970.

Carlson, Earl R. *Born That Way.* New York: J. Day, 1941.

The life story of a physician and therapist who is also a spastic.

Christoph, Franz. *Krüppelschläge: Gegen die Gewalt der Menschlichkeit.* Reinbek bei Hamburg: Rowohlt, 1983.

The author, physically handicapped since birth, directs this polemic at all those who pity "cripples."

Cleland, Max. *Story at the Broken Places: A Personal Story.* Lincoln, Va.: Chosen, 1980.

The author lost both legs and one arm in an explosion. Poignantly, he describes his search for a way out of his crisis.

Drescher, Peter. *Birkenhof.* East Berlin: Evangelische Verlagsanstalt, 1981.

An autobiographical story. From the perspective of a 22-year-old man, the author writes about changes he experiences, living at a retreat center for the physically disabled.

Hobrecht, Jürgen. *Du kannst mir nicht in die Augen sehen.* Berlin: März 2001, 1981.

A 24-year-old man comes to terms with his congenital, quadriplegic disability, and in particular, with his sexuality.

Hofbauer, Friedl. *Federball.* Freiburg: Herder, 1981.

Autobiographical novel.

Knop, Jürgen. *Sie werden uns doch bemerken müssen . . . Geschichten aus einem behinderten Leben.* Hannover: SOAK, 1981.

Stories from a "disabled" life.

Lefranc, Alain. *Le courage de vivre.* Paris: Editions du Cerf, 1975.

During a break in a swimming meet, this 17-year-old swimmer-athlete is paralyzed as the result of a dive.

Leuprecht, Winfried. *Der Versuch, aufrecht zu stehen.* Stuttgart: Radius, 1980.

A 10-year-old must learn to live with his progressive paralysis (Friedrich's ataxia).

Liebscher, Siegfried. *Der Behinderte ist normal, "wenn man ihn normal behandelt."* Hamburg: Claudius, 1971.

Maass, Siegfried. *Keine Flügel für Reggi.* 2d ed. East Berlin: Verlag Neues Leben, 1986.

A man in a wheelchair deals with re-entry problems after leaving a rehabilitation center.

Marshall, Alan. *I Can Jump Puddles.* Cleveland: World, 1957.

Segal, Patrick. *The Man Who Walked in His Head.* New York: Morrow, 1980.

Viscardi, Henry. *. . . A Letter to Jimmy.* New York: Eriksson, 1962.

Twelve letters to a disabled youth, from another affected person.

c) Affected individuals

Schöler, L., Lindenmeyer, J., and Schöler, H. *Das alles soll ich nicht mehr können? Sozialtraining für Rollstuhlabhängige.* Weinheim & Basel: Beltz, 1981.

Thom, Wilhelm and Elfriede. *Rückkehr ins Leben.* 5th ed. East Berlin: Verlag Neues Leben, 1986.

> The author, a competitive athlete and army officer, is paralyzed in an accident. With his wife, he learns to live "differently."

PARENTS

a) Mothers

Burton, Josephine. *Crippled Victory.* New York: Sheed & Ward, 1956.

> The story of a child with dysmelia.

Carette, Jeanine. *Te mettre au monde.* Paris, 1973.

> A mother—a factory worker—has lived for 12 years knowing that her son will die of muscular dystrophy.

Carson, Mary. *Ginny: A True Story.* New York: Popular Library, 1971.

> A six-year-old girl suffers brain damage in a car accident.

Killilea, Marie. *Karen.* New York: Dell, 1983.

> A mother suffers the birth of her cerebral palsied daughter, and fights to establish, from the first parents' self-help groups, the United Cerebral Palsy Association.

Krüger, Barbara. *Mein Sohn Andi: Tagebuch einer Mutter.* Freiburg: Herder, 1979.

Völling, Kornelia. *Ich danke Dir Gott für Lydia.* Neukirchen-Vluyn: Schriftenmissionsverlag, 1984.

b) Fathers

no entries

c) Parents, together

Aly, Monika and Götz, and Tumler, Molind. *Kopfkorrektur oder der Zwang, gesund zu sein: Ein behindertes Kind zwischen Therapie und Alltag.* Berlin: Rotbuch, 1981.

PARTNERS

No entries

PROFESSIONALS

a) Professional women

Herrera, Hayden. *Frida: A Biography of Frida Kahlo.* New York: Harper & Row, 1983.

> Life story and extensive analysis of the works of Frida Kahlo.

Immendorf, Ruth. *Ich sage ja: Körperbehinderte in der Bewältigung ihres Lebens.* East Berlin: Evangelische Verlagsanstalt, 1983.

> Professional women tell about preschoolers and correspondence students. Their accounts are supplemented by the autobiographies of six severely disabled students.

Teilhard de Chardin, Marguerite-Marie. *L'energie spirituelle de la souffrance! escrits et souvenirs recueillis par Monique Givelet*. Paris: Editions du Seuil, 1951.

On illness and suffering.

Wilson, Dorothy Clarke. *Take My Hands: The Remarkable Story of Dr. Mary Verghese*. New York: McGraw-Hill, 1963.

This doctor was paralyzed after a car accident.

Wilson, Dorothy Clarke. *Handicap Race*. New York: McGraw-Hill, 1967.

A husband is paralyzed in a sports accident.

Ziesche, Marie. *Calasanz: Die letzte Freiheit*. Ludwigsburg: Süddeutsche Verlagsanstalt, 1982.

The monk of Reichenau, Hermann of Altershausen, composer of "Salve Regina."

b) Professional men

Fischer, Bernhard. *Mein Geheimnis gehört mir*. Stuttgart: Freies Geistesleben, 1974.

Excerpts from world literature.

Petzold, Heinz-Joachim. *Anerkennung statt Mitleid*. 2d ed. Rudolstadt: Greifenverlag, 1983.

With the help of 11 young people, a journalist describes the education, work and life-styles, and rehabilitation of the disabled in the German Democratic Republic.

Piechowski, Joachim. *Der Mann ohne Arme: Dokumentar-Roman über Carl Herrmann Unthans*. Hamburg: Matari, 1967.

Schröder, Mathias. *Linda*. Munich: Langen-Müller, 1978.

An autobiographical novel.

c) Professionals, together

Wallace, Marjorie, and Robson, Michael. *On Giants' Shoulders: The Story of Terry Wiles*. London: Corgi, 1977.

Stunted growth, the result of thalidomide.

LEARNING DISABILITY

Affected individuals

PARENTS

No entries

PARTNERS

No entries

PROFESSIONALS

No entries

a) Professional women

Kreye, Ulrike. . . . *betroffen: Sonderschüler erzählen.* Wetter: Freundeskreis der Sonderschule Wetter, no date.
 Based on her personal involvement, a special-education teacher writes about the problems of students with learning disabilities.

b) Professional men

No entries

c) Professionals, together

No entries

PSYCHOLOGICAL AND EMOTIONAL DISORDERS

Affected individuals

a) Women

Atwood, Margaret E. *The Edible Woman.* New York: Popular Library, 1976.
 On the verge of loss of self.
Barnes, Mary. *Two Accounts of a Journey through Madness.* New York: Ballantine, 1973.
 The famous case from Kingsley Hall. Chronicled by Mary Barnes, with commentary by her psychiatrist Joseph Berke.
Brender, Irmela. *In Wirklichkeit ist alles ziemlich gut.* Munich: Knaur, 1986.
Cardinal, Marie. *The Words to Say It: An Autobiographical Novel.* Cambridge, Mass.: Van Vactor B. Goodheart, 1984.
 Autobiographical novel of a psychoanalysis.
Conti, Adalgisa. *Manicomio 1914.* Milan: G. Mazzotta, 1978.
 On life in a mental institution.
Erlenberger, Maria. *Der Hunger nach Wahnsinn.* Reinbek bei Hamburg: Rowohlt, 1983.
Fell, Alison. *Every Move You Make.* London: Virago, 1984.
 In London Jane Guthrie lives through the politically tense 70s. Her inner turmoil finally burst forth in a breakdown.
Ferguson, Sarah. *A Guard Within.* New York: Penguin, 1976.
 Before her suicide, a 40-year-old, psychologically disabled woman tries to come to terms with the death of her psychotherapist of many years.
Gerlinghoff, Monika. *Magersüchtig.* Munich: Piper, 1985.
Goldmann-Posch, Ursula. *Tagebuch einer Depression.* Munich: Kindler, 1985.
Graf, Andrea. *Die Suppenkasperin.* Frankfurt: Fischer, 1985.
Green, Hannah. [pseud.] *I Never Promised You a Rose Garden.* New York: New American Library.
 Joanne Greenberg's autobiographical novel about the healing of her schizophrenia through the work of the therapist Dr. Fried, first wife of Erich Fromm.

Hayden, Torey L. *Sheila*. Bern and München: Scherz Verlag, 1981.
  A child caught in fear and loneliness becomes a gifted, life-affirming person.
Hayden, Torey L. *Somebody Else's Kids*. New York: Putnam, 1981.
  The exemplary story of a small group of disadvantaged children who, thanks to their teacher, are restored to a place in the community.
Lair, Jacqueline, and Lechler, Walter H. *I Exist. I Need. I'm Entitled*. Garden City, N.Y.: Doubleday, 1980.
Langsdorff, Maja. *Die neimliche Sucht, unheimlich zu essen*. Frankfurt: Fischer, 1985.
  Bulimia eating disorder.
Lavant, Christine. *Kunst wie meine ist nur verstümmeltes Leben*. Salzburg: Otto Müller, 1978.
  Poems, prose, and letters, posthumous or previously published in various places.
Lawrence, Marilyn. *The Anorexic Experience*. New York: P. Bedrick, 1987.
  Identity-crisis and an addiction to becoming thin (anorexia).
MacLeod, Sheila. *The Art of Starvation: A Story of Anorexia and Survival*. Schocken, 1982.
  An autobiographical account of an addiction to thinness (anorexia).
Margolis, Karen. *Die Knochen zeigen*. Berlin: Rotbuch, 1985. Originally published in English.
  A woman protests against her own compulsion.
Moser, Annemarie E. *Vergitterte Zuflucht*. Graz: Styria, 1983.
  A young woman tells the story of her depression and her stay in a psychiatric clinic.
Muhr, Caroline. *Depressionen: Tagebuch einer Krankheit*. Frankfurt: Fischer, 1978.
Noy, Gisela. *Zerstörungen*. Reinbek bei Hamburg: Rowohlt, 1986.
  The story of a woman who, having survived a psychological crisis, finds the courage to live again.
Opitz, Elisabeth. *Horch in das Dunkel*. Frankfurt: Fischer, 1981.
Prinzen, Helma. . . . *aber sonst geht's mir gut*. Munich: Knaur, 1986.
  Auguste Herzog suffers from a neurotic compulsion.
Sechehaye, Marguerite. *Journal d'une schizophrène: Auto-observation d'une schizophrène pendant le traitement psychothérapique*. Paris: Presses universitaires de France, 1969.
Valère, Valérie. *Le pavillon des enfants fous*. Paris: Editions Stock, 1978.
  A 13-year-old girl becomes anorexic. Two years later the 15-year-old describes the experience of her healing.

b) Men

Augustin, Ernst. *Raumlicht: Der Fall Evelyne B*. Frankfurt: Suhrkamp, 1976.
  Autobiographical novel about schizophrenia.
Blanton, Smiley. *Diary of My Analysis with Sigmund Freud*. New York: Hawthorn, 1971.
Döll, Hermann K. A. *Philosoph in Haar: Tagebuch über mein Vierteljahr in einer Irrenanstalt*. 2d. ed. Frankfurt: Syndikat Autoren-and Verlagsgesellschaft, 1981.
  Diary of his three months in an institution for the mentally ill.
Ebner, Ferdinand. *Schriften in 3 Bänden*. Munich: Kösel, 1963.
  A philosopher lives through depression, suicide attempts, and fear.
Kardiner, Abram. *My Analysis with Freud: Reminiscences*. New York: Norton, 1977.
Kipphardt, Heiner. *März:* Munich: Bertelsmann, 1976.
  Autobiographical novel by a physician about the schizophrenia of Alexander März. Author used psychopathological texts by psychiatrist Leo Navratil.

Mesrine, Jacques. *L'instinct de mort*. Paris: J. C. Lattès, 1977.

Sutherland, Stuart. *Breakdown*. St. Albans: Granada, 1977.

An experimental psychologist describes his nervous breakdown and his healing through psychoanalysis.

Werner, Frank. *Herzland*. Munich: List, 1983.

A 40-year-old man withdraws from his profession because he suffers from cardiac neurosis. He becomes "rootless: a man without a home," then begins to regain his footing when he discovers the realm of imagination.

c) Affected individuals

No entries

PARENTS

a) Mothers

Clement, Barbara. *Ein Kind wird gesund . . . Der Weg einer psychologischen Behandlung.* "Psychologisch gesehen" 41. Ed. by Hildegund Fischl-Carl. Fellbach: Bonz, 1982.

Fredet, Francine. *Mais, Madame, vous êtes la mère*. Paris: Le Centurion, 1979.

Gauchat, Dorothy. *All God's Children*. New York: Ballantine, 1985.

The story of a foster family.

Muthesius, Sibylle. *Flucht in die Wolken*. 4th ed. East Berlin: Buchverlag Der Morgen, 1984.

A mother tells the story of the psychological illness of her daughter, based on her daughter's letters, entries from her daughter's diary, and her daughter's painting, and supplemented by the mother's own experiences.

Park, Clara C. *The Siege: The First Eight Years of an Autistic Child*. Boston: Little, Brown, 1982.

A mother and teacher describes her attempts over many years to open a way to conscious life for her autistic child.

Pinney, Rachel. *Bobby: Breakthrough of a Special Child*. New York: McGraw-Hill, 1986. Autism.

Thieme, Gerda. *Dirk lernt verstehen: Ein Bericht über weitere vier Lebensjahre*. Lüdenscheid: Gerda Crummenerl, 1974.

Thieme, Gerda. *Leben mit unserem autistischen Kind: Möglichkeiten und Grenzen einer Hilfe im Elternhaus. Ein Bericht über die ersten 12 Lebensjahre*. 4th ed. Lüdenscheid: Gerda Crummenerl, 1975.

Life with an autistic child. Possibilities and limits of helping at home.

A report on the first 12 years of an autistic child's life.

b) Fathers

Conrad, Klaus. *Dauerndes Glück: Chris*. Frankfurt: Fischer, 1980.

Autobiographical novel about life with an autistic child.

Gagelmann, Hartmut. *Kai lacht wieder: Ein autistisches Kind durchbricht Seine Zwänge*. Munich: Droemer-Knaur, 1986.

An autistic child breaks through.

Hundley, Joan M. *The Small Outsider*. New York: Ballantine, 1973.

The story of an autistic child.

Kaufman, Barry N. *Son-Rise.* New York: Warner, 1977.

c) Parents, together
no entries

PARTNERS

a) Female partners
No entries

b) Male partners
Bulgakov, Mikhail. *Aufzeichnungen eines Toten.* Neuwied: Luchterhand, 1986.
When Maksudov commits suicide, Bulgakov receives a letter the man wrote him
before killing himself. Originally published in Russian.
Reed, David. *Anna.* New York: Bantam, 1979.
A husband accompanies his schizophrenic wife, describes R. F. Laing's treatment
methods, and experiences abandonment when his wife takes her own life.

c) Partners, together
Gotkin, Janet and Paul. *Too Much Anger, Too Many Tears: A Personal Triumph over
Psychiatry.* New York: Quadrangle, 1975.
Jan, Edmund; Marlis, Eva; and Doktor, S. *End-täuschung: Dokumente einer Trennung.*
Frankfurt: Extrabuch, 1983.
Documents of a separation. A family tells its own story, supplemented by the report
of their therapist.
Weber-Gast, Ingrid. *Weil du nicht geflohen bist vor meiner Angst: Eine Ehepaar durchlebt
die Depressionen des einen Partners.* 6th ed. Mainz: Matthias Grünewald, 1984.

PROFESSIONALS

a) Professional women
Axline, Virginia M. *Dibs: In Search of Self.* Harmondsworth: Penguin, 1981.
A mentally disturbed child gets well in psychotherapeutic treatment.
Dieke, G. *Todeszeichen.* Neuwied: Luchterhand, 1981.
Texts by and about people who have committed or attempted to commit suicide.
Dolto, Françoise. *Dominique: Analysis of an Adolescent.* New York: Outerbridge &
Lazard, 1973.
A report of the analysis of a child.
Isaksson, Ulla. *The Blessed Ones.* Washington, D.C.: R. B. Luce, 1970.
The psychiatrist Dettow comes to terms with the suicide of a married couple, and
discovers that he never understood his own dead wife.

Jürgensen, Geneviève. *La folie des autres.* Paris: R. Laffort. 1973.

    About working with Bruno Bettelheim as a child therapist.

Lindenberg, Nita. *Sich selber fremd.* Stuttgart: Brachhaus, 1981.

    Accounts of mentally ill people.

MacCracken, Mary. *Lovey: A Very Special Child.* New York: New American Library, 1977.

The transformation of a "difficult" child through the liberating power of love. The concern of a teacher for a child with severe behavior problems.

Mannoni, Maud. *Un lieu pour vivre: les enfants de Bonneuil, leurs parents et l'équipe des "soignants."* Paris: Editions du Seuil, 1976.

Meves, Christa. *Ich will mich ändern: Geschichte einer Genesung.* Freiburg: Herder, 1986.

Schwarz, Jutta-Ute. *Gegenseitigkeit.* Neukirchen-Vluyn: Neukirchener Verlag, 1982.

    Ten stories from a diary. Experiences of a pastor in a state-run psychiatric hospital.

Simonton, Stephanie. *The Healing Family: The Simonton Approach for Families Facing Illness.* New York: Bantam, 1984.

Ude, Anneliese. *You Must Always Be Good.* Palo Alto, CA: Science and Behavior Books, 1977.

    Treatment of an autistic child.

Ude-Pestel, Anneliese. *Ahmet—Geschichte einer Kindertherapie, ". . . weil ich nicht weiss, wohin ich gehöre."* 2d ed. Munich: Piper, 1983.

    Ahmet is the son of a Turkish foreign worker in West Germany.

Whitaker, Carl A. and Napier, Augustus. *The Family Crucible.* New York: Bantam, 1980.

    Example of successful child therapy.

b) Professional men

Ambrosio, Richard d'. *Der stumme Mund.* 3d ed. Bern, Munich, Vienna: Scherz, 1973.

    Muteness as trauma after parental abuse at the age of 18 months, diagnosed as schizophrenia and feeblemindedness. Documented healing process of 14-year-old Laura through the efforts of the psychotherapist, D'Ambrosio, who had been affected in his own life by the same kind of situation.

Beck, Dieter. *Krankheit als Selbstheilung.* Frankfurt: Suhrkamp, 1986.

    How physical illnesses can represent an attempt at mental healing. With an afterword by E. Kübler-Ross.

Bettelheim, Bruno. *Truants from Life: The Rehabilitation of Emotionally Disturbed Children.* New York: Free Press, 1964.

Bolland, John, and Sandler, Joseph. *The Hampstead Psychoanalytic Index: A Study of the Psychoanalytic Case Material of a Two-Year-Old Child.* New York: International University Press, 1966.

    With a foreword by Anna Freud.

Ekstein, Rudolf. *The Challenge: Despair and Hope in the Conquest of Inner Space.* New York: Brunner/Mazel, 1971.

    Clinical studies of the psychoanalytic treatment of severely disturbed children.

Goetz, Rainald. *Irre.* Frankfurt: Suhrkamp, 1986.

    A physician describes work in his psychiatric clinic.

Hesse, Jürgen and Schrader, Hans Christian. *Auf einmal nicht mehr weiter wissen.* Frankfurt: Fischer, 1987.

    Pastoral ministry by telephone—a mirror of our problems.

Kellner, Jakob. *Zwiesprache mit Ziwjah: Das Werden einer neuen Identität.* Freiburg: Lambertus, 1972.

The evolving of a new identity. Diary of a treatment. Originally published in Hebrew.

Lane, Robert. *A Solitary Dance.* New York: New American Library, 1984.

A psychologist struggles for the soul of an autistic child.

Lennhof, Friedrich Georg. *Problem-Kinder.* Munich: Reinhardt, 1967.

On the work of a therapeutic boarding school.

Maas, Hermann. *Der Seewolf.* Olten: Walter, 1984.

Description of a psychoanalytic method using case studies.

Mehringer, Andreas. *Verlassene Kinder.* Munich: Reinhardt, 1985.

Experiences of the director of a home for mentally disturbed and deprived small children.

Moser, Tilman. *Das Erste Jahr.* Frankfurt: Suhrkamp, 1986.

Redl, Fritz. *Children Who Hate: The Disorganization and Breakdown of Behavior Controls.* New York: Free Press, 1965.

Rey, Karl Guido. *Neuer Mensch auf schwachen Füssen: Erfahrungen eines Psychotherapeuten mit Gott.* 2d ed. Munich: Kösel, 1984.

A psychoanalyst's experiences with God.

Tobias, Karl-Heinz. *Damit ich wieder normal leben kann.* Recklinghausen: Psychiatrie Verlag, 1984.

Tombino, Mario. *Die Frauen von Magliano.* Zurich: Unionsverlag, 1986.

A physician in a mental hospital.

Wendeler, Jürgen. *Autistische Jugendliche und Erwachsene.* Weinheim, Basel: Beltz, 1984.

Conversations with parents.

Winnicott, Donald W. *The Piggle: An Account of the Psychoanalytic Treatment of a Little Girl.* Madison, Conn.: International Universities Press, 1977.

Changing relationships between a child, her parents, and her analyst.

c) Professionals, together

Bettelheim, Bruno, and Karlin, Daniel. *Liebe als Therapie,* Munich: Piper, 1986.

Conversations about the emotional life of a child.

Eckstaedt, Anita, and Klüwer, Rolf, eds. *Zeit allein heilt keine Wunden: Psychoanalytische Erstgespräche mit Kindern und Eltern.* 2d ed. Frankfurt: Suhrkamp, 1980.

Initial psychoanalytic conversations with children and parents.

Fréderic, Hélène, and Malinsky, Martine: *Martin.* Boston: Routledge & Kegan Paul, 1981.

Herzog, G. and Barnea-Braunstein, R. *Beroschim.* Reinhardt, 1980.

Original Hebrew title: *"Beroschim."*

"Beroschim" is a school for emotionally disturbed children.

McKnew, Donald H.: Cytryn, Leon; and Yahraes, Herbert C. *Why Isn't Johnny Crying? Coping with Depression in Children.* New York: Norton, 1985.

Meyer, Willi, and Wydler, Gertrud. *Anja: Abenteuer einer Kindertherapie.* Olten: Walter, 1982.

SENSORY DISABILITY
(Blindness, visual impairment/Deafness, hearing impairment)

Affected individuals

a) Women

Blatchford, Claire H. *All Alone (Except for My Dog Friday)*. Elgin, Ill.: Chariot, 1983.
Blauensteiner-Stephan, Yvonne. *Das Stille Jahr*. Vienna: Kurt Kleber, 1986.
Diderot, Denis. *Lettres sur les aveugles pour ceux qui voient*. Geneva: Droz, 1970.
Dyer, Donita. *Strahlende Hoffnung*. Asslar: Schulte und Gert Verlag, 1983.
  The author, blinded at age six, describes her difficult journey through school and
  advanced study to become a physician.
Golinski, Edith. *Der Blick nach innen*. 2d ed. Kiel, 1971.
  Experiences of a blind woman.
Gösling-Geske, Rauthende. *Blüten und Abgründe*. Isernhagen (self-published), 1982.
  The autobiography of the lifelong partnership between a teacher and her husband,
  blind and mute as a result of World War II.
Hocken, Sheila. *Emma and I*. New York: New American Library, 1979.
  The amazing experiences of a young blind woman and her dog.
Keller, Helen. *Midstream: My Later Life*. New York: Greenwood, 1968.
Keller, Helen. *The Story of My Life*. Rahway, N.J.: Watermill, 1980.
  With a selection from her letters from 1887 to 1901 and a description of her education
  as a blind and deaf-mute writer.
Keller, Helen. *Teacher: Anne Sullivan Macy*. Westport, CT: Greenwood, 1985.
Marx, Annemarie. *Die heile Insel*. Hamburg: Rauhes Haus, 1975.
  Life story of a visually and hearing-impaired pastor.
Pla, Frieda le. *Blicke in eine verborgene Welt*. Duisburg: Deutsches Blindenhilfswerk,
  no date. Originally published in English.
Schaumann, Ruth. *Das Arsenal*. Freiburg: Kerle, 1968.
  This reflection about an experience on the edge of death, written by a painter who
  became deaf at the age of six as a result of scarlet fever, is a wedding gift from the
  painter (at age 25) for her husband, with whom she now has five children.
Schwarz, Hildegard. *Mit Träumen leben: Träume einer Erblindeten*. Darmstadt: Verlag
  Darmstädter Blätter, 1981.

b) Men

Bjarnhof, Karl. *Das gute Licht*. Gütersloh: Bertelsmann, 1958. Original Danish edition
  published by Güldendahl, Copenhagen.
Gohn, Ludwig. *Ein Weg zum Glück*. Rotterdam: van Witsen, 1957.
Haebler, W. *Mein Dorf zwischen den Wäldern*. Karlsruhe: Hans Thoma, 1965.
  The account of a teacher, born blind.
Haebler, W. . . . *Wir haben einen Hund, einen Vater und eine Mutter*. Karlsruhe: Hans
  Thoma, 1967.
Haun, Ernst. *Jugenderinnerungen eines blinden Mannes*. Stuttgart, 1918.
Krents, Harold. *To Race the Wind*. New York: Bantam, 1973.

Lusseyran, Jacques. *And There Was Light.* New York: Parabola, 1987.

The author, blinded as a schoolboy, becomes a French resistance fighter, and later, a professor of literature and a father. He reflects on his "inner sight."

Lusseyran, Jacques. *Le monde commence aujourd'hui.* Paris: La Table Ronde, 1959.

Mansfeld, F. C. *Die Lichtbringer.* Vienna: Kurt Kleber, 1953.

Meyer-Auhausen, Otto. *Als das Dorf noch meine Welt war.* Oettingen: Fränk.-Schwäb. Heimatverlag, 1963.

Meyer-Auhausen, Otto. *Wenn auch das Licht erlosch.* Leipzig: Koehler und Amelang, 1936.

A manufacturer tells his story.

Narbesher, Maximilian. *Weg ins Licht.* St. Florian: Verlag Stiftsbuchhandlung, 1949.

Ostrowski, Nikolai. *Wie der Stahl gehärtet wurde.* East Berlin: Verlag Neues Leben, 1986. Originally published in Russian.

This autobiography, which has become famous, provides insights into the author's lifelong attempt to cope with the injuries and blindness he suffered as a 15-year-old in the Russian civil war (1914–1922).

Rupp, H. *Schlag die Hand nicht aus: Blindsein, Mit Blinden lernen.* Haan: Brockhaus, 1981.

Suggestions, opinions, information, from the point of view of an affected pastor.

Russel, Robert. *To Catch an Angel: Adventures in the World I Cannot See.* Leicester, England: Ulverscroft, 1965.

An account of a man, blinded at age five, who is now a university professor and father living in the U.S.

Schah-Mohammedi, Abbas. *Bis die Nacht vergeht: Erfahrungen und Erkenntnisse eines Blinden. Denkanstösse für Sehende.* Berlin: Hass & Co., 1981.

Smithdas, Robert. *Mit Händen ergriffen.* Stuttgart: Engelhorn, 1960.

A deaf and blind American describes his life.

Stoeckel, Alfred. *Von Homer bis Helen Keller.* Bonn: Verlag des Deutschen Blindenverbandes, 1984.

"Without light and yet full of light": this legend of Homer's on the portal of a school for the blind led the then 24-year-old young man, who because of an accident at 16 gradually became blind, to investigate the lives of significant blind personalities of world literature.

Sullivan, Tom, and Gill, Derek. *If You Could See What I Hear.* New York: New American Library, 1976.

A blind man triumphs over his fate.

Twersky, Jacob. *The Face of the Deep.* Cleveland: World, 1953.

Vajda, Albert. *Lend Me an Eye.* New York: St. Martin's, 1975.

A blinded writer works through his illness and later healing.

Vogel, Robert. *Zwischen hell und dunkel.* Vienna, 1982.

Vuillemier, John Friedrich. *Der letzte Tunnel.* Wiesbaden: Walter, 1970.

The transformation of a man who is confronted by the challenge to move forward into his life as a blind person.

Wright, David. *Deafness.* New York: Stein & Day, 1975.

The life story of a deaf man.

c) Affected individuals, together

Panara, R. F.; Denis, T. B.; and McFarlane, J. H., eds. *Taubheit: Du Schicksal. Verband ehemaliger Studenten des Gallaudet-College zu Washington, D.C.* Essen: Gehörlosen-Verlag, 1976. Originally published in English.

PARENTS

a) Mothers

Lucas, Christel. *Silke—ein blindes Kind: Anregungen für Elternhaus und Kindergarten.* Stuttgart: Kösel, 1979.
A foster mother and teacher tells her story.

Stüssi, Rosmarie. *Aufzeichnungen aus dem Leben mit einem blinden Kind.* Bern: Hans Huber, 1982.
Notes from life with a blind child.

b) Fathers

Möckel, Klaus. *Hoffnung für Dan: Ein Bericht.* 4th ed. East Berlin: Verlag Neues Leben, 1986.
Dan's father, a writer, gives an account—from Dan's mother's perspective—of his wife's lifelong efforts on behalf of Dan, then 14 years old, deaf, brain-damaged, and unable to speak. The struggle includes confrontations with representatives of government agencies.

c) Parents, together

No entries

PARTNERS

a) Female partners

Wallisfurth, Maria. *Sie hat es mir erzählt.* Freiburg, Basel & Vienna: Herder, 1979.
The daughter of deaf-mute parents tells about her mother.

b) Male partners

No entries

c) Partners, together

No entries

PROFESSIONALS

a) Professional women

Green, Hannah [pseud.]. *In This Sign.* New York: Avon, 1984.
Love, marriage, and the destiny of a deaf-mute couple.
Schmitz, Marlies. *Kati lernt hören.* Berlin: Marhold, 1986.
A disability and its treatment using the Delacato method.
Skorokhodova, Olga. *Jenseits der Nacht.* East Berlin: Verlag Kultur & Fortschritt, 1951.
Wilson, Dorothy C. *Er brachte ihnen das Licht.* Wuppertal, Oncken Verlag, 1983.
Dr. Victor Rambo, an eye doctor, takes on the task of helping the blind in India.

b) Professional men

Bodenheimer, Ronald A. *Doris: Die Entwicklung einer Beziehungsstörung und die Geschichte ihrer Behebung bei einem entstellten taubstummen Mädchen.* Basel, Stuttgart: Schwabe, 1968.
The development of a behavior disorder in a disfigured, deaf and mute girl, and the story of its healing.
Düren, T.; Hauser, H.; and Neugebauer, H., eds. . . . *aber sie können nicht sehen.* Cologne: Rheinland, 1977.
An illustrated book to encourage and help those involved with blind and visually impaired children.
The life stories of five children.
Düren, T.; and Strehle, W. *Die besten Jahre.* Cologne: Rheinland, 1979.
Help given early to visually impaired children. Letters from parents, from blind and visually impaired teachers and physicians, to parents of blind and visually impaired children.
Düren, T.; Hauser, H.; and Neugebauer, H., eds. . . . *aber sie geben nicht auf.* Cologne: Rheinland, 1983.
The life stories of five children.
Guibert, Hervé. *Des aveugles.* Paris: Guillimard, 1985.
Johansen, Otto. *Ridderspranget: Erling Skordahl og hans verden.* Oslo: Gyldendal Norsk, 1972.
The life of Erling Stordahl, for blind and disabled people.
Loewy, Alfred. *Blinde grosse Männer.* Zurich: Kommissionsverlag Rascher, 1935.
Fawcett, Rodenbach, Saundersen and Euler, Eberhardt, Planck, Plateau, Javal, Huber, Händel—great blind men.
Pause, Walter. *Helen Keller: Das Leben triumphiert.* Gütersloh: G. Mohn, 1960.
Reuss, Alexander. *Verlorenes Licht.* Heilbronn: Eugen Salzer, 1933.
Ruderisch, Gustav. *Ist der Weg auch weit . . .* Munich: Kindler, 1956.
Wanacek, Ottokar. *Licht im Dunkel.* Vienna, 1960.
Blind musicians, then and now.
Wengrow, N., and Efras, M. *Ein Mensch wie Du: Das Leben des Nikolai Ostrovski.* East Berlin: Verlag Kultur & Fortschritt 1950. Original Russian title: *Zizn Nikolaja Ostrowskogo.*
Wengrow's biography of the Soviet writer Nicolai Ostrovsky. Compare Wengrow's autobiography.

c) Professionals, together

No entries

SPEECH DISABILITY

Affected individuals

a) Women

Tropp-Erblad, Ingrid. *Katt böjar pa S.* Stockholm, 1982.
  On aphasia, or the loss of words.
Whitehouse, Elizabeth S. *There's Always More.* Valley Forge, Pa.: Judson, 1968.
  A woman after a stroke; she suffers from a speech disorder, memory loss, and
  paralysis.

b) Men

Dirks, Walter. *Der singende Stotterer.* Munich: Kösel, 1983.
Lenz, Siegfried. *Der Verlust.* Hamburg: Hoffman & Campe, 1981.
  An autobiographical novel. A man suffers from a fundamental speech disorder and
  is therefore isolated from those around him.
Rother, Thomas. *Der plötzliche Verstummen des Wilhelm W.* Bern, Munich & Vienna:
  Scherz, 1981.
  A journalist loses his power of speech.
Walter, Otto F. *Der Stumme.* Reinbek bei Hamburg: Rowohlt, 1984.

c) Affected individuals, together

Bacher, Ingrid. *Das Paar.* Hamburg: Hoffman & Campe, 1981.
  Martin loses his power of speech in a car accident. The love of his wife helps him
  to accept this challenge.

PARENTS

a) Mothers

No entries

b) Fathers

Hill, Archie. *Closed World of Love.* New York: Avon, 1976.
  Record of a stepfather's steadily deepening relationship with his paralyzed and speech-
  impaired son.

c) Parents, together

No entries

PARTNERS

No entries

PROFESSIONALS

a) Professional women

Carsten, Catarina. *Wie Thomas zum zweiten Mal sprechen lernte*. Vienna: Herder, 1985.
Dr. Martin Schwartz and his work with stutterers.

b) Professional men

Feldenkrais, Moshe. *The Case of Nora: Bodily Awareness as Healing Therapy*. New York: Harper & Row, 1977.
The story of the therapy of a 60-year-old woman who wakes up one morning with a severe speech impairment.
Hayden, Torey L. *Murphy's Boy*, New York: Avon, 1983.

c) Professionals, together

No entries

CANCER

Affected individuals

a) Women

Atwood, Margaret. *Verletzungen*. Munich: Knaur Taschenbuch, 304.
A mastectomy changes the life of Rennie Wilford.
Bellvré, Katharina. *Durch den Tunnel der Angst*. Heidelberg: Verlag für Medizin Dr. Ewald Fischer, 1985.
From the diary of a woman with cancer.
Bleimann, Annemarie. *Leben ist die Alternative*. Munich: Tomus, 1985.
Learning about cancer.
Bok, Sissela. *Lying: Moral Choice in Public and Private Life*. London, New York: Quartet, 1980.
The daily compulsion to lying.
Boppert, Lieselotte. *Der Knoten*. Reinbek bei Hamburg: Rowohlt Verlag, 1979.
Trust and responsibility in the physician-patient relationship, portrayed in a breast cancer case.
Brodhage, Barbara. *Caroline, lass dir an meiner Gnade genügen*. Moers: Brendow, 1981.
Brunnengräber, Richard. *Christiane: An Leukämie erkrankt und geheilt*. Munich: Meyster, 1984.
Bruns, Ingeborg. *Das wiedergeschenkte Leben: Tagebuch über die Leukämieerkrankung eines Kindes*. Frankfurt: Fischer, 1987.
A child becomes ill with leukemia, and daily life changes dramatically for the child's family.
Burnham, Elizabeth Dean. *When Your Friend Is Dying*. Lincoln, Va.: Chosen, 1982.
Expectations of a patient who knows his suffering cannot be alleviated.
Cameron, Jean. *For All That Has Been: Time to Live and Time to Die*. New York: Macmillan, 1982.
As a social worker, the author spent years serving cancer patients, many of them terminally ill. Now she herself is diagnosed with cancer, and must find her way.

Cunéo, Anne. *Une cuillerée de bleu.* Zurich: Limat, 1982.

Fuchs, Rosemarie. *Stationen der Hoffnung.* Stuttgart: Kreuz, 1984.

A pastor accompanies six children and their parents through various stages of life-threatening cancer.

Fulda, Edeltraud. *. . . und ich werde genesen sein.* Vienna: Zsolnay, 1983.

Autobiography of a woman cured of an incurable disease at Lourdes.

Heyst, Ilse van. *Das Schlimmste war die Angst: Geschichte einer Krebserkrankung und ihrer Heilung.* Frankfurt: Fischer, 1982.

The author of many children's books describes her crisis with cancer.

Klein, Norma. *Sunshine.* New York: Avon, 1982.

Autobiographical novel taken from a taped journal. A 20-year-old journalist with cancer writes her story for her two-year-old daughter.

Lee, Laurel. *Walking through the Fire.* New York: Bantam, 1978.

A young woman is stricken with Hodgkin's disease, has her fourth child, deals with illness, divorce, the certainty of death, and gives her children her diary.

Lenker, Christiane. *Krebs kann auch eine Chance sein.* Frankfurt: Fischer, 1984.

A teacher is stricken with breast cancer. She describes her personal transformation.

Moster, Mary B. *Living with Cancer.* Wheaton, Ill.: Tyndale, 1985.

A nurse, Nell Collin, has lived since 1971 with the certainty that she will die of cancer. Journalist Mary Moster tells the story of Collin's experiences, her decision to start a ministry with cancer patients, and her problems.

Netherly, Susan. *One Year and Counting: Breast Cancer, My World, and Me.* Grand Rapids, MI: Baker, 1978.

Piechota, Ulrike. *Trauert nicht wie die, die keine Hoffnung haben.* Stuttgart: Radius, 1983.

A woman accompanies an older, hopeless man, sick with cancer, until his death.

Prévost, Françoise. *Ma vie en plus.* Paris: Stock, 1975.

A victory over cancer.

Prollius, Helga. *Die Angst liegt hinter mir: Frauen und Krebs.* 2d ed. Freiburg, Basel & Vienna: Herder, 1980.

Women and cancer.

Reimann, Brigitte. *Die Geliebte, die verfluchte Hoffnung.* Neuwied: Luchterhand, 1986.

Diaries and letters (1947–1972) of this writer, stricken with cancer, who died at age 40.

Roman, Joe. *Exit House.* New York: Seaview, 1980.

A defense of suicide from the perspective of a woman sick with cancer.

Sandkorn, Anemone. *Das Signal oder die Entfernung des Knotens.* Frankfurt: Fischer, 1986.

Sarton, May. *A Reckoning.* South Yarmouth, Ma.: J. Curley, 1985.

When she discovers that she does not have much longer to live, Laura Spelman decides to experience her death consciously and in her own way.

Scheresky, Jeanne. *Diagnosis, Cancer: Where Do We Go from Here?* Old Tappan, N.J.: Revell, 1977.

A family lives through the cancer suffered by husband, son, and father.

Sontag, Susan. *Illness as Metaphor.* New York: Farrar, Strauss and Giroux, 1988.

The author investigates, through her own involvement, the metaphorical dimensions of illness, so that by coming to terms with her own cancer, she may find the strength to resist and to free herself.

Tausch, Anne-Marie. *Gespräche gegen die Angst.* Reinbek bei Hamburg: Rowohlt, 1981.

Wander, Maxie. *Leben wär' eine prima Alternative: Tagebuchaufzeichnungen und Briefe (Part 1)*. Wander, Fred, ed. *Die Geschichte einer Krebskrankheit (Part 2)*. Darmstadt: Luchterhand, 1984.

Zeun, Renate. *Betroffen: Bilder einen Krebserkrankung*. East Berlin: Verlag Volk & Gesundheit, 1986.

> This photographer presents the story of her own struggle with breast cancer through photographs and a short text. A series of photos describes her experience in portraits, interviews, landscapes, still lifes, and documents.

Zierling, Elfriede. *Das Mass des Lebens*. East Berlin: Verlag Neues Lebens, 1984.

> Diary of a young woman who dies from lymphatic cancer at age 21.

b) Men

Becker, Klaus Peter. *Ich habe meinen Krebs besiegt*. Unterhaching: Luitpold Lang, 1982.

Cousins, Norman. *Anatomy of an Illness as Perceived by the Patient: Reflections on Healing and Regeneration*. New York: Bantam, 1979.

Diggelmann, Walter Matthias. *Schatten: Tagebuch einer Krankheit*. Frankfurt: Fischer, 1981.

> Diary entries from a hospital stay during two difficult cancer operations. The author gradually learns to accept death as a part of life.

Formaz, Casimir. *A l'ecole du Christ souffrant: journal de malade*. Paris: Editions du Cerf, 1975.

> Entries from the diary of a young Augustinian monk consciously facing death.

Gots, Anton. *Das "Ja" zum Kreuz*. 8th ed. Vienna, Linz & Passau: Veritas, 1984.

> The author struggles to find meaning in his apparently senseless existence, and faith in the presence of God in the face of incurable illness.

Noll, Peter. *Diktate über Sterben und Tod mit Totenrede von Max Frisch*. Munich: Piper, 1987.

> Professor Peter Noll discovers that he has cancer of the bladder, and resolves to experience his dying consciously.

Weber, Walter. *Jenseits der Nacht: Erfahrungen im Krankenhaus*. Stuttgart: Kreuz, 1981.

Zorn, Fritz. *Mars*. New York: Knopf, 1982.

> A university instructor tells about his difficult childhood and youth, and relates his struggle with cancer to his own history.

c) Affected individuals, together

No entries

PARENTS

a) Mothers

Fredriksson, Dorrit. *Lennart dog ung*. Stockholm, 1973.

> A mother accompanies the death of her son, stricken with cancer.

Lamla, Gertraud. *Muss ich auch wandern in finsterer Schlucht*. Freiburg: Herder, 1985.

> A mother experiences the death of her leukemia stricken child.

Ludwig-Klein, Elisabeth. *Krebs-Kinder-Tagebuch: Wagnis einer Hoffnung*. Stuttgart: Radius, 1980.

Lund, Doris. *Eric.* New York: Dell, 1979.

Reflections of a mother, who accompanies her son, sick with cancer, through study, friendship, and love.

Schiff, Harriet S. *The Bereaved Parent.* New York: Penguin, 1978.

Parents anticipate for 10 years the death of their son, ill with cancer, and seek to work through their loneliness.

Woelfing, Marie Luise. *Komm, gib mir deine Hand.* Düsseldorf: Erb Verlag, 1985.

A mother describes her experience with her tumor-stricken son.

b) Fathers

Kadenbach, Hans. *Requiem für Sabrina.* Halle, Leipzig: Mitteldeutscher Verlag, 1986.

A father tells the story of the life and death of his daughter, who dies of cancer at the age of 18.

Klee, Falk-Ingo. *Jasmin K. (3 Jahre): Diagnose: Krebs.* Rastatt: Moewig, 1986.

Parents describe their successful struggle against their three-year-old daughter's cancer.

c) Parents, together

Claypool, John; Walter, Karl-Heinz. *Spuren der Liebe: Von der Kraft, das Leid zu tragen.* East Berlin: Evangelische Verlagsanstalt: 1982.

Author and coauthor, both of whom are also translators, have each lost a child to leukemia. Claypool, a theologian, describes in four sermons what he has learned.

Zorca, Victor and Rosemary. *Away to Die.* New York: Knopf, 1980.

Parents accompany their 25-year-old, incurably ill daughter; their fearfulness in facing death is transformed into trust.

PARTNERS

a) Female partners

Joesten, Renate. *Stark wie der Tod ist die Liebe: Bericht von einem Abschied.* Stuttgart: Kreuz, 1985.

A wife accompanies her cancer-stricken husband.

Stephan, Lydia. *Du hattest so gern noch ein bisschen gelebt.* Frankfurt: Fischer, 1986.

A wife accompanies her husband, sick with lung cancer.

Weidenhöfer, Margit. *Du führst mich hinaus ins Weite.* Frankfurt: Knecht, 1984.

A wife accompanies her husband, suffering from tumors.

Worgitzsky, Charlotte. *Heute sterben immer nur die anderen.* East Berlin: Buchverlag Der Morgen, 1986.

The author accompanies a friend, ill with cancer, until her death.

b) Male partners

Ragsdale, Grady. *Steve McQueen, the Final Chapter.* Ventura, Calif: Vision House, 1983.

"I have run away my whole life; now I must face up to it."

Rodman, F. Robert. *Not Dying.* New York: Norton, 1988.

A psychotherapist lives through the death of his wife, ill with cancer.

Sinninger, Michel. . . . *aber die Liebe bleibt: Zeugnis einer Ehe.* Freiburg: Herder, 1980.
Originally published in French.
A husband suffers through the death of his wife from cancer.

Weyrich, Walter. *Wir haben gewusst, dass Du früher gehst: Drei Jahre Zeit zum Sterben und Leben.* Zurich: Gotthelf, 1980.
Notes by a pastor on the last few years of his cancer-stricken wife's life.

c) Partners, together

Lair, Jess and Jacqueline. *Hey God, What Should I Do Now?* New York: Ballantine, 1982.
A couple lives through crisis, a heart attack, the certainty of death.

Martini, Werner, and Schroif, Angelika. *Der Tod wird keine Grenze für uns sein: Wir begleiten Martin beim Sterben.* 2d ed. Mainz: Matthias Grünewald, 1981.
A priest and the wife of a man dying of cancer give the man their support.

Tausch, Anne-Marie and Reinhard. *Sanftes Sterben: Was der Tod für das Leben bedeutet.* Reinbek bei Hamburg: Rowohlt, 1985.

Tibbe, Trudi and Johann. *Leben an der Grenze des Todes.* 6th ed. Brecklum: Neukirchener, 1981.

PROFESSIONALS

a) Professional women

Fabre, Jacqueline. *Die Kinder, die nicht sterben wollten: Bericht aus einer Leukämie-Kinderklinik.* Düsseldorf: Econ, 1982.
Report from a clinic for children with leukemia.

Franck, Barbara. *Trotzdem leben: Reportagen über die Angst.* Hamburg: Hoffman & Campe, 1983.
Ten pieces about the spiritual working through of the fear of death and the fear of life. Pieces about people who have a disease—cancer—that is considered sure death.

Haas, Gisela. *Ich bin ja so allein: Kranke—krebskranke—Kinder zeichnen und sprechen über ihre Angste.* Ravensburg: Otto Maier, 1981.
Illustrated with drawings, the following situations and aids to overcoming them are depicted: fear of separation from family; fear of hospitals and schools; problems of parents and siblings; and how children deal with death.

Hahn, Mechthild. *Lebenskrise Krebs.* Hannover: Schlütersche Verlagsanstalt, 1981.

Herrmann, Nina. *Go Out in Joy!* New York: Pocket, 1978.
Notes by a hospital chaplain.

Kelly, Petra K., ed. *Viel Liebe gegen Schmerzen.* Reibek bei Hamburg: Rowohlt, 1986.
Parents, children, nurses, and doctors relate their fears and hopes in the struggle against cancer.

Philips, Carolyn E. *Michelle.* New York: New American Library, 1982.
A girl is stricken with bone cancer. Her leg is amputated. In this book, the rest of her life is depicted.

Sharkey, Frances. *A Parting Gift.* New York: Bantam: 1984.
A pediatrician describes her experiences with children who have cancer.

Zickgraf, Cordula. *I Am Learning to Live Because You Must Die: A Hospital Diary.* Philadelphia: Fortress, 1981.

A nurse in in-patient treatment experiences the death from cancer of a 17-year-old copatient.

b) Professional men

Drescher, Peter. *Montag fange ich wieder an.* 2d ed. East Berlin: Evangelische Verlagsanstalt, 1980.

The author provides the channel for a boy who has undergone an operation to remove a brain tumor, to tell the story of his ordeal and his triumph over it.

c) Professionals, together

Parker, Merren, and Mauger, David. *Children with Cancer: A Handbook for Families and Helpers.* London: Cassell, 1979.

The experiences—feelings and problems—of parents of children with cancer.

Schwartzenberg, Léon, and Viansson-Ponté, Pierre. *Changer la mort.* Paris: S. Michel, 1977.

A journalist and a physician tell the life stories of 16 severely ill cancer patients. They take up one of the most controversial and strongly tabooed issues of euthanasia—"actively" helping someone to die.

MULTIPLE SCLEROSIS

Affected individuals

a) Women

Ahrens, Hildegard. *Ist es Schicksal?* Bad Rothenfelde: Rompf Druck (self-published), no date.

The lifelong struggle against progressive deterioration.

Deiss, Elfriede. *Diamant wächst im Dunkel.* 5th ed. Stuttgart: Christliches Verlagshaus, 1984.

The author is struck by multiple sclerosis at 20, and must break off her professional training. Bedridden for three years, she learns through her faith to live with an incurable illness.

Graham, Judy. *Multiple Sclerosis: A Self-Help Guide to Its Management.* Rochester, Vt.: Thorsons, 1984.

Hauch, Gerta. *Der Aufschrei: Warum?* Eupen: Grenz Echo, 1984.

Lipke, Cordula. *Lauf, solange du kannst! Bericht über eine Krankheit.* Regensburg: Habbel, 1980.

A 21-year-old describes her struggle against multiple sclerosis.

b) Men

Ireland, David. *Letters to an Unborn Child.* New York: Harper & Row, 1974.

Thirteen letters based on taped sketches, recorded by a father dying of nervous disease, to his as yet unborn child.

Schweppenhäuser, Ekkehard. *Multiple Sklerose: Ein Weg zur Heilung. Eigene Erfahrungen mit einer schubförmigen MS.* 2d ed. Freiburg: Verlag Die Kommenden, 1982.

c) Persons affected, together

No entries

PARENTS

No entries

PARTNERS

No entries

PROFESSIONALS

a) Professional women

No entries

b) Professional men

Liebscher, Fred. *Multiple Sklerose: Eine Krankheit, mit der man leben kann*. Heidelberg: K. F. Haug, 1982.
> MS: An illness with which one can live.

Menninger, Dieter. *Belügt uns nicht!* Berlin, Stuttgart: Kreuz, 1978.
> Reports on MS, cancer, paralysis.

c) Professionals, together

No entries

ADDICTIONS

Affected individuals

a) Women

Atkinson, Sandy A., and Markel, Jan. *Somebody Loves Me!* Wheaton, Ill.: Tyndale House, 1979.
> A young woman struggles desperately against her addiction.

Bayer, Ingeborg. *Trip ins Urgewisse*. 4th ed. Munich: Deutscher Taschenbuch, 1982.
> Experiences of a 17-year-old narcotics addict.

Bryant, Lee. *The Magic Bottle*. Philadelphia: A. J. Holman, 1978.
> The author recounts how, as an adoptive child, she experienced rejection and hate— which led her to begin drinking and to become an alcoholic.

Gordon, Barbara. *I'm Dancing as Fast as I Can*. New York: Bantam, 1981.
> Within a matter of weeks, the prize-winning television producer loses her husband, her career, herself. She describes how she became completely dependent on Valium, and how she struggled desperately to free herself from this addiction.

Harpwood, Diane. *Tea and Tranquillisers: The Diary of a Happy Housewife.* London: Virago, 1981.

An autobiographically shaped account of the drama of an ordinary housewife.

Hermann, K., and Rieck, H. *Christiane F.: Wir Kinder vom Bahnhof Zoo.* Hamburg: Gruner & Jahr, 1978.

The life of a drug-addicted girl. Written by two journalists, based on a tape-recorded account.

Joachim, Doris J. *Entzug: Oder die Angst vor der Angst.* Frankfurt: Frauenliteraturvertrieb, 1982.

Johannes, Ingrid. *Das siebente Brennesselhemd.* Berlin: Verlag Neues Leben, 1986.

Keeping a journal after a drug treatment program as a help in preventing recurrence of the addiction.

Johansen, Margaret. *Du kan da ikke bare gå—.* Oslo: Tiden, 1981.

Kavan, Anna. *Who Are You?* London: Peter Owen, 1975.

The drug-addicted poet Anna Kavan writes this novel.

Kerremans, Helen. *Abschied von Angst.* Bergisch Gladbach: Bastei-Lübbe, 1987.

Lukasz-Aden, Gudrun. *Tiefer kannst du nicht fallen.* Munich: Heyne, 1986.

Women and addiction.

Martell, Inge. *Morgen-Grauen.* Berlin: Frauenbuchvertrieb, sisi, 1982.

Women depict their experiences and problems with alcohol.

Rauchfuss, Hildegard Maria. *Schlusstrich.* Halle, Leipzig: Mitteldeutscher Verlag, 1986.

Autobiographical novel about alcohol dependency.

S., Nina. *Und der Jones ist immer pünktlich: Eine Fixerkarriere—ein authentischer Bericht.* Munich: Goldmann, 1983.

Stier, Karin. *Ich wollte immer grösser sein: Geständnisse einer Ausgeflippten.* Asslar: Schulte & Gerth, 1984.

Ward, Mildred M. *Liza.* Anderson, Ind.: Warner, 1976.

The life story of a black woman who grows up unloved in the slums of New Orleans. After an escape into a short marriage, she uses alcohol as a way to forget; later, she seeks and finds a fulfilled life.

Weber, Monika. *Die dunkle Seite meines Lebens: Überwindung einer Selbstzerstörung.* Frankfurt: Fischer, 1983.

b) Men

Arndt, Ralf. *Spiegelbilder: Eine Antwort an die Kinder vom Bahnhof Zoo.* 5th ed. Asslar: Schulte & Gerth, 1983.

Life story of a junkie, born in 1954. From 1972 on, he is part of the drug scene, arrests, suicide attempts, drug treatment programs; from 1980 on, a drug counselor for Teen Challenge in Berlin, West Germany.

Baily, Faith C. *These, Too, Were Unshackled: Fifteen Dramatic Stories from the Pacific Garden Mission.* Grand Rapids, Mich.: Zondervan, 1962.

Billisch, R. Franz. *Süchtig: Aufstieg und Fall des Fotomodells Doris W.* Rastatt: Moewig, 1986.

The life story of the internationally known top model Doris Weiss.

BK Erzählung. *Befreit von der Sucht.* Wuppertal, Bern: Blaukreuz, 1981.

Women and men tell the story of their experiences with alcohol.

Burroughs, William S. *Junky.* New York: Ace, 1973.

Capote, Truman, and Grobel, Lawrence. *Conversations with Capote.* New York: New American Library, 1986.

Interviews from the last two years of Capote's life.

Duval, Aimé. *One More Tomorrow.* New York: Berkley, 1984.

Feid, Anatol F. . . . , Ingo. *Wenn du zurückschaust, wirst du sterben: Protokoll einer Phase im Kampf gegen das Heroin.* Mainz: Matthias Grünewald, 1981.

Account of a phase in the struggle against heroin. Both authors—the youth F., who seeks escape from drug addiction, and the priest—document outer and inner stations in the struggle: the Frankfurt (West German) train station, two jails, therapy sites, as well as "supply-side criminality" as a consequence of total physical and mental dependency.

Frank, P. Helmut. *Kinder ohne Perspektive.* Rastatt: Moewig, 1986.

They are still children—dependent on drugs that they earn through prostitution.

Gabel, W. *Fix und fertig.* Weinheim: Beltz & Gelberg, 1978.

The true story of a drug-addicted young man. As a resident of a small town he becomes a victim of his inability to communicate his problems.

Georg, Hans. *Ich suchte das Glück.* Wuppertal: Blaukreuz, 1982.

Alcohol became the undoing of the author.

Hahn, Reinhardt. *Das letzte erste Glas.* Halle, Leipzig: Mitteldeutscher Verlag, 1986.

The author, an alcoholic, gives an account of the circumstances and compulsions of his illness.

Hurter, C. *Und ein bisschen glücklich sein.* Haan: Oncken, 1981.

Kris, *Weil ich leben will.* 2d ed. Haan: Brockhaus, 1983.

Küster, Hermann. *Nachrufe.* Bern: Blaukreuz, 1977.

Who is responsible for Raul Walther's becoming an alcoholic—and therefore, for his death in a car accident? The testimonies of his family, friends, his physician, and his pastor, make clear how alone and misunderstood an alcoholic can be.

Lake, Alexander. *You Need Never Walk Alone.* Anderson, Ind.: Warner, 1973.

An attorney begins to have problems with alcohol.

Loosen, Werner. *Neuanfang.* Bern, Wuppertal: Blaukreuz, 1982.

Diary of a journalist during his six-month stay in a special clinic for alcoholics.

Mein Name ist Adam. Munich: Mosaik, 1980.

A member of Alcoholics Anonymous takes stock of his life.

Moore, Walter. *Set Me Free.* London: Pickering & Inglis, 1980.

Murphy, Robert. *Christianity Rubs Holes in My Religion.* Houston: Hunter Ministries, 1976.

Nussbeck, Norbert. *Der Ausstieg des Norbert N.* Asslar: Schulte und Gerth Verlag, 1983.

A drug addict tells his story.

Quincey, Thomas de. *Confessions of an English Opium-Eater.* Harmondsworth: Penguin, 1986.

Raymond, Jean. *L.* Paris: Editions du Seuil, 1982.

Narration as authentic witness. The narrator, destined to die, describes the stages of his descent.

Saint-Dizier, Jean. *Ich bin geheilt.* 3d ed. Wuppertal: Blaukreuz, 1981.

The painful progress of an alcoholic who learns, finally, to rebuild his relationship with God and those around him.

Seibt, Rainer. *Ich möchte in Eurer Liebe baden! Eine Knast- und Heroin-Biographie.* Bensheim: Päd-extra Buchverlag, 1981.

Souter, John C. *The Pleasure Seller,* Wheaton, Ill.: Tyndale, 1979.

Wackernagel, Christof. *Bilder einer Ausstellung.* Reinbek bei Hamburg: Rowohlt, 1986.

Wallburg, Hans-Dieter. *Endlos schien die Nacht.* Wuppertal, Bern: Blaukreuz, 1983.

The author, a journalist, finds help for his alcoholism; he then becomes a counselor to addicts.

Wecker, Konstantin. *Und die Seele nach aussen kehren: Ketzerbriefe eines Süchtigen. Uns ist kein Einzelnes bestimmt. Neun Elegien.* Reinbek bei Hamburg: Rowohlt, 1983.

Wiesner, Wolfgang. *Ich bin clean.* Munich: Heyne, 1987.

Drug addicts help themselves and each other.

Wochele, Rainer. *Der Absprung.* Reinbek bei Hamburg: Rowohlt, 1981.

A documentary novel about a young drug addict who finally breaks out of the vicious circle of dependency, withdrawal, and relapse.

c) Affected individuals, together

No entries

PARENTS

a) Mothers

Leroyer, Micheline. *Me: Mother of a Drug Addict.* Belfast: Christian Journals, 1981.

Minwegen, Hiltrud. *Mario: Von der Sucht zur Hoffnung. Eine Mutter sucht im Rom ihren drogensüchtigen Sohn.* Frankfurt: Fischer, 1983.

A mother searches in Rome for her drug-addicted son.

b) Fathers

Guillon, Jaques. *Cet enfant qui se drogue, c'est le mien.* Paris: Editions du Seuil, 1978.

c) Parents together

Madeisky, Uschi, and Werner, Klaus. *Flucht in die Sucht: In Selbsthilfegruppen finden Eltern ein neues Verhältnis zu ihren Kindern.* Reinbek bei Hamburg: Rowohlt, 1983.

The authors are affected parents and producers of the film by the same name.

PARTNERS

a) Female partners

No entries

b) Male partners

No entries

c) Partners, together

Nullmeyer, Heide. *Ich heisse Erika und bin Alkoholikerin: Betroffene und Angehörige erzählen.* Frankfurt: Fischer, 1983.

Examples of overcoming an illness.

PROFESSIONALS

a) Professional women

No entries

b) Professional men

Hofmann, Albert. *LSD, My Problem Child.* Los Angeles: J. P. Tarcher, 1983.
Mühlbauer, Helmut. *Kollege Alkohol.* Munich: Kösel, 1986.
Noack, Hans-Georg. *Trip: Roman mit Sachinformation zum Thema "Rauschgift und Jugend."* Ravensburg: Otto Maier, 1975.
   Novel with factual information on the theme "Drugs and Youth."
Shipp, Tom. *Kummer mit dem Alkohol: Begegnungen und Erfahrungen mit Alkoholkranken.* Wuppertal & Bern: Blaukreuz, 1980.
   A parish pastor reports on his encounters with alcoholics.

c) Professionals, together

Merfert-Diete, Christa, and Soltau, Roswitha, eds. *Frauen und Sucht.* Reinbek bei Hamburg: Rowohlt, 1986.
   The daily entanglement in dependency.

OTHER

Affected individuals

a) Women

Anders, Renate. *Grenzübertritt.* Frankfurt: Fischer, 1984.
Arcy, Paula d'. *Song for Sarah.* Wheaton, Ill.: Harold Shaw, 1979.
   Diary of a young woman who loses both husband and child in an accident.
Axt, Renate. *Und wenn du weinst, hört man es nicht.* Bergisch Gladbach: Bastei-Lübbe, 1986.
   A shocking account of women behind bars.
Cooke, Susan. *Ragged Owlet.* London: Arrow, 1979.
G., Katharina (pseud.). *Die Geschichte der Katharina G.: Aus dem Tagebuch einer Strafgefangenen.* Asslar: Schulte & Gerth, 1984.
Giudice, Liliane. *Die Kraft der Schwachen: Über das Kranksein.* Berlin: Kreuz, 1979.
   Drawing from literature and from the cases of a number of incurably ill people, the author provides accounts of those whose daily lives have been changed by illness, and who in spite of their own suffering have helped others to love life.
Kast, Verena. *"Trauern."* Stuttgart: Kreuz, 1982.
   Elena, a 25-year-old student, unexpectedly loses her boyfriend to a heart attack.
König, Hera. *Der tödliche Hunger—Erfahrungen einer Diabetikerin.* Frankfurt: Fischer, 1983.
Königsdorf, Helga. *Respektloser Umgang.* East Berlin: Aufbau, 1986.
   A fictional encounter—two women in crisis: an atomic physicist dealing with fascism, a scientist dealing with multiple sclerosis.

Neidhart, Kristel. *Niemand soll mich so sehen.* Berlin: Rotbuch, 1983.
    A daughter takes care of her senile mother. Account of a healing.
Oberthür, Irene. *Mein fremdes Gesicht.* 3d ed. East Berlin: Buchverlag Der Morgen, 1986.
    The author survives an accident, but—supported by psychotherapy—must learn to live with her disfigured face.
Schine, Cathleen. *Alice in Bed.* New York: Berkley, 1984.
    Alice is only 19 when rheumatic fever renders her hips completely stiff.
Schlag, Evelyn. *Die Kränkung.* Frankfurt: Fischer, 1987.
    A woman finds the wherewithal to live within her pain.
Schwartz, Lynne Sharon. *Disturbances in the Field.* New York: Bantam, 1985.
Wagner, Gesine. *Im Feuer ist mein Leben verbrannt.* 2d ed. Gütersloh: GTB Siebenstern, 1986.
    The author survived a plane crash for 81 days.
Weber, Marianne. *Lernprozess: Leben mit einem neuen Gesicht.* Frankfurt: Fischer, 1985.
    A woman must learn to live with a face altered by burns.
Woodson, Meg. *If I Die at Thirty.* Grand Rapids, Mich.: Zondervan, 1979.
    With her mother, the girl Peggy lives through all the stages from denial of death to acceptance of death from the hereditary glandular disease, cystic fibrosis.
Yurtdas, Barbara. *Einen Mondmonat lang.* Munich: Frauenoffensive, 1985.
    The death of her husband throws a German woman living in Turkey into an existential crisis.

b) Men

Berg, Thomas. *Aufs Spiel gesetzt.* Königstein/Ts: Athenäum, 1984.
    The author describes his life and, as autotherapy, reflects on the consequences of his heart attack.
Bernhard, Thomas. *Die Kälte.* Munich: Deutscher Taschenbuch, 1984.
    The author's memories of his youth in the isolated world of a sanatorium.
Blieweis, Theodor. *Wer ein Warum zu leben hat, erträgt fast jedes Wie! Beispiele von Persönalichkeiten in Krankheit und Leid.* Vienna, Linz, Passau: Veritas, 1979.
Breinersdorfer, Fred. *Notwehr.* Reinbet bei Hamburg: Rowohlt, 1986.
    A nurse struggles to save the life of her daughter, who suffers from meningitis, through the use of a clinically experimental drug.
Fingerhut, R., and Manske, C. *Ich war behindert an Hand der Lehrer und Ärzte.* Reinbek bei Hamburg: Rowohlt, 1984.
Hock, Kurt. *Die Heimkehr.* Freiburg: Herder, 1983.
    A son experiences the death of his father.
Hudson, Rock, and Davidson, Sarah. *Rock Hudson: His Story.* New York: Avon, 1987.
    An account of life in the face of death.
Jankowich, St. von. *Ich war klinisch tot.* Munich, 1984.
    Death: the most wonderful experience I have had.
Karasek, Horst. *Blutwäsche.* Neuwied: Luchterhand, 1986.
    Karasek describes eight years of incurable kidney disease.
Kupferschmidt, Alfred. *In des Töpfers Hand.* Bern: Blaukreuz, 1986.
Lagercrantz, Olaf. *Mein erster Kreis.* Frankfurt: Insel, 1984.
    Originally published in Swedish.
    The author depicts his own evolution in the face of two burdens: his depressive mother and his own lung disease, contracted at the end of high school.

Lewis, C.S. *The Problem of Pain*. New York: Collier, 1986.

Observations by the author on the death of his wife.

Mey, Daniel. *Stahlbein*. Zurich: Pendo, 1986.

Mathematics student Daniel Mey presents his "report on surviving an accident."

Minahan, John. *Mask*. New York: Berkley, 1985.

A 15-year-old, disfigured by an hereditary disease, lives out his life.

Nouwen, Henri J.M. *Sterben um zu Leben*. Freiburg: Herder, 1983.

Pilgrim, Volker Elis. *Die Elternaustreibung*. Düsseldorf: Claasen, 1984.

Autobiographical novel about the relationship between two men.

Roth, Joseph. *Job: The Story of a Simple Man*. Woodstock, NY: Overlook, 1985.

The difficult destiny of a Jewish family with a disabled child.

Wiesenhütter, Eckart. *Blick nach drüben: Selbsterfahrungen im Sterben*. Gütersloh: Gutersloher Verlag, 1977.

An account by a physician of living through two experiences of pulmonary infarction.

Wola, Frank. *Sebastian, ich will es dir erklären*. Frankfurt: Fischer, 1985.

A man who does not need a shirt, steals one. It is only through his conversations with a psychologist that the psychological conflicts that brought about the apparently senseless act come to light.

Affected individuals, together

Hampe, Johann Christoph. *To Die Is Gain: The Experiencing of One's Own Death*. Atlanta: John Knox, 1979.

Those who have been revived from their own deaths report on their experiences.

PARENTS

Eickstedt, Schieche von, ed. *Ist Auföpferung eine Lösung?: Mütter behinderter Kinder berichten*. Berlin: Frauenbuchvertrieb, 1981.

Mothers of disabled children tell their stories.

Jackson, Marjorie. *The Boy David*. London: British Broadcasting Corporation, 1985.

The child with two faces.

Scotson, Linda. *Doran: How a Mother's Love and a Child's Spirit Made a Medical Miracle*. New York: New American Library, 1986.

Shortly after the death of her husband, Scotson gives birth to a brain-damaged son; after years of therapy, he is healed.

Seidick, Kathryn. *. . . Or You Can Let Him Go*. New York: Bantam, 1984.

Seidick's son becomes a dialysis patient at the age of 8.

Steiner, Erika, and Geissler, J. *Neurodermitis*. Stuttgart: Hippocrates, 1986.

A mother's attempt to treat neurodermitis is successful.

Steller, Odile. *Un espoir infini*. Paris: Presses de la Renaissance, 1985.

Reflections on the death of her child.

Terlan, G. *Zwölf Monate sind mehr als ein Jahr*, 2d ed. Wuppertal: Oncken, 1979.

b) Fathers

Bodelschwingh, F. von. *Vom Leben und Sterben vier seeliger Kinder*. 32d ed. Bielefeld-Bethel, no date.

Kushner, Harold. *When Bad Things Happen to Good People.* New York: Avon, 1983.
  A rabbi loses one of his children to an incurable disease (progeria). While still a
  small child, Aaron is diagnosed with "early aging" and is told he will not live longer
  than 12 years. Aaron dies at age 14. The father and rabbi begins to rethink his
  relationship to God and to life.
Schmidt, Klaus-Jürgen G. *Mein Kind ist behindert.* Rheinstetten-Schindele, 1986.
  Advice for parents of handicapped children.

c) Parents, together

No entries

PARTNERS

a) Female partners

Beauvoir, Simone de. *Adieux: A Farewell to Sartre.* New York: Pantheon, 1984.
Bronnen, Barbara. *Die Überzählige.* Munich: Droemer-Knaur, 1986.
  A mother expects that her daughter will take care of her in her old age.
Johansen, Margaret. *Damenes vals.* Oslo: Tiden, 1978.
  Kristina's husband becomes prematurely senile, and must be cared for.
Meulenbelt, Anja. *Alba.* Amsterdam: Van Genrep, 1984.
  A daughter takes care of her mother on her deathbed.
Philipe, Anne. *No Longer Than a Sigh.* New York: Atheneum, 1964.
Philipe, Anne. *Je l'ecoute respirer.* Paris: Gallimard, 1984.
  A daughter comes home, to the still house of her dying mother.
Rollin, Betty. *Last Wish.* Harmondsworth: Penguin, 1987.
  The account of a daughter about helping her mother to die a dignified death.

b) Male partners

Schreiner, Robert. *Wach auf, kleine Annette.* Zurich: Kreuz. 1984.
  A grandfather tells the story of his epileptic grandchild.

c) Partners, together

No entries

PROFESSIONALS

a) Professional women

Bartholomäus, *Ich möchte an der Hand eines Menschen Sterben.* Mainz: Matthias Grün-
  wald, 1981.
  The story of a German student who works in a London hospice.
Cermak, Ida. *Ich klage nicht.* Zurich: Diogenes, 1983.
Frisch, Helga. *Tagebuch einer Pastorin.* Frankfurt: Fischer, 1981.
  The author writes about what a pastor working in a "hot-line center" must confront.

Jun, Gerda. *Kinder, die anders sind.* 4th ed. East Berlin: VEB Verlag Volk & Gesundheit, 1986.

A report by a medical specialist and 11 parents of affected children, supplemented by expert advice and legal considerations.

Kübler-Ross, Elisabeth. *On Children and Death.* New York: Collier, 1985.

Through letters, drawings, and conversations, the reader gets an idea of the intuitive insights of those affected, dying children and youth, in relation to the mystery of dying and death.

Palmer, Lilli. *Um eine Nasenlänge.* Munich: Droemer-Knaur, 1984.

On the utopian expectations of a cosmetic operation, and the hard path to the recognition that good fortune cannot be bought.

Wyss, Laure. *Ein schwebendes Verfahren.* Frankfurt: Fischer, 1983.

Suppositions about the background of a family tragedy. A documentary.

b) Professional men

Burch, Jennings Michael. *They Cage Animals at Night.* New York: New American Library, 1985.

The story of a child who learns to survive.

Lindenberg, Vladimir. *Schicksalsgefährte sein . . .* 3d ed. Munich, Basel: Reinhardt, 1970.

Originally published in Russian.

Lindenberg, Vladimir. *Gespräche am Krankenbett.* Munich, Basel: Reinhardt, 1983.

Originally published in Russian.

Fifteen conversations this doctor has had with those affected.

Maier-Gerber, Hartmut. *In der Hoffnung auf das Jenseits.* Munich: Kösel, 1985.

A physician accompanies a young patient on the last part of her life's path.

Meyer-Hörstgen, Hans. *Hirntod.* Frankfurt: Suhrkamp, 1985.

The account of a neurosurgeon.

Moser, T., ed. *Gespräche mit Eingeschlossenen.* Frankfurt: Suhrkamp, 1974.

Moser, T. *Romane als Krankheitsgeschichten.* Frankfurt: Suhrkamp, 1984.

Pray, Lawrence M., and Evan, Richard. *Journey of a Diabetic,* New York: Simon & Schuster, 1983.

Schultz, Hans Jürgen, ed. *Letzte Tage.* Stuttgart: Kreuz, 1983.

Stories of death from the past 2000 years. (See also Experts, together.)

Wedler, Hans-L. *Gerettet?* Neuwied: Luchterhand, 1979.

Encounters with others after suicide attempts.

Zink, Jörg. *Vielleicht ist es noch nicht zu spät.* Stuttgart: Kreuz, 1983.

All those who refuse to resign themselves should read this book.

AFFECTED INDIVIDUALS, TOGETHER WITH PROFESSIONALS

a) Professional women

Beuys, Barbara. *Am Anfang war nur Verzweiflung.* Reinbek bei Hamburg: Rowohlt, 1984.

How parents of disabled children learn to live in a new way.

Kübler-Ross, Elisabeth. *Befreiung aus der Angst.* Stuttgart: Kreuz, 1983.

The author here presents reports from those affected, from her seminar "Life, Death, and Passing-over": she describes the feelings elicited out of regular contact with illness and death.

Lohner, Marlene. *Plötzlich allein.* Frankfurt: Fischer, 1984.
   Conversations of an ill woman with women whose husbands have died.
Schuchardt, Erika, ed. *Jede Krise ist ein neuer Anfang: Aus Lebensgeschichten lernen.*
   3d ed. with contributions by Hans-Bernhard Kaufmann, Marlies Winkelheide, et al.
   A publication of the Comenius Institut. Dusseldorf: Patmas, 1987.
   Thirteen of our affected contemporaries offer their accounts within the framework
   of a call for biographies: "We write about . . . ourselves."
Schuchardt, Erika. *Krise als Lernchance: Analyse von 331 Lebensgeschichten aus unserer
   Zeit.* With an introduction by Horst Siebert. A publication of the Comenius Institute
   Düsseldorf: Patmos, 1985.
   The systematic research that resulted from the call for biographies for the book,
   "Every Crisis Is a New Beginning" (previous entry).
Schuchardt, Erika. *Geschwister kann man sich nicht aussuchen: Wir gehören doch zu-
   sammen.* Hamburg, 1988.

b) Professional men

Hambrecht, Martin. *Das Leben neu beginnen: Wenn Therapie zur Lebensschule wird.*
   Munich: Kösel, 1983.
   Case studies from a clinic for psychosomatics; crisis treatment alternatives are de-
   scribed.
Kratzmeier, Heinrich, ed. *Behinderte aus eigener und fremder Sicht.* Heidelberger son-
   derpädagogische Schriften, vol. 14. Rheinstetten: Schindele, 1980.
Kronenberg, Martin, ed. *Behindertenschicksale.* Wolfenbüttel: Kallmeier, 1980.
Sporken, Paul, ed. *Was Sterbende brauchen.* Freiburg: Herder, 1982.
   Thoughts about dying from various points of view; includes, among others, a con-
   versation with a cancer-stricken woman.

c) Professionals, together

Deutscher Paritätischer Wohlfahrtsverband (DPWV), ed. *Unser Alltag: behinderte
   Menschen, ihre Eltern und Familienangehörige berichten* Frankfurt, 1981.
Gabel, Claudia & Wolfgang. *Hindernisse oder Wir sind keine Sorgenkinder.* Zurich:
   Benziger, 1981.
   Those who have been affected—the disabled, their friends, family members, and
   helpers—try to counteract "problem-children" attitudes in writing.
Ring, Kenneth. *Life at Death: A Scientific Investigation of the Near-Death Experience.*
   New York: Quill, 1982.
   Discoveries and experiences of people who have been on the threshold of death and
   have survived.
Schmitt, Christian, ed. *Reise ans Ende der Angst.* Munich: Bertelsmann, 1983.
   In stories and poems, 27 authors describe their experiences with the fear of death.
Schultz, Hans Jürgen, ed. *Letzte Tage: Sterbegeschichten aus zwei Jahrtausenden.* Stutt-
   gart: Kreuz, 1983.
   Without exaggeration, without conclusions, various authors from the past two millenia
   write about death.
Tausch, Anne-Marie and Reinhard. *Wege zu uns.* Reinbek bei Hamburg: Rowohlt, 1983.
   A husband-and-wife psychotherapist team gives many people the opportunity to have
   their say.